Avoiding Mid-Air Collisions

TAB
PRACTICAL
FLYING SERIES

Avoiding
Mid-Air Collisions

Shari Stamford Krause, Ph.D.

TAB Books
Division of McGraw-Hill, Inc.
New York   San Francisco   Washington, D.C.   Auckland   Bogotá
Caracas   Lisbon   London   Madrid   Mexico City   Milan
Montreal   New Delhi   San Juan   Singapore
Sydney   Tokyo   Toronto

Notice to the reader

The National Transportation Safety Board recently issued Safety Recommendation A93-127-132, which calls for the Federal Aviation Administration to assume a more active role in instructing the flying community on the numerous factors that can cause mid-air collisions. This book addresses those factors in depth and provides the reader with the practical information and applications that have been emphasized by the NTSB in the current safety recommendation.

Disclaimer

The information presented in *Avoiding Mid-Air Collisions* by Shari Stamford Krause, Ph.D., is for reference only. Pilots should discuss any techniques or opinions expressed in this book with a qualified Certified Flight Instructor (CFI) prior to use. The pilot assumes all responsibility for using any technique contained herein.

© 1995 by **Shari Stamford Krause.**
Published by TAB Books.
TAB Books is a division of McGraw-Hill, Inc.

pbk   1 2 3 4 5 6 7 8 9 FGR/FGR 9 9 8 7 6 5
hc   1 2 3 4 5 6 7 8 9 FGR/FGR 9 9 8 7 6 5

Library of Congress Cataloging-in-Publication Data

Krause, Shari Stamford.
    Avoiding mid-air collisions / by Shari Stamford Krause.
      p.   cm.
    Includes index.
    ISBN 0-07-035944-X   ISBN 0-07-035945-8 (pbk).
    1. Airplanes—Collision avoidance.   I. Title.
  TL696.C6K73   1994
  629.132'52—dc20   94-4699
                                       CIP

Acquisitions editor: Jeff Worsinger
Editorial team: Charles Spence, Editor
                 Susan W. Kagey, Managing Editor
                 Joanne Slike, Executive Editor
                 Joann Woy, Indexer
                 Nancy Mickley, Proofreading
Production team: Katherine Brown, Director
                  Jan Fisher, Desktop Operator
Design team: Jaclyn J. Boone, Designer
              Brian Allison, Associate Designer
Cover photographs: Bender & Bender, Waldo, Oh.   PFS
Cover copy writer: Cathy Mentzer   0359458

Contents

5 Pilot judgment and decision making   117

6 Distraction: Confusion and chaos in the cockpit   143

7 Welcome to the world of stress management   163

8 Traffic-alert and collision-avoidance systems   173

Acknowledgments

THIS TEXT IS THE CULMINATION OF YEARS OF DEDICATION AND RESEARCH. But without the help, guidance, and insight of the many knowledgeable aviation professionals who assisted me, the pages of this book would be nearly blank. I extend my sincerest thanks and appreciation to:

    Gerry Brown, National Aeronautics and Space Administration
    Joe Ceasar, Bendix-King, Allied-Signal Aerospace Company
    Pablo Santa Maria, Air Line Pilots Association
    Robin Dam, Air Line Pilots Association
    Steve Schallhorn, M.D., U.S. Navy
    Joe Walsh, Federal Aviation Administration
    Otto Keesling, Federal Aviation Administration
    Barney Rahal, Aircraft Data, Inc.

The staffs of:

    Air Line Pilots Association Air Safety Library
    National Aeronautics and Space Administration Library
    Federal Aviation Administration Library
    University of Nevada—Las Vegas, Government Document Library
    Aviation Safety Reporting System, Ames Research Center
    National Transportation Safety Board, Public Inquiries Office
    Lockheed Aircraft Corporation—Burbank Library

Very special acknowledgments:

To my wonderful husband, Merrick, for always supporting and encouraging me to reach for my dreams. I especially thank him for the sleepless nights and hundreds of hours that he put into creating the illustrations for this book. If it weren't for his talent and devotion to this project, you would be looking at pages filled with stick figures.

To my parents, Alberta Stamford and the late Walter Stamford, and to my sister Shirley, for their unselfish love and endless support.

To my in-laws, Doctors Marvin and Helen Krause for their generosity in providing the computer and printing equipment on which this book was produced.

Introduction

FIFTEEN YEARS AGO, AS A STUDENT PILOT, I WAS THE CAUSE OF A NEAR-miss. The flight started out innocently enough. A little, uncontrolled field about 10 miles due east of my home airport wasn't in the practice area and I thought I would be able to shoot touch and go landings in peace. I informed the controller of the departure field of my intended eastwardly heading. After my departure from runway 27, I made my left turn. I flew a few miles parallel to the runway, careful not to interfere with the traffic pattern. After about 10 miles, thinking I was clear of any conflict with the landing traffic, I began a turn towards the northeast.

Once on my desired heading of 090 degrees, I began looking for the uncontrolled airport. The next moment, a light twin-engine airplane (I have no idea what type) made a banking, diving descent beneath me. My immediate reaction was to gasp and apply the standard student-pilot death grip on the yoke! Shaken and bewildered, I quickly decided that the best thing for me, and for all pilots flying in the skies of Pittsburgh that day, was to get on the ground as soon as possible.

As I circled back to my base airport, the tower controller called: "Grumman 26401, what's your position and altitude?" This didn't sound good, so I meekly answered: "401's 10 miles east of the airport at 3000, inbound for landing."

"Roger 401, you're flying the localizer for 27. Fly to the south and report downwind," I sort of knew what the localizer was, but I really didn't understand the seriousness of it until much later.

I was relieved that the, "Hi, I'm with the FAA, and I'm here to help you" representative didn't meet me at the plane, but as I walked through the door of my flight school, the secretary handed me the phone and said: "The tower supervisor wants to talk with you." I thought my career—if a 20-hour pilot actually has a career—was over, finished, done. I was lucky, though, and the first words I heard were, "Shari, dear . . . do you know what a localizer is . . .?" I somehow managed to squawk out a barely audible, "No." After a few minutes of counseling, the phone call ended. I had no idea that the approach to that runway started more than 30 miles away. And it never dawned on me that although it was VMC, IFR traffic might be landing on 27. Stunned by my stupidity and unintentional mistake, yet relieved that I hadn't been banned from the airport, I began to think of what could have happened.

As instructors started to inch their way towards me I heard everything from, "Well, now you know better and you learned something in the process," to "Hey, stuff happens." (They really didn't use the word "stuff," but this is a family book). "All student pilots do stupid things . . .." Well, this student pilot never did unsafe, stupid things that endangered other people's lives.

I was mortified, but I did learn something. All it takes is one mistake. There was nothing wrong with my general flying skills that day, I communicated my intentions to

ATC fairly well, I had pretty good situational awareness (at least I thought I knew enough to stay away from the traffic pattern and final approach), and I diligently looked for other traffic. My one little mistake was a lack of knowledge. I didn't understand instrument procedures. At the time I wasn't expected to but I was still sharing airspace with IFR traffic.

Time goes by

Fast forward ten years. I'm in graduate school at Embry-Riddle, and I need to write a paper on "any safety topic" for my accident investigation class. Without thinking twice, I decided to research mid-air collisions. I eagerly read every scrap of information I could get my hands on, and soon began to realize that collision avoidance is not just looking out the window or being content that your airplane is depicted as a flickering blip on a radar scope. Collision avoidance is much, much more. It's the culmination of that research and those ideas, that led to the concept of this book.

Avoiding mid-air collisions is a safety issue that has plagued the aviation community for as long as pilots have wanted to slip the surly bonds of earth. Today the threat is even greater, as more flights and aircraft than ever launch skyward. The FAA estimated in 1983 that by 1995 takeoffs and landings, just from tower-controlled U.S. airports alone, would rise more than 67 percent. Thus, the FAA projects a 300 percent increase in mid-air collisions over the next twenty years. Now there's a statistic no pilot or air traffic controller should take lightly!

Don't kid yourself. This is not a low-time pilot or inexperienced-controller problem. Every pilot and controller is at risk of either causing a mid-air collision or being involved in one.

The magnitude of the situation can best be illustrated by looking at some data. From 1968 to 1989 there were 608 mid-air collisions in the United States. Although 85 percent of those accidents were between two general-aviation aircraft, the airline industry was far from being immune (Fig. I-1). Between 1958 and 1988 there were 40 airliners in the United States involved in mid-air collisions, resulting in 908 deaths. And the general-aviation figures were even more startling, with an average of 50 deaths per year.

There was a potential for even more accidents. The government doesn't keep records on the number of pilots that almost landed short, or those that almost stalled on climbout. But there are data on how many almost had collisions. The numbers are staggering. From 1983 to 1989, there were 3536 pilot-reported near-misses, which includes only the critical, potential, and unclassified classes of hazards. And between 1981 and 1987 the sum of near-misses reported by air traffic control totaled 3088.

So what's the point?

Now that I've wowed you with the obligatory statistics, let's get down to the real objective of this book, and that is to provide some practical guidelines for collision avoidance. There are no quick answers or guaranteed solutions to the problem. How-

Fig. I-1. *Mid-air collisions 1968–1989.*

ever, the information, ideas, and techniques discussed in this book are guidelines that can be applied to decrease the potential of a mid-air collision.

The basis of this book is to view each element of collision avoidance as a resource: see and avoid, air traffic control services, cockpit resource management, which applies to general aviation as well as airline operations, human factors, and Traffic Alert and Collision Avoidance Systems (TCAS). With the exception of TCAS, each of these resources is directly available to us every time we go fly. The catch is that when these practices or concepts are used separately, they have varying degrees of limitations and failure rates. However, when every available resource is used collectively, the margin for error significantly decreases.

Humans do the darndest things

Because we humans (pilots and controllers) are intimately involved with every aspect of any given flight, it is no surprise that there's the potential for countless things to go wrong. When it comes to collision avoidance, these factors are often overlooked. Take my story, for instance. If I had been in a mid-air, what would most likely have been the official probable cause? "The failure of each pilot-in-command to see and avoid the other aircraft . . .." And a contributing factor would have included: "The failure of the student pilot to remain clear of the localizer course on runway 27 . . .." But those were the end results, not the originating causes. What started this near-miss scenario in motion? Very simply, my lack of knowledge over instrument procedures and systems.

Collision avoidance is a concept that encompasses every aspect of flying—physical, emotional, and mechanical. Additionally, when the characteristic and inevitable limitations and deficiencies of each area are then added to a situation, the possibilities for mid-air incidents are endless.

Let's put all this in perspective. The facts of my near-miss are clear. First, I should not have been flying outbound on the localizer approach to 27, although I didn't know at the time that's what I was doing. Second, I had been watching for traffic but my attention had been momentarily diverted to finding the airport. And third, it was obvious that the other pilot saw me well before I saw the other airplane.

Let's suppose this other pilot was fatigued (physical) from a long cross-country and just wanted to get home (emotional). The pilot glances down to finish a pre-landing checklist . . . doesn't expect another airplane to be directly in front and . . . impact! One diversion is sometimes all that it takes. Now add a few more common pilot problems like trouble-shooting a system malfunction (mechanical), feeling stressed (emotional) and distracted (physical-emotional) over the malfunction, and the sun being in the eyes (physical). The list could go on, but nevertheless, a mid-air could have occurred.

Breaking your error chain, by using all available resources

Every time we go flying, we have the potential of adding links to that proverbial "deadly chain of events." Just like every other type of accident, the events that lead to a mid-air collision can begin before you get to the airport. Those elements can, subsequently, intensify in flight. Stress, boredom, "get-home-itis," lack of knowledge, fatigue, poor judgment, physical limitations, distractions, task saturation, communication, complacency, decision-making, lack of skill, and low situational awareness are all potentially deadly links. How you handle those links is what a total mid-air collision-avoidance concept is all about. We can break an error chain simply by effectively using all of our available resources.

And finally

Although we can never completely wipe away the threat of a mid-air collision, we can reduce the potential of one occurring. That is the best news we in the aviation community could ever hope for. I sincerely hope that some of the techniques found in this book, along with sound instruction and rigorous study and practice, will increase safety awareness of all who participate in aviation. No single guide can provide all the answers and this volume is not a final, exclusive reference. Please read with an open mind, and use what works for you. I don't expect that my short book will stop all accidents, that's up to every pilot, controller, and maintainer. I do, however, hope that the many gems of information I've found in my research will assist students and instructors alike in promoting aviation safety.

Please read on. You might find some information to put into your "clue-bag" that you carry in flight.

1
Mid-air collision avoidance: Myths and realities

T O FULLY UNDERSTAND HOW YOU CAN IMPLEMENT A COMPREHENSIVE mid-air collision-avoidance concept into your own flying regime, you must begin with the basic premise that myths and realities exist in a collision-avoidance environment. Few professions require as much continuous study and practice as flying, yet certain facts and general knowledge are frequently overlooked. The acceptance of myths as realities are routinely passed on from one generation of aviator to the next. Therefore, this chapter was written to dispel these misconceptions of see and avoid and provide a realistic insight to collision avoidance.

SEE AND AVOID: THE MYTH

See and avoid is an integral part of collision avoidance and can neither be taken lightly nor disregarded in any flight scenario. Unfortunately, severe physical limitations and deficiencies are intrinsic to the practical practice of seeing and avoiding other aircraft. Although we are unable to change the inherent flaws, which I will discuss shortly, it is helpful to understand what the human body can and cannot do in a collision-avoidance environment. By first learning the myths behind see and avoid, we can develop a sound foundation in which the realities of this resource can truly be enhanced.

Quick, off the top of your head, what does see and avoid mean to you? "Well, when I see an airplane, I avoid it." Perhaps you had a more sophisticated answer than that, but if you didn't, you're not alone. Remember your primary flight training days? Like many of us, you probably fell into one of four categories concerning see and avoid.

One, you didn't want to die, so if looking out the window and seeing other aircraft prevented such catastrophes, you were more than happy to oblige, even though you were never quite sure what you were looking for.

Two, your instructor told you it was very important to keep your head out of the cockpit. Of course, you were immediately turned off by the idea when the first few times you tried it, you went into a 2000 fpm climb.

Three, while you were cramming for the written, you stumbled across the Federal Aviation Regulation (FAR) that requires you to see and avoid. "Wow! I guess it's really important if there's a specific FAR on the subject. Next time I go flying, I'll try real hard to find my traffic."

Or four, if you were lucky, your instructor discussed a visual scanning technique or two and discussed the importance of a solid visual search.

Whatever way you were introduced to see and avoid, you were at least somewhat aware of the significance the Federal Aviation Administration (FAA) placed on this collision-avoidance technique. Here lies part of the problem. Without a thorough knowledge of see and avoid and its inadequacies, you can easily get a false sense of security.

For instance, FAA clearly states its position in FAR 91.67:

> When weather conditions permit, regardless of whether an operation is conducted under instrument flight rules or visual flight rules, vigilance shall be maintained by each person operating an aircraft so as to see and avoid other aircraft.

As you read further in this chapter, you will understand how certain physical limitations inhibit your ability to see and avoid. However, they do not hinder a state of vigilance that should always be maintained during a flight. Keep that in mind as the myths of see and avoid are explored.

You might also be familiar with FAA's recommendation in the following Aviation Circular (AC) 90-48C:

> Effective scanning is accomplished with a series of short, regularly spaced eye movements that bring successive areas of the sky into the central visual field. Each movement should not exceed 10 degrees, and each area should be observed for at least one second to enable detection. Although horizontal back-and-forth eye movements seem preferred by most pilots, each pilot should develop a scanning pattern that is most comfortable and then adhere to it to assure optimum scanning.

Once again, sounds like great advice, but just how should you come up with this optimum-scanning technique? When you read this AC for the first time—and it could have been just now—were you confused by the whole concept or did you go ahead and create a personalized version of these scanning patterns? If you fell into the former group, you might have just dropped the whole idea and decided to look out the window as best you could. However, if you were one of those conscientious new pilots who absorbed every scrap of information you read, it's likely that you thought you had mastered the art of scanning. Unfortunately, while you found yourself flying off into the sunset with a smile on your face and a warm, fuzzy feeling in your stomach, that old false sense of security had crept in to stay.

Behind the myth: physical limitations

The myth behind see and avoid is based solely on our physical limitations. Therefore, it's important to understand how each problem area affects the collision-avoidance environment and how it relates to scanning ability.

Let's begin by looking first at the myth behind the recommended scanning techniques mentioned in AC 90-48C. Remember, we aren't discarding these techniques altogether, but rather looking at the limitations that are associated with these methods. You'll see them again at the end of the chapter.

The side-by-side (Fig. 1-1A) and front-to-side (Fig. 1-1B) scanning methods are both based on the theory that traffic detection can be made only through a series of eye fixations at different points in space. For each technique, the pilot is to break down the field of vision in blocks of 10 to 15 degrees, totaling 9 to 12 blocks in the scan area.

Fig. 1-1A. *Side-by-side scanning method. The pilot is to start at the far left of the visual area and make a methodical sweep to the right, pausing in each block one or two seconds. At the end of the scan, the pilot is to refocus to the instrument panel.*

Notice any similarities between these methods and your own? Most likely yes. But what are you really seeing with these scanning techniques? Not as much as you think or have been led to believe.

Fig. 1-1B. *Front-to-side scanning method. The pilot is to start in the center block of the visual field [center of windshield] and move to the left while focusing in each block one or two seconds. Pilot is to then quickly shift back to the center block after reaching the last block on the left. The pilot should scan instrument panel before repeating the process in the right blocks.*

What you see is not what you get

Because these limitations center around our vision, it's important to start with the basics on how the human eye works. Figure 1-2 illustrates the primary parts of the eye.

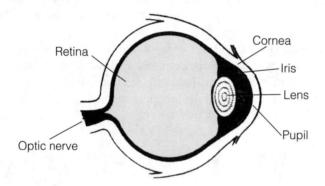

Fig. 1-2. *A cross-section of the human eye.*

Flashback to your ninth-grade biology class. Perhaps you remember that it takes both the cornea and the lens to create an image on the retina. The iris forms the pupil, which protects the eye from changes in light by widening in the dark and contracting in brighter light. The retina is a delicate, multilayer membrane that provides the vital link between the eye and the brain. It consists of a network of minute receptors, known as *rods* and *cones*. The rods are used for night or low-intensity-light vision. They inhibit depth perception and supply no detailed acuity or color (only shades of gray) capability. The cones, however, are used in day or high-intensity-light vision. They give us the greatest level of visual acuity (the ability to detect small objects and distinguish fine detail) and depth perception, as well as the

4

ability to see color. A combination of rod and cone vision is used at light intensities equivalent to dusk and dawn.

These specialized nerve endings (rods and cones) convert the light from the image that is on the retina into neural impulses. These impulses are then transmitted to the brain through the optic nerve. In essence, your brain, not your eye, processes and interprets the images that are displayed on your retina.

The center of the optic field, in the retina, is called the *fovea.* This extremely small region covers slightly less than two degrees of visual field in which only cones are present. This point is where our visual acuity is at its peak. When we look directly at an object, we are actually moving the image of that object onto the central fovea. Because that area provides us with the most lighted (cones) imagery, our best vision, theoretically, should be what appears directly in front of us. This theory, however, does not always hold true for aircraft detection, which I'll discuss later in the chapter.

The natural blind spot

The eye also has a natural blind spot in the visual field of the retina through which the nerve fibers leave the retina to join the optic nerve. It is usually about 5 to 10 degrees in width. Refer to Fig. 1-3 and follow the directions. You might be surprised to see how wide your blind spot is.

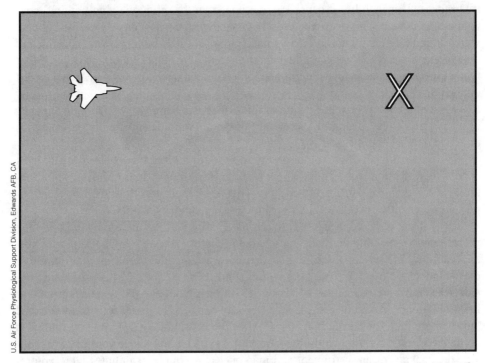

U.S. Air Force Physiological Support Division, Edwards AFB, CA

Fig. 1-3. *Blind-spot exercise. Cover your right eye and focus your left on the X. Move the diagram toward you until the airplane disappears.*

Because the blind spot is on opposite sides of the visual field in the two eyes, each eye compensates for the other. This compensation is why we are generally unaware of its existence; however, it does create a certain degree of visual deterioration.

I can see clearly now

Now that you have a general idea of how the different parts of the eye function, it's important to understand how the eye actually focuses. The muscles that control the curvature of the lens tighten when there is a visual stimulus—i.e., an airplane. The lens adjusts, or accommodates, for the retina to focus on these objects. When an image is created on the retina, the muscles tighten, which results in a focused vision of the target. Without this stimulus, these muscles tend to relax, eliminating the ability to adequately focus on the object.

In 1966, Lockheed Aircraft Company conducted a study to determine the physical limitations of pilots in a dynamic environment. Although the research is not recent, it is classic and still provides valuable information concerning our visual scanning abilities. In part, the report stated that viewing targets at infinity creates an empty visual field myopic (nearsighted) effect. According to the science of ophthalmology, infinity is any unlimited area of space greater than 20 feet. Because the eye does not have a sufficient visual stimulus, it tends to remain in constant movement, eliminating the ability to focus. This inability is caused by the image on the retina viewing nothing more than a blank space. The brain, therefore, is unable to process a clearly defined image, which ultimately results in blurred vision. Flying in total darkness, fog, a uniformly overcast sky, or a cloudless sky, all create the potential for this situation to occur. Other factors include frequent focusing on near objects, such as the instrument panel or dirt on the windshield.

Most of the time we aren't aware of this effect occurring, so we continue our scan of what seems to be several miles forward of the airplane when actually our search is effective only a short distance off the nose.

How does this all relate to our ability to scan for aircraft? Very simply: Our eyes cannot focus from a close-range object like the instrument panel to infinity of a featureless sky, then back inside the cockpit. That is a conclusion from the Lockheed report and a recently conducted U.S. Air Force study on visual acuity.

Let's discuss the connection between the findings of the air force study and the recommended scanning methods. Here's the scenario: You've just checked your altitude and heading while sitting in a shaded cockpit. You then look up and out into a clear-blue, cloudless sky (or a gray-white, solid-overcast sky). You begin a side-by-side scan. What are you actually looking at? Infinity. Nothing. With no background or line of reference in which an airplane, especially one on a collision course, could stand out, you are literally staring into space. After the recommended 9 to 12 seconds you complete your scan of the wild-blue—or white—yonder and lower your eyes back inside the cockpit for an instrument and map check. A couple of minutes later, you repeat the process.

Sounds like a fairly routine flight, one that all of us have experienced countless times before. It is, however, one of the more detrimental myths of see and avoid. Clearly, we are unable to rapidly—at one- to two-second intervals—focus from an intricate object that's two feet in front of us to a blank sky several miles away.

Another myth exposed

Often pilots go to the other extreme and stare too long at objects or blocks of sky in hopes of enhancing their ability to spot traffic. According to the same U.S. Air Force study, approximately 60 seconds after looking at a distant object, the focal point of the eyes slips to less than 10 feet. Take the previous scenario and add a radio tower at your 12 o'clock position. You know the tower is about 10 miles away and is near an uncontrolled airport. You realize that there's potential traffic in the vicinity, but you're also concerned about avoiding the tower. As you try to remain focused on the airspace above the tower, your sight becomes blurred and your field of vision quickly shifts from 10 miles to just off the nose of the airplane. Not good!

Seeing is still not believing

The Lockheed report examined the fact that human eyes cannot physically scan in a smooth rhythm. Rather, when searching for a target, they jump from one focal point to another in a number of fixations or *saccades*. Saccadic eye movement, as illustrated in Fig. 1-4, is actually a combination of four different types of eye motion ranging from very slow (2 to 5 times/second) to extremely rapid (30 to 70 times/second). The distance between each saccade is varied, extending from only 1 minute of arc to as much as 26 minutes of arc. While the eyes are in saccadic motion, visual acuity is sharply decreased, leaving large gaps in the distant field of vision. From this evidence, the study concluded that during saccadic eye movement there is only a 35 percent probability of detecting another aircraft, even when the location of the target is known.

Not until the eyes have focused on an object and begin to track it does the saccadic eye movement suppress and do the eyes automatically shift to a smoother scan. A U.S. Navy study on visual search used the following example. Hold up your index finger and have someone focus on it while you move it horizontally. You'll see that their eyes move smoothly as they follow your finger. Now, have the same person guide their eyes over the identical path, this time without focusing on any one object. Although your friend cannot physically feel the saccadic movement in the eyes, you can see that person's eyes make a series of discrete "jumps." Apply this example to scanning for other aircraft and you can begin to understand how these gaps in visual acuity occur.

This visual phenomenon obviously creates a real problem for the pilot searching for traffic. A mere one- or two-second scan is not sufficient time for proper focusing or saccadic suppression. This short scan, therefore, further deteriorates our ability to see objects at distances greater than two miles.

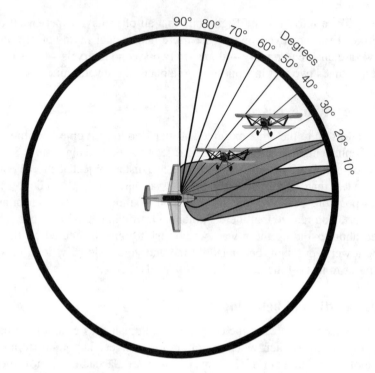

Fig. 1-4. *Saccadic eye movement. The shaded areas are the field of vision while scanning. The spaces between the tips of the cones are the visual gaps during saccadic motion. The gaps can be as much as 10 degrees, and at a distance of only one to two seconds.*
Naval Aerospace Medical Research Laboratory

I saw it coming out of the corner of my eye

Visual acuity is at its highest level when we are viewing objects directly in front of us. Since the fovea is only about two degrees in width, up to 178 degrees of detection range are available only through peripheral vision, which is why we tend to spot traffic or obstacles out of the corner of our eyes. Now think back to those times you have spotted traffic out of the corner of your eye. How close was that other airplane?

Although acuity steadily drops the farther a target is from the central visual axis, detecting traffic from the periphery occurs primarily for one of two reasons. First, the target is closer, therefore bigger and easier to see. There's an obvious caveat to that, which I'll discuss later. The second explanation is that an aircraft in a head-on, or overtaking, encounter is much more difficult to detect simply because less square footage of metal can be seen. More of the aircraft is visible when it's flying at an angle and you are able to see a partial view of the fuselage.

To visualize these differences, refer to Fig. 1-5. The U.S. Navy study included research on the relationship between acuity and central and peripheral vision. The visual detection lobe depicts this relationship and represents the range where visual percep-

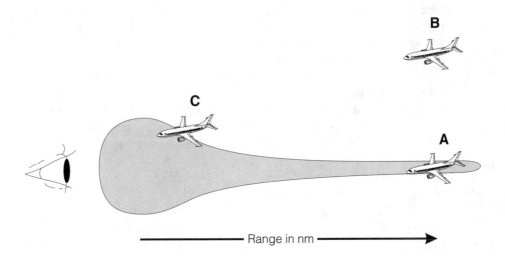

Range in nm

Fig. 1-5. *The visual detection lobe. The three positions—A, B, C—are of the same type of aircraft. Target A theoretically can be seen because it lies within the lobe, in the central field of vision. Target B is outside of the detection lobe but at the same range as Target A. Because it is not being directly viewed and acuity decreases rapidly once off the visual axis, the target cannot be detected at that angle and distance. Target C is at the same degree off the axis as Target B, but because it is closer it can theoretically be seen in your peripheral vision.* Naval Aerospace Medical Research Laboratory

tion of a target can occur. It's important, however, to understand that the lobe represents the probability of detection, not a guarantee of detection.

Although the study concluded that peripheral vision is the key to rapid detection, it emphasized that peripheral vision does not have the detection range of central vision. Remember: The primary reason we are able to see the other airplane peripherally is because it is closer and obviously a larger target—but the probability that we would be able to avoid it decreases sharply.

Just how close to a target do we need to be before we have a chance of seeing it? First you must know that peripheral vision is measured in degrees off the fovea. According to the Lockheed findings, at only six degrees off the fovea, an object must be about twice as large as that seen in the central field of vision. At 20 degrees, the target must fill the width of a 10-minute arc, and at 70 degrees from the fovea the aircraft must fill the width of a 100-minute arc in order to be seen. In all three examples the threat aircraft must be uncomfortably close.

Eyes like a hawk, or blind as a bat?

The condition of your eyesight is yet another factor concerning your overall ability to detect other aircraft. Over the years several studies have been conducted, primarily by the U.S. military, that have found pilots with normal 20/20 vision are twice as likely to spot targets as those with 20/30 or 20/40 vision. Additional evidence suggests that 20/10 or 20/15 vision further improves aircraft detection. There's no question that the better eyesight you have, the better chance you have to see other aircraft. Let's put this in perspective. If you were taking an eye test with the chart placed one nautical mile away, the letters on the 20/20 line would have to be about nine feet tall! That's just three inches shorter than the tail of a Cessna 182. Now imagine trying to read those letters on the 20/20 line in two seconds, after first focusing on a chart on your knee. Having 20/20 vision does not guarantee collision avoidance.

Also, eyesight deteriorates with age. According to a U.S. Air Force study, peripheral vision can be up to 180 degrees when we're 20 years of age, but can drop to about 140 degrees by the time we're around 50.

Let's do a quick experiment. Look up and straight ahead. Is your peripheral vision close to 180 degrees? If so, place your hands at chin level and above your shoulders. Now slowly bring them forward and stop at approximately the 140 degree point. At a certain age, and it's different for everyone, your peripheral vision from where your hands are currently positioned to back where they started at the beginning of the experiment would be lost. It's easy to see what a big chunk of sky you would be missing if, or when, your peripheral vision drops 40 degrees. Our ability to detect targets peripherally is obviously reduced substantially.

The Lockheed study also examined the connection between the eye and the brain. As we know from earlier discussion, the brain interprets the images that are displayed on the retina. Without the brain to process this information, we simply can't see. Sometimes, however, the brain gets fooled by the projected image or might take a long time to evaluate the data. It's in these cases that valuable seconds, which should be spent scanning, can be wasted.

Optical illusions and other visual phenomena

Just like a mirage in the middle of the desert, optical illusions and other forms of visual phenomena are very common in a flight environment. In the air, these illusory images can easily create erroneous aircraft attitude orientation. By not being aware of these potential hazards, you can quickly find yourself in a turn when you think you're straight and level or following traffic that doesn't exist. Therefore, your attempts at see and avoid can become totally ineffective.

Most illusions are day or night specific, so it's important to know what kind of phenomena can appear when.

Daylight illusions

False reference. According to the Lockheed study, the most frequently observed daytime illusion is slanting cloud layers. This illusion includes cloud formations, ceilings, or decks that have sloping lines that are mistaken for horizontal. Here is what can happen: You have a widely spread cloud layer directly in front of you that looks level with the horizon. You check your ADI and notice you're in a steady, slow turn. You look out front again, and the cloud reference still appears horizontal. But then you look out the side for a more panoramic view to discover the true horizon is not in the same position as the one straight ahead. The cloud formation that you've been using as a reference is actually slanted, but the illusion makes it appear as a level horizon. Before you caught this error and corrected for it, what were you unknowingly doing? Turning off course and possibly off altitude. Not a good situation.

Oculogyral. As you experience relatively fast acceleration and at the same time rotate your head, objects can appear to shift slightly away from their actual position. This illusion can occur while you're scanning and rapidly increasing your speed at the identical moment. The airplane that you have spotted might seem to move to a different location. Once you have stopped rotating your head, even if you're still accelerating, your eyes will refocus and the airplane will once again be seen at its true position.

Oculogravic. This illusion is observed mostly while flying in a high performance (jet) aircraft. Viewed objects can appear to rise from their exact positions during moderately high acceleration speeds. This effect is similar to an oculogyral illusory motion, but the acceleration speeds must be much greater. Instead of objects shifting laterally, they appear to slightly gain altitude. Although this illusion is not that common, even among fighter pilots, it is a visual phenomena that can skew an otherwise effective scan.

Night illusions

Autokinesis. This illusory effect occurs when a single stationary light appears to be moving. Here's the scenario: You are flying at night, feeling like you could strap any airplane to your posterior and enter into the Aviation Hall of Fame by day's end. ATC has told you to "follow traffic" and you replied "traffic in sight," when suddenly you realize that the aircraft you've been flying chase with for the past five miles is a blinking red light on top of a radio tower. After you recover from your ego bursting into a million pieces, you have a second to ponder, "How could I have mistaken a stationary light for that of a moving, anti-collision light?" You just experienced an autokinetic illusion. Now the really important question: "If that light wasn't my traffic, then where is my traffic?"

False reference. It's not clouds this time that create the illusion at night, but rather stars or lights near the horizon. Because of atmospheric interference, stars tend to twinkle or appear in motion when they are near the horizon and can easily be mistaken for aircraft lights. This is a common occurrence, especially in the winter, when Sirius, the brightest star in the northern hemisphere, appears over the entire continental U.S. at one to three fist-widths above the horizon. On a night with scattered clouds, all you might see is a shaky bright light peeking in and out of the clouds, looking just like an aircraft, when it's actually Sirius.

Another similar event can occur at dusk. Venus is quite prominent at that hour, and pilots have mistakenly reported seeing everything from airplanes to satellites to UFOs.

Night visual illusions have also led fighter pilots, who believed that they were rejoining their leader to a fingertip formation, to attempt to rejoin a train or the light of an isolated house. Also eye-watering is the example of the general-aviation pilot who landed on a road with streetlights. He thought it was a runway.

Oculogyral. The effects of this illusion at night are identical to those that occur during the day. However, the acceleration needed to induce the illusory motion is much lower.

Night myopia. You can experience this visual phenomena even with normal eyesight. According to the Lockheed report, the cause of night myopia is involuntary accommodation and a distortion of the retinal image due to the largely dilated pupil. Although the effects are not as severe as those experienced with empty-field myopia, night myopia still inhibits your ability to properly focus on objects.

Flash blindness. You're minding your own business, sound asleep in bed, when someone walks in and turns on the lights. Dazed and just a little cranky, you wonder who changed the 60-watt light bulb from the lamp that you had been quietly reading by an hour before to a Three Rivers Stadium light. You're lying there blinded with flashing blue spots, which is fortunate for the culprit, who can make a fast exit. The same effects apply while night flying, prompting Lockheed to study the causes. Research found that it takes up to 30 minutes for our eyes to adapt to darkness, but that ability can be totally lost after only 5 seconds of exposure to a bright light. Just a glance at the moon or city lights—especially stadium lights—can be enough of a flash to blur your vision and temporarily blind you. You could experience inferior vision for the next 30 minutes. Not a good situation to be in, especially at night.

If you must turn on the lights while flying, the general rule of thumb to follow is to close or cover one eye so you can still retain some night vision capability. This idea presents quite the dilemma. Omitting about 90 degrees of visual field—central and peripheral—when you close one eye or running the risk of seeing nothing but blurry bright spots if you keep both eyes open does not create an optimum see and avoid environment. Take a small flashlight, preferably with a red lens, with you while night flying. You eliminate the need to turn on the cabin lights to read a map, change a frequency, or cross-check a darkly lit instrument panel. Your night vision can then stay intact.

It takes more than a pair of good eyes

Let's break down the recognition and reaction times in a see and avoid situation. The left bar graph in Fig. 1-6 clearly shows that the see and avoid concept encompasses three physical elements: eye perception, three neuron-reflex arc, and muscle reflex. A fourth element includes the limitations of the aircraft.

For the eye to see—but not recognize—an object takes 0.1 seconds. The three neuron-reflex arc, a fancy way to say how fast the brain is able to determine the object is truly a threat, is a disturbing 10 seconds. That time includes recognizing that the object you see is actually an aircraft, realizing that you're on a collision course, and making a decision about how to avoid it. Let's first take a look at the significance of these numbers. It takes slightly more than 10 seconds to visually and mentally process the situation—and here's the kicker—you haven't even begun to move your airplane out of harm's way. Add 0.4 seconds for muscle reflex time—and that's on a good day—for a grand total of 10.5 seconds.

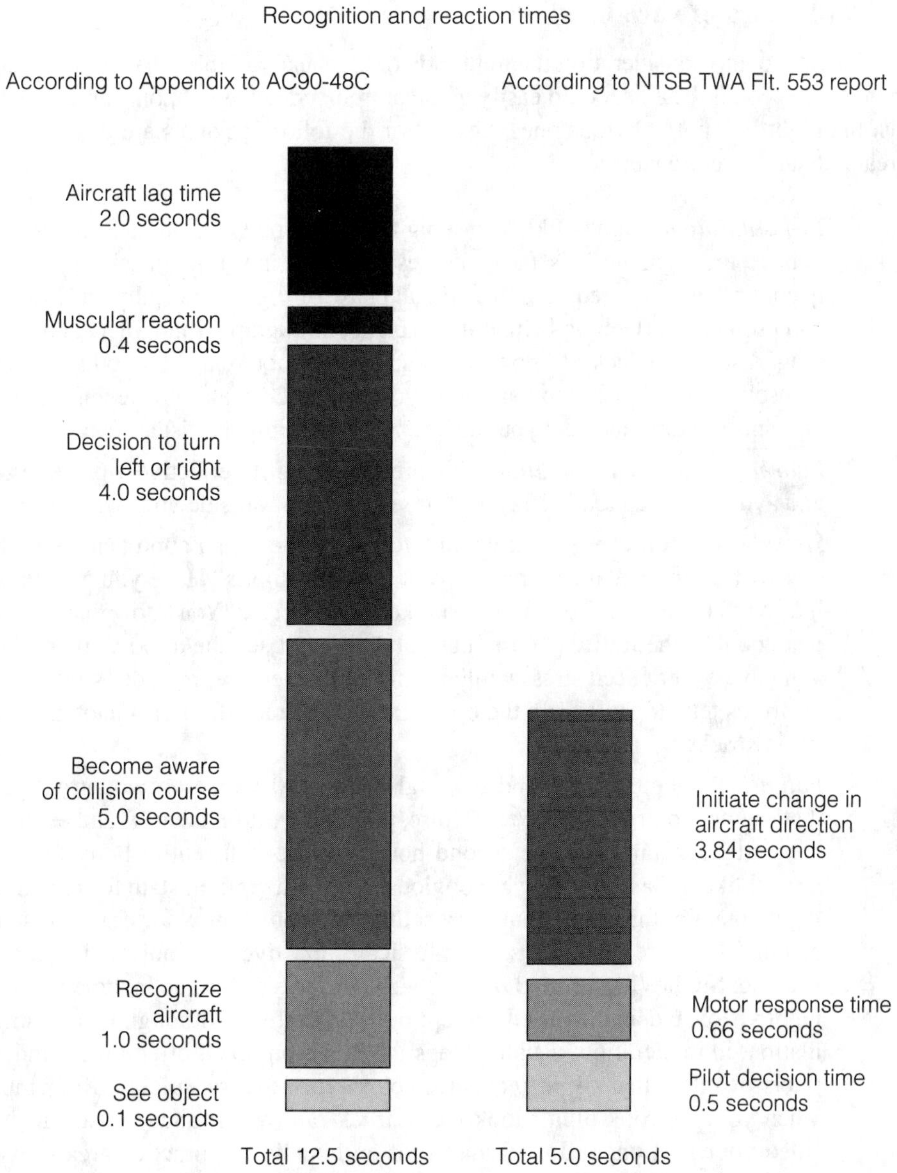

Recognition and reaction times

According to Appendix to AC90-48C

According to NTSB TWA Flt. 553 report

Aircraft lag time
2.0 seconds

Muscular reaction
0.4 seconds

Decision to turn
left or right
4.0 seconds

Become aware
of collision course
5.0 seconds

Initiate change in
aircraft direction
3.84 seconds

Recognize
aircraft
1.0 seconds

Motor response time
0.66 seconds

See object
0.1 seconds

Pilot decision time
0.5 seconds

Total 12.5 seconds   Total 5.0 seconds

Fig. 1-6. *Breakdown of recognition and reaction times in a see and avoid environment. According to the Lockheed study, the left bar graph shows the minimum time necessary to recognize and react to a threat aircraft. The right bar graph is derived from the TWA Flight 553 NTSB accident investigation.* Lockheed Corporation/NTSB

A plethora of variables

Let's take into consideration the multitude of physical variables that could extend those 10.5 seconds. The list could easily go on at tremendous length, but for now, let's just highlight the more obvious ones. Several of the following areas are discussed in greater detail in later chapters.

1. *Task saturation.* High workload is a big factor that prevents pilots from looking outside the cockpit. This factor comes into play any time checklists or frequency changes are required in a critical phase of flight, especially on climbout and pre-landing. Getting behind the airplane, through poor judgment and planning, distraction, lack of knowledge and skill, or not being able to handle that "muscle" plane you rented to impress your friends, can also create unnecessary amounts of work that take your attention away from your visual scan.

2. *Poor meteorological conditions.* It's pretty difficult to effectively practice see and avoid when a cloud or layer of haze hangs just outside your window.

3. *Stress.* Have you ever gotten behind your airplane on an approach when the crosswind component is almost at your aircraft's limits? Have you ever tuned into ATIS to hear, ". . . two miles, smoke and haze . . .." You know that you are just about in the traffic pattern, but you still can't see the airport? If so, then you have experienced stress while flying. And when you're under stress, your priorities tend to shift from the normal to the distracted, to the chaotic, to the panic-stricken.

4. *Fatigue.* Remember those endless single-prop, 100-knot cross-country flights that seemed to drone on forever? Sure, you felt great on takeoff, and even for the first hour, but after the second hour or more your entire body felt and moved like molasses. You were obviously not in a vigilant state for recognizing a potential threat and making a sound decision about your next course of action. The more time you spend physically inactive, the more fatigued you become. Studies have found that the visual effects of fatigue include reduced night vision and an increased susceptibility to vertigo. Although mental stimulation, in moderation, usually keeps the blood pumped, often times student pilots or pilots that fly infrequently get overtaxed very quickly. Remember when your logbook didn't look like a truck ran over it and you still hadn't filled your first page? Just flying .8 of an hour in the practice area proved physically and mentally exhausting. Getting used to a flight environment requires a certain level of stamina, and before you achieve that you can easily become fatigued.

5. *Sleep deprivation.* Try looking for traffic between yawns while your eyes are half opened. That is not a good situation. There is, of course, quite a bit more that can be said about lack of sleep and circadian rhythms—but for this exercise, I'm sure you get the picture.

6. *Age.* As we already know from a previous discussion, physical prowess declines as we age. Among other things, our reflexes and eyesight, two very important qualities for pilots, might fade over the course of time.

7. *Smoking.* The most important reactions to smoking is the loss of sensitivity to light and a restriction of the visual field. According to a Lockheed study, the carbon monoxide inhaled saturates the blood 210 times more than oxygen. The carbon monoxide also takes between 6 and 24 hours to actually leave the bloodstream. Because the supply of available oxygen is decreased, the effects of smoking closely parallels those of hypoxia. Even a mild case of hypoxia is detrimental to vision, especially at night. There is a five percent loss of night vision as low as 4000 feet; at 6000 feet the loss increases to 10 percent, and at 10,000 feet the visual loss jumps to 20 percent.

8. *Alcohol.* The same study also concluded that alcohol reduces depth perception, inhibits the ability to distinguish different brightnesses, and produces similar effects as hypoxia. At times, the only chance we have to detect other aircraft is through observing a target in our peripheral vision—a time when depth perception becomes important—or in a luminescent environment where it would be best if we could still differentiate levels of contrast. Remember, we only have two degrees of foveal area to begin with, and drinking or smoking further shrinks our overall visual field.

9. *Legal drugs and medications.* The Lockheed report also found that certain over-the-counter drugs and prescription medications can affect vision. Antihistamines and sulfonamides, a sulfa-based antibiotic used for broad-range illnesses such as upper respiratory infections and bladder infections, can negatively affect depth perception and acuity. They can also enlarge our natural blind spot, which can limit our peripheral vision and hinder our ability to focus by creating a loss of muscular coordination of the eyes. Additionally, aspirin used in excessive quantities can have these same negative effects on your vision. For example, people with painful arthritis might take three times the amount of aspirin as one would normally take for a bad headache.

Now to move the beast

The study allotted a minimum of two seconds for aircraft lag time. Again, this time is measured under ideal conditions. Of course, numerous factors could easily prolong that lag time. The size and wingspan (the bigger the airplane, the greater the chance of it not completely clearing the threat aircraft), the turn radius (don't expect every airplane to be able to turn on a dime), and the condition of the aircraft (an older and ill-maintained airplane is not going to maneuver like it did when it was new).

The study concluded that it takes a minimum of 12.5 seconds to recognize a threat (see) and react to it (avoid). Sometimes in life 12.5 seconds feels like an eternity, such as when you're waiting in traffic, sitting through TV commercials, or on hold with the cable company. But looking up to notice that the smudge on the windshield you thought was the remains of a bug has suddenly turned into a 120-knots airplane coming straight at you with 250 knots of closure makes 12.5 seconds seem but a blink of an eye.

CASE 1: COLLISION OF FLIGHT 553 AND A BARON

Just one year after the Lockheed study came out, a TWA DC-9 collided with a twin-engine Beechcraft Baron near Urbana, Ohio. The National Transportation Safety Board (NTSB) determined that the airline crew should have been able to recognize and react to the Baron in a mere five seconds. According to Lockheed's research, however, that would have been physically impossible. Fig. 1-6 illustrates the difference between the Lockheed study and the NTSB investigation of this accident.

The following is a brief discussion of the events prior to the mid-air. You'll find nothing unusual or unique about either flight. Both were very ordinary and routine, which, in itself, makes this accident all the more noteworthy. No blatant errors were made on the part of either pilot. It was simply a matter of a high workload in the cockpit and not being able to see and avoid.

Background information

9 March 1967: TWA Flight 553, a DC-9, collided with a twin-engine Beechcraft Baron, 25 nautical miles northeast of the Dayton, Ohio, Municipal Airport at 4525 feet.

Reported weather at time of accident: High, thin, scattered clouds. Visibility six to seven miles. Haze. Ground was 80 to 90 percent snow covered.

Experience of the pilots. TWA captain: 9832 total flight hours with 193 in the DC-9. TWA first officer: 1560 total flight hours with 15 in the DC-9. Beechcraft pilot: 4074 total flight hours, 575 in the Baron.

Probable cause

The NTSB determined that the probable cause of this accident was the failure of the DC-9 crew to see and avoid the Beechcraft. Contributing to this cause were physiological and environmental conditions and the excessive speed of the DC-9, which reduced the crew's visual-detection capabilities.

The accident

At approximately 1153 Eastern Standard Time, Flight 553 was cleared to descend out of 6000 feet to 3000 feet for its approach into the Dayton Municipal Airport. About the same time, the pilot of the Baron radioed the Springfield, Ohio, airport UNICOM that he would be landing shortly. He was flying VFR and was not in contact with any ATC facility, nor was he required to be. In those days it was not necessary to turn on your transponder.

Immediately after the controller gave Flight 553 the clearance to descend, he observed an identified radar target—the Baron—ahead and slightly to the right of Flight 553. He quickly issued the following traffic advisory: "TWA five fifty-three . . . traffic at twelve-thirty, one mile, southbound, slow moving." By the time the captain of Flight

553 acknowledged the transmission with a "Roger", the two aircraft were only 14 seconds away from colliding.

According to the cockpit voice recorder (CVR) tape, the crew never indicated that they ever saw the Baron, and for the final four seconds before impact, the crew concentrated on the pre-landing checklist.

At 1153:50, as Flight 553 was descending and in an overtaking position, it struck the level Baron in the left rear quarter of its fuselage. The Beech disintegrated instantly, and the DC-9 entered into an uncontrollable dive. The Baron pilot and the TWA crew died, along with the 21 passengers on board the DC-9.

The investigation

Ironically, several important points evolved from the investigation that defended the findings of the Lockheed study. What you must remember, however, is that this accident took place in 1967, light years away from present-day investigative concepts. What is apparent to us now about some limitations to see and avoid was not the prescribed way of doing things back then.

The cockpit visibility study

According to the NTSB, for approximately two minutes prior to the mid-air, the Beechcraft would have been visible to the DC-9 captain in the center windshield. The DC-9 has a side, front, and center windshield set-up for each pilot. The captain's eye reference point, however, was at his front windshield. The view for the first officer would have been partially obscured by the right side of his front windshield post. The pilot of the Beechcraft would have had to look to his left between 92 and 108 degrees and between 6 and 14 degrees up in order to see the DC-9.

There's a distinct difference between an object appearing in a windshield and an object that is easily detectable. The Baron did not fall into the latter category. Neither did the DC-9. Just on the basis of see and avoid, none of the three pilots was able to recognize and react to the threat in time.

We can only speculate

In piecing together the bits of information derived from the CVR and ATC tapes, a possible scenario can be formed as to the activities of the pilots just prior to the collision.

The TWA crew would have had a busy workload in preparation for landing. The first officer was flying the aircraft and, according to sounds from the CVR, was making power adjustments along with several heading changes. The captain was occupied with the radios. At the time, TWA had a company operating procedure that required the pilot flying the airplane go over the checklist silently before requesting the other pilot to read the list aloud. Just before impact, the first officer said, "Ready on the checklist, Cap'n." It was assumed that he had already completed the checklist items and was asking the captain to read the preliminary landing checklist. Therefore, some time during the descent the first officer would have diverted his attention to inside the cockpit.

Because the captain never indicated to the controller that he had the traffic in sight or that the crew had any discussion over the matter, the Board assumed that after the crew failed to see the aircraft initially they went back to their cockpit duties.

Meanwhile, moments before the accident, the pilot of the Baron had radioed to the Springfield UNICOM. He was most likely preparing for landing and could have been concentrating on his own checklists and navigation.

Refer back to Fig. 1-6 while keeping this TWA incident in mind and again review the impact of the difference between the conclusions of the Lockheed study and NTSB investigation. It is apparent that various credible sources cannot agree on the exact amount of time the see and avoid concept takes to occur. Obvious, however, are the limitations of relying upon the seeing in see and avoid.

THE OLD DISAPPEARING ACT

Perhaps you might take for granted that, at the very least, you'd be able to recognize an object as that of an airplane. That depends on whether the view behind the target aircraft has a distinct and clear contrast or one that is complex and not uniform.

Flying against a clear contrast

It's important to understand how and why contrast affects ability to recognize a target. The scientific reason is that contrast is a ratio between the difference in luminance of an object and the background it's viewed against and the luminance of the background itself. The Lockheed study proved that the threshold contrast—the least contrast required for an object to be detected against its background—decreases as luminance increases. In other words, the ability of the eye to observe changes in the brightness of objects increases as illumination increases. That finding—it's easier to see in the light than the dark—was, of course, expected. But when a color contrast was added to the experiment, notable data was collected. When there is a high brightness contrast composed of different colors between the target and the background, visual acuity improves only slightly. However, when the brightness contrast is low, color contrast can improve visual acuity appreciably. Brightly colored aircraft are easier to notice in an overcast sky and white aircraft are best detected in a darkened sky. A white- or tan-colored airplane can be extremely difficult to detect against a bright, sunny sky.

Flying against a complex background

Visual search of an aircraft over a heavily populated area or downtown sections of a city is extremely difficult. At times the image of the target can disappear altogether. These regions have the greatest diversity in background and contrast. They are filled with varying building heights, houses, streets, shadows, reflections, and a plethora of other city landscapes. Unlike the previously discussed conditions in which a pilot has a chance of noticing a discontinuity against a more uniform background, flying amidst buildings and in and out of shadows makes recognizing an aircraft on a collision course nearly impossible.

18

A further consideration is that helicopters frequently fly in a complex background in and around cities. They have unique shapes and flight characteristics and not necessarily a form with which you are familiar. For a different, yet realistic, look at how difficult, and sometimes impossible, it is to recognize aircraft against complex backgrounds, let's take a look at the following illustrations.

Figure 1-7A depicts the baseline image of a helicopter at ½ mile against a bluish-gray sky with a bright contrast level (100 mL) of luminosity. Although we can't identify any specific details unless there's bold lettering on the side, we can recognize the object has an outline of a helicopter. Vertical flight buffs could even venture to guess the make and model of the target.

3000 ft

Fig. 1-7A. *Image of a helicopter against a bright contrast at a distance of 3000 feet.*

Figure 1-7B shows the same helicopter flying in the same conditions at 1 mile away. All detail has been lost, but the rotor-wing characteristics are still marginally evident and the general shape is intact. Therefore, the image can be perceived as that of an helicopter.

6000 ft

Fig. 1-7B. *Image of a helicopter against a bright contrast at a distance of 6000 feet.*

Figure 1-7C illustrates the same helicopter viewed at 2 miles. This image, at best, would be observed as a discontinuity against the background sky. With that in mind, you could take measures to monitor the path of this potential traffic. Once the target

Fig. 1-7C. *Image of a helicopter against a bright contrast at a distance of two nm*

got closer, it would be likely that you could recognize the shape as a helicopter, and most importantly, its course of flight.

You'll be reading more about using communication as an effective collision-avoidance resource throughout the book, but I feel compelled now to get in my first plug. The reasons just mentioned, and those that are about to be addressed, are why I can't stress enough the importance of requesting traffic advisories when flying in and around metropolitan areas.

Figure 1-8A illustrates that same helicopter at ½ mile, but this time it's set against a complex-patterned background of two buildings with shadows casting near the helicopter's tail rotor and behind the fuselage. You might be able to identify this target if you catch a glimpse of movement or if the sun happens to reflect off the aircraft at just the right angle. What is most likely to occur, however, is that the helicopter will blend in with the buildings. Don't even hope to see a white aircraft against a white building. A detection of relative motion is lost, and the sun reflects off not only the aircraft but every other piece of glass and metal structure.

With those glad tidings, take a look at Figs. 1-8B and 1-8C. Again, they depict the aircraft at 1 and 2 miles, respectively. Either image only remotely resembles a heli-

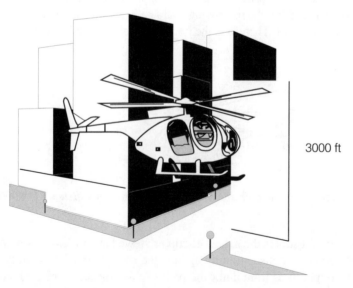

Fig. 1-8A. *Image of a helicopter against a complex background at a distance of 3000 feet.*

6000 ft

Fig. 1-8B. *Image of a helicopter against a complex background at a distance of 6000 feet.*

2 nm

Fig. 1-8C. *Image of a helicopter against a complex background at a distance of two nm.*

copter. Remember, we need a visual stimulus in order for our eyes to focus. Do we have one? No. Instead, we have a blob looking like an ink spot that wouldn't trigger any eye-brain response, and therefore, would go undetected during our visual search. Likewise, there are no distinct discontinuities against a complex background because everything is viewed as a discontinuity.

From these illustrations we can better understand why it takes a minimum of 10 seconds to recognize that an object is an aircraft, realize it is on a collision course, and make a decision about what to do about it.

THE FINAL MYTH

The Lockheed study also presented analyses concerning the two primary visual detection principles. The Minimum Visual Detection *Angle* theory (myth) and the Minimum Visual Detection *Area* theory (reality) have been debated over the years as to which is the more accurate in a see and avoid environment. The evidence, however, that evolved from this research can logically support only one theory.

A practical look at visual detection

Geometry 101: Because these theories are founded on rudimentary principles of geometry, it might be best to have a quick review. Figure 1-9 illustrates degrees, minutes, and seconds of arc and how they relate to seeing close or distant objects.

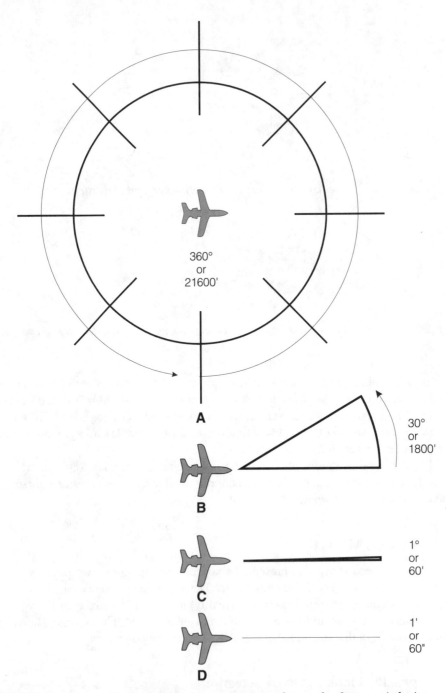

Fig. 1-9. *The relationship between degrees, minutes, and seconds of an arc. A depicts a circle of 360 degrees. B illustrates an arc (or "wedge") of 30 degrees from the 360 degree circle. C shows 1 degree of arc. D represents 1 minute of arc.*

Now, let's apply this concept to real life. Without getting too cosmic, visualize the above diagrams in relation to flying. We already know that there are 360 degrees in a full circle of arc. As you sit in your airplane, you have a 360-degree view of the sky. The wedges in Fig. 1-9 A, B, C, and D are progressively smaller amounts of sky you can see within in that 360-degree circle around your aircraft. As you can see, 1 minute of arc is a very small piece of sky; 1 second of arc is even smaller. With this information, let's discuss the visual detection theories.

The Minimum Visual Detection Angle theory (Fig. 1-10A) is measured as a single dimension. This simply means that an object is viewed as a straight line without any depth or height. Obviously, a real airplane is not two-dimensional and cannot be referred to as simply as a drawing, therefore, this theory loses credibility. However, it's important to understand why this principle falls into the category of a see and avoid myth.

Minimum
Visual Detection Angle
(~12' or 0.2 degrees under ideal conditions)

Fig. 1-10A. *Minimum Visual Detection Angle theory. According to the theory, in a head-on or overtaking encounter, the opposing pilot should detect the threat aircraft when its wingspan fills 12 minutes (0.2 degrees) of arc.* Lockheed Corporation

The illustration in Fig. 1-10A shows a general-aviation aircraft in a head-on encounter. According to the theory, we would have a high probability of seeing this airplane as soon as it fills a visual angle of 12 minutes (0.2 degrees) of arc. Now, quickly refer back to Fig. 1-9C to see just how small 12 minutes of arc is. Then, visualize that area of sky in relation to your 360-degree field of view.

To make this concept even easier to understand, let's do a little exercise right where you're sitting. Make a circle with your thumb and forefinger (an okay sign), and look through it at arm's length. That's about a 3-degree circle. According to the Angle theory, you should be able to spot an entire airplane in a head-on encounter at 0.2 degrees. That equates to ¼ the size of your okay sign. Here's a good example of what ¼ of 3 degrees would look like. Take a typical ball-point pen, turn it upside down, and hold it at arm's length. Spot a distant object that is the same size as the pen's clicker. Amazingly small, isn't it? According to the Angle theory, that is the size target we are expected to see of an airplane on a head-on collision course.

You can make numbers mean anything you want

The numbers used to support the Angle theory can be quite misleading. For this example, I've used the dimensions of a Grumman Cheetah. The aircraft's wingspan is

32 feet and the width of the fuselage, including prop clearance, is 6 feet. After doing a little calculation, you should expect to see the threat at 9169 feet (1.5 nm), or at 120 knots for each plane (240 knots closure), and a time to impact of 22.6 seconds.

Does that amount of time sound reasonable to you? You know it takes at least 12.5 seconds to recognize and react to an object. In this scenario you're supposed to have a time to impact of 22.6 seconds. That seems right. No, it isn't. This is one of those "gotchas" that can sneak up on us when we're in a see and avoid environment. Remember how small your object was in the ball-point pen exercise, even though you probably chose something quite substantial, like a house on a hill, or a gigantic oak tree? So just think of how much more difficult it would have been to spot your object if you had chosen a high-tension wire. However, that's exactly what an airplane looks like as it appears motionless off your nose. The thickness of wings are so narrow it makes them nearly invisible to detect at a safe distance. And the width of the fuselage, still using the Cheetah as an example, is approximately one-fifth the size of the wingspan. Just being aware of your physical limitations gives you the knowledge and insight needed to be a safer pilot.

SECTION REVIEW

Thus far we have discussed the myth. Before moving to the realities, let's review.

See and avoid
- Evolves from FAR 91.67.

Scanning methods
- Stated in AC 90-48C. Side-by-side method. Pilot is to start at far left of visual area, and make a methodical sweep to the right, pausing in each block one or two seconds. Pilot ends each round of scan by refocusing on instrument panel.
- Front-to-side method. Pilot is to start at center of windshield, move left of visual field, focusing in each block one or two seconds. Pilot ends each round of scan by refocusing on instrument panel.

Physiology of the human eye
- Cornea and lens create image on retina.
- Iris forms pupil.
- Pupil protects eye from changes in light by widening when it's dark and contracting when it's bright.
- Retina provides eye-brain connection.
- Retina consists of receptors (specialized nerve endings) known as rods and cones.
- Rods are used for night or low-intensity-light vision.

- Visual acuity is the ability to detect small objects and distinguish fine detail.
- Rods inhibit depth perception and supply no detailed visual acuity or color capability.
- Cones are used in day or high-intensity-light vision.
- Cones provide the greatest level of visual acuity, depth perception, and the ability to see color.
- The combination of rods and cones are used at light intensities equivalent to dusk and dawn.
- Rods and cones convert the light from the retinal image to neural impulses.
- The brain processes and interprets the retinal images.
- Fovea is the center of the optic field in retina.
- Fovea is about two degrees in width.
- Only cones are present in fovea, which produces the best level of vision and acuity.
- Natural blind spot exists in the retina where the nerve fibers leave the retina to join the optic nerve.
- Natural blind spot is usually 5 to 10 degrees in width.
- Eye focuses when the muscles that control the curvature of the lens tighten due to a visual stimulus.
- Accommodation occurs when the lens adjusts to permit retinal focus of images of objects at different distances.
- Without a visual stimulus, the eye cannot properly focus.
- Infinity is any unlimited area of space greater than 20 feet.
- Empty visual-field myopia is caused by viewing objects at infinity.
- Flying in total darkness, fog, a uniformly overcast sky, or a cloudless sky, creates the potential for empty visual-field myopia to occur.
- Frequent focusing on the instrument panel or dirt on the windshield can also produce empty visual-field myopia.
- Eyes cannot focus from a close range object to infinity and back to a close-range object instantly.
- Staring at a distant object for one minute allows the eyes' focal point to drop to under 10 feet.
- Saccadic eye movement occurs when the eye "jumps" from one focal point to another while searching for a target on which to focus.
- Saccadic eye movement sharply decreases visual acuity and leaves large gaps in the distant field of vision.

- During saccadic eye movement, there is only a 35 percent chance of target detection, even when the location of the threat aircraft is known.
- Saccadic eye movement is suppressed when the eye is focused on an object.
- Peripheral vision is measured in degrees off of the fovea.
- Visual acuity drops farther away from the fovea.
- Peripheral vision aids in rapid detection of target because the threat aircraft is closer [appears bigger] and is flying at an angle.
- Visual detection lobe represents the relationship between acuity and central and peripheral vision.
- 20/20 eyesight enhances visual search by twice as much as 20/30 or 20/40.

Optical illusions and other visual phenomena
- False reference (day) includes cloud formations, ceilings, and decks with slanting cloud layers.
- False reference (day) creates the illusion that a sloped horizon is level.
- Oculogyral (day) occurs when pilot is accelerating and rotating head simultaneously. Objects appear to shift laterally.
- Oculogravic (day) occurs when pilot is rapidly accelerating and rotating head simultaneously. Objects appear to rise vertically.
- Autokinesis (night) occurs when a single stationary light appears to be moving.
- False reference (night) occurs when stars or lights near the horizon are mistaken for aircraft.
- Oculogyral (night) occurs when pilot is accelerating at a moderate speed and rotating head simultaneously. Objects appear to shift laterally.
- Flash blindness (night) occurs when the dark adaptation of the eye is interrupted by bright lights.
- The eye can take up to 30 minutes to adapt to darkness and lose it after only 5 seconds of exposure to bright lights.
- When night flying, use a flashlight (red if possible) for cockpit tasks.

Recognition and reaction factors
- Seeing an object is not the same as recognizing the object.
- Three physical elements: eye perception, three neuron-reflex arc, and muscle reflex.
- Fourth element: Aircraft limitations.
- Minimum recognition and reaction time for physical elements is 10.5 seconds.

Other factors that could increase the 10.5 second baseline are:

- Task saturation
- Poor meteorological conditions

- Stress
- Fatigue
- Sleep deprivation
- Age
- Smoking
- Alcohol
- Medications
- Minimum aircraft lag time (limitation) is two seconds.

Background and contrast
- Contrast is a ratio between the difference in luminance of an object and the background it is viewed against and the luminance of the background itself.
- Brightly colored aircraft are easier to detect in an overcast sky.
- White aircraft are easier to detect in a darkened sky but more difficult to detect against a bright background.
- Distant aircraft might be detected as discontinuities against a clear or uniform background.
- Aircraft viewed against complex backgrounds are extremely difficult to detect and could entirely disappear from view.

Geometry
- 1 minute of arc equals 60 seconds of arc.
- 1 degree of arc equals 60 minutes of arc.
- 0.2 degrees of arc equals 12 minutes of arc.
- 360 degrees is equal to a full circle of arc.

Minimum Visual Detection Angle Theory
- Theory is measured in a single dimension, therefore, an object is viewed as a straight line.
- Theory states that entire threat airplane can be seen when it fills a visual angle of 12 minutes of arc.
- Calculations can be misleading.

SEE AND AVOID: THE REALITY

Now the good news. Awareness of potential hazards is a key to becoming a safer pilot. Understanding how to compensate for those hazards will further enhance your ability to avoid mid-air collisions.

The minimum visual detection area theory (Fig. 1-10B) is based on measuring a circle with the diameter of the Minimum Visual Detection Angle. Very simply, it states that the fuselage—not the entire airplane—of the threat aircraft must fill 12 minutes of

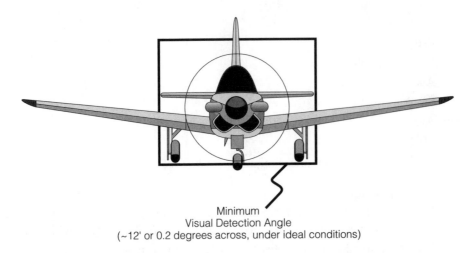

Minimum
Visual Detection Angle
(~12' or 0.2 degrees across, under ideal conditions)

Fig. 1-10B. *Minimum Visual Detection Area theory. According to the theory, in a head-on or overtaking encounter, the opposing pilot should detect the threat aircraft when its fuselage fills 12 minutes (0.2 degrees) of arc.* Lockheed Corporation

arc before there is a high probability of seeing it. By using a Cheetah again as an example, we can determine just how terrifyingly close it has to be for you to recognize the seriousness of the situation. As we discussed earlier, the wingspan is not a practical variable when calculating the range of visual detection. Therefore, using the six-foot diameter of the fuselage and prop-clearance area, the distance between both airplanes equates to approximately 1720 feet.

Now let's put that 1720-feet range into perspective. If each general aviation aircraft is traveling at 120 kts head-on, at the same altitude, their closure rate is 240 kts, or 405 fps. An aircraft that size, with that closure, is 4.2 seconds away from impact. If it takes slightly more than 10 seconds to recognize and react to an object, you can see you'd respond to this threat 6 seconds after impact.

The scanning techniques: a revised version

It's clear and a million. Maybe a lone puffy-white cloud or two dot an otherwise pristine blue sky. It should be unbelievably easy to see another plane buzzing away this Saturday morning doing Lazy-8s. Right? Wrong. The next thing you know, the windscreen is filled with a Tomahawk in a hard right turn. How did that happen?

A clear sky, without features upon which to focus the eye, is frequently a challenging environment for maintaining a disciplined visual lookout. With no outstanding visual reference at a distance, our eyes refocus to a position about 10 to 20 feet away. When we glance back inside the cockpit for an instrument or map check, our eyes once again must refocus, this time at only 1 to 2 feet. Not only do our eyes have to focus and refocus between our scanning and flying the airplane, but plenty of common annoyances redirect our attention, like the unrepentant bug that smashed on the windscreen directly in front of our faces. Even that can cause us to refocus our eyes. It also holds true that when we bring the aircraft's wings, or cowling, into focus, distant objects lose their detail. It's no wonder that our eyes can be in an almost constant focus-refocus mode throughout an entire flight.

A good example often presents itself on vacations. Imagine a trip to the Grand Tetons, and we stop for a picture. I'm driving, and you decide it's a bit too breezy to step outside, so you want to take a picture from the car window. You grab the camera from the back seat, down comes the window and out comes the camera. Depending upon f-stop and other factors of course, when you focus on a mountain, the mountain produces a good picture. However, the corner of the headrest that you didn't see in the viewfinder is a blurry blob in the corner of the frame as is the bear you didn't see standing just outside the window by the back seat. Noticing the bear, you decide that photographing that cute berry-eating grizzly bear just outside of the car is a good idea. The mountain is now out of focus in the background as you focus in on the bear's cute little smile. You notice this just before the bear swipes the camera out of your hand while trying for that bologna sandwich on the dash. I speed away while you yell at me for not warning you about the dangers inherent in the sport of photography.

In each case there is a compromise. Besides the poor judgment with the bear, there is a limit to the focusing ability of the camera. A balance must be met with seeing both distant and very near objects. Similar limits appear in the focusing of human eyes.

The constant refocusing is not bad. If we didn't refocus, an instrument cross-check would be impossible. But to ensure safe separation from other aircraft, that all-important visual scan must also be tuned to the appropriate range to be most effective. Refer once again to Fig. 1-1. The FAA says that these patterns can be accomplished in about 10 seconds. Conversely, a navy study on visual acuity says that 5 seconds are needed for each block of the scan. Obviously, there is a discrepancy. This difference of opinion becomes quite apparent when scanning in a featureless sky.

It is possible to do complete and disciplined scan patterns in every 10 to 20 seconds, as the FAA recommends. However, because the eye isn't focused beyond the length of the plane, a long-range visual contact on a relatively small object is unlikely without the assisting cue of motion. That head-on Tomahawk, not moving on the canopy because it is on a collision course, keeps closing in range, unnoticed.

So how can we conduct a focused but complete and rapid scan pattern in a disciplined manner? How can we follow both FAA guidelines and respect the research done on scanning and focusing? One possible solution is a technique taught to air force fighter pilots, who frequently rely on their "Mark-1 Eyeballs" for detecting enemy planes. It is simple enough for any student pilot, or even any crush-capped, crusty 747 captain, to use.

Figure 1-11 demonstrates graphically the technique of using clouds, cultural features, or man-made objects to focus the eye during a scan pattern. In each scan block, note an object such as a cloud, train, or a pond. Pick an object several miles away, about the distance you want to search for other planes. The faster your plane goes, the farther away in front of your plane you want to look. A compromise dis-

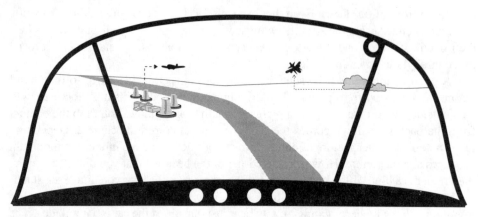

Fig. 1-11. *Example of a scan pattern in a clear, featureless sky.*

tance for light, general aircraft is 5 to 10 miles. According to the navy study, this should take three to five seconds, after which you immediately scan your block. Move to the next block, find an object, and repeat the procedure. Vary distances to ensure a thorough scan and to reduce fatigue. Remember to also look both above and beneath your altitude.

A common mistake made by civilians and fighter jocks alike is to concentrate too long on only the horizon. The reason we fly with a stick or yoke instead of a steering wheel is because planes operate in three dimensions. This concept is very important because the "big-sky" theory breaks down without warning. Even fighter planes hit one another, and they have multi-million dollar radars to avoid each other. There is no substitute for looking out the windows and scanning correctly and intently.

Another problem with a featureless sky is that it is usually associated with a nice day. On nice days, the air is calm, the sun is bright, and everything is wonderful and trouble-free at 4500 feet. It's time to relax, like on a lawn chair in the backyard. Have a soda, listen to the radio. Then . . . BAMM! It's called complacency, and must be guarded against. Performing a disciplined, visual search pattern provides ample opportunity to look around, but it also prevent mid-airs.

Entering the pattern of an airfield, particularly an uncontrolled airport on a clear day, is notoriously hazardous. More aircraft are airborne in fine weather than on a dreary day, which means more complacent, unfocused pilots flying carelessly. Use proper focusing and scanning techniques to enter the pattern. Focus on the runway or tower from a distance, then look up to pattern altitude for your initial entry. Also look for high-to-low and low-to-high planes on takeoff or landing. Expect the occasional but usually unexpected blundering pilot who stumbles through the pattern without ever realizing other planes are aloft. Proper scanning, particularly in fine, clear weather, avoids unpleasant surprises caused by unfocused eyes and complacency.

More on scanning techniques

The Naval Aerospace Research Laboratory Study, NAMRL Monograph 41, March 1990, noted that the fixations that occur during a scan require about ⅓ of a second. And as we saw in Fig. 1-5, the closer a target is to your plane the fewer fixations you need to scan due to the larger visual detection lobe. So, besides the fact that closer planes are bigger than distant ones, fewer scans are required, and a visual pick-up is much more likely than during a long-range acquisition process.

The naval study goes further to recommend that visual search should be spaced widely apart to help cover a large area of the sky in a minimum of time. This recommendation agrees with the FAA's basic premise of rapid scanning. But the navy study tells us to not expect long-range visual contacts; inside of two nautical miles is more likely. To help make the most of the eyes we have, a systematic visual search is recommended.

A *sector scan* is one method of breaking up the sky. Although a scan pattern recommended by the FAA appears in Figs. 1-1A and 1-1B, the navy study divides the sky into horizontal and vertical sectors (Fig. 1-12). Even though all aircraft do not have two sets of eyes, a bubble cockpit, and the ability to roll upside down to scan 360 degrees in all directions, it is possible to see how we might divide the sky into more manageable sections to concentrate our scan patterns.

The FAA Aviation News reported that:

> You can generally avoid the threat of an inflight collision by scanning 60 degrees to the left and right, and 10 degrees up and down.

Figure 1-13 graphically depicts the areas recommended by the FAA to concentrate your visual search. By combining the naval sector idea (Fig. 1-12) with the side-to-side or front-to-side scanning patterns (Figs. 1-1A and 1-1B) with a concentration of scanning in the direction of your flight path ±60 degrees azimuth and ± degrees elevation), you might develop a scanning technique for yourself. Be sure to include or try techniques presented by qualified instructor pilots, and build habit patterns for yourself. The best technique in the world does no good if you forget to use it.

Clearing turns, S-turns on final or after takeoff to look under your nose, and belly checks—rolling out of bank part way through a turn to see if someone is going to hit your plane's belly—are all techniques to add to your usual scan. Check behind yourself as well as up and down at least once per critical phase of flight. I prefer to look much more frequently. This could prevent that fast twin from descending on top of you during a localizer approach or let you see that jerk trying to cut you off on final when you do a belly check.

After acquiring traffic

Scan techniques are great, but seeing the other guy is only half of the equation. Illusions might cause you to hesitate in taking evasive maneuvers. For instance, an aircraft at more than a mile distant might appear above you in altitude when it is actually

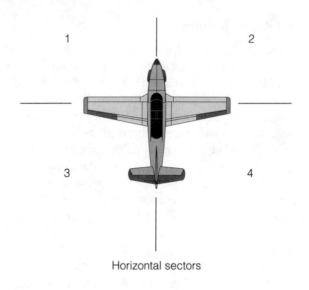

Horizontal sectors

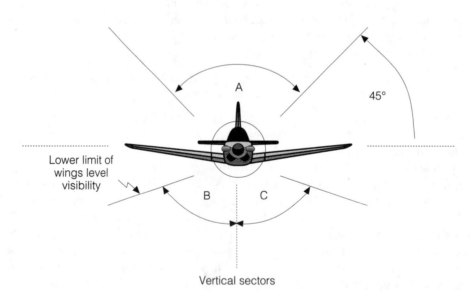

Vertical sectors

Fig. 1-12. *U.S. Navy recommended visual search sectors. Divide the sky into horizontal and vertical sectors.* Naval Aerospace Medical Research Laboratory

level. Also, a plane on a collision course might appear to be remaining the same size, and not closing, until those final few seconds when it gets big really fast. An early evasive maneuver to cause the traffic to begin moving on your canopy can help ensure a greater miss distance. If an aircraft remains motionless for several seconds in the same position on your windscreen, then it probably is on a collision or near-collision course. Remember: An early maneuver to avoid traffic is better than a late one.

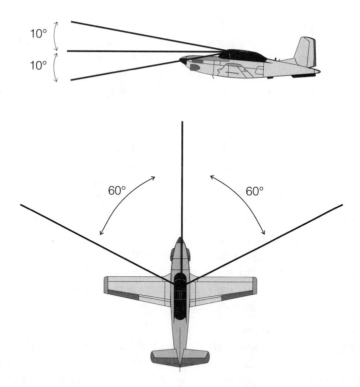

Fig. 1-13. *FAA-recommended visual search sectors. Scan 60 degrees to the left and right and 10 degrees up and down.* Federal Aviation Administration

Putting it all together: a collision-avoidance checklist

The FAA has some good ideas to prepare and execute safe collision-avoidance techniques. After some adaptation, I've compiled a simple guide to think about using before your next flight. In fact, I would incorporate many of these questions and points into all flight planning. As you get more questions, or if you have a more detailed guide, consider adding some of the following items. These are techniques only, not a be-all, end-all checklist.

1. Self-check

   How is your physical and emotional condition? Did you get enough sleep? Are you in the mood to fly? Are you prepared mentally? Are your glasses or contacts cleaned? Did you eat breakfast? Are you under a lot of personal stress?

2. Preflight planning—accomplish

   Did you get weather and Notices to Airmen (NOTAMs)? Do you have all the correct maps and publications? Have you highlighted your route on the maps and folded them neatly? Have you calculated gas? Do you know information about unfamiliar airfields? Have you checked frequencies? Have you called ATC if you are planning multiple approaches to avoid bad timing? Have you checked for student flying areas? Will you be crossing military low-level flying routes or active military operating areas (MOAs)? Doing these activities on the ground, before the flight, saves heads-down time in the cockpit while airborne.

3. Aircraft preflight—accomplish

Obviously you should follow all published aircraft checklists. Pay special attention, when considering avoiding mid-airs, to a clean canopy. It isn't going to get any cleaner than before you start up that engine. Get good sunglasses, polarized and clean. Avoid solid sun visors and shades because they block areas of the sky from your now-practiced scan pattern.

4. FARs and Standard Operating Procedures (SOPs)—know and follow

In your planning, you researched the SOPs for your airfield and any you might fly to. Use ATC to the maximum extent available, and file a flight plan when possible. Know how to enter patterns at strange fields, and consider avenues where conflict aircraft might appear.

5. Congested areas—avoid

When planning, or when flying, expect VORs, major landmarks (highways, rivers, etc.) and local attractions to have other traffic in the area. Avoid military airfields by as much as 25 miles. Many fighters have waivers to operate at more than 250 knots below 10,000 feet, and during climbout they might be going as fast as 400 knots. Avoid the extended approach areas for fields with instrument approaches. Don't even try to do multiple patterns at very busy commercial fields.

6. Aircraft limitations—review

Every plane, besides having 20 airspeeds to memorize, has certain characteristics that aid or limit a visual search. Know these limits for your plane and create a strategy for compensation. For instance, when flying a Cessna 152, you might have trouble seeing into turns, but looking down is no problem. For a 90-degree turn, it helps to roll out of bank every 30 degrees or so, to clear the flight path. Conversely, when flying a low-wing Grumman Tiger, it is easy to scan into a turn. However, I might do more belly-checks when entering a pattern to check under that low-wing for unannounced traffic.

7. Lights—on

For the most part, lights are a gimme. No one will charge you more if you turn them on, so consider it. The FAA reports that high-intensity strobes could increase your plane's contrast by up to 10 times, day or night. Turn them all on if it won't drain your battery too much.

8. Transponder—on

Use Mode-3 and -C, both the four-digit code and the altitude function activated. When possible, file a flight plan or at least pick up flight following for traffic advisories. Ask ATC to give you a discrete transponder code to highlight yourself, particularly in a busy area. ATC wants to help you, so you help them.

9. Radio—use

Learn how to talk and listen to a VHF radio. If you can afford a headset, it could be worth the price by allowing you to keep scanning while you talk, instead of hunting around with your head inside the cockpit looking for a mike to respond to a traffic call. Call airports with a radar service early. If flying to an airport with only a UNICOM, tune the frequency early and listen to the traffic. Put together a mental picture of where every airplane is, and use that situational awareness (SA) to plan your scan for entry into the pattern. Tell people where you are, precisely, with altitude.

10. Scan—accomplish

Learn and practice scan techniques. Try new ones. Talk with old heads about their close calls, and chair-fly how you would handle the situation. Build a scanning-habit pattern, so you concentrate on scanning in all phases of flight. It must be a conscious effort before you strap on that aircraft. Remember: If you are wondering what you need to do next, or feel like you finally got all your ducks in a row, then you are wrong. If you are not doing something at all times in a plane, then you must be forgetting to do something. If the task at hand is done, don't just look out the windows—SCAN!

SECTION REVIEW: THE REALITY

Minimum Visual Detection Area theory states that the fuselage of the threat aircraft must fill 12 minutes of arc.

Featureless sky:

Aircraft are very difficult to detect in a clear, featureless sky. Our eyes are almost in a constant state of focus and refocus.

Scan patterns in a featureless sky include:

- Focus on distant object, then immediately scan block in that area.

- The faster your plane flies, the farther in front you must scan.

- Vary distances to ensure thorough scan and to reduce fatigue.

- Always scan above and beneath your altitude.

- Don't stay focused on one object for too long.

- Maintain vigilance and don't get complacent.

- Maintain proper focusing and scanning techniques when entering the pattern.

Scan techniques
Sector scanning

- 60 degrees off nose
- 10 degrees above/below

After acquiring traffic
- Illusions
- S-turns
- Belly checks

Putting it all together
- Checklist

Chapter 1 references

Edwards, Gerald, James Harris, Sr. 1972. "Visual Aspects of Air Collision Avoidance: Computer Studies on Pilot Warning Indicator Specifications". NASA.

George, Fred. April 1991. "Can You See in Time to Avoid?" *Flying:* 81-4.

Hanff, G.E. 1966. Collision Avoidance Visibility. Lockheed Corporation.

Harris, Randall, Bobby Glover, Amos Spady. 1986. "Analytical Techniques of Pilot Scanning Behavior and Their Application". NASA.

Howell, Wayne. 1957. "Determination of Daytime Conspicuity of Transport Aircraft. Civil Aeronautics Administration".

Proctor, Paul. 27 April 1987. "FAA Investigators Seek Pattern in Near Midair Collisions". *Aviation Week and Space Technology:* 63-4.

Rosdahl, C. 1985. *Textbook of Basic Nursing, 4th ed.* Philadelphia: J.B. Lippincott: 118.

Schallhorn, S., K. Daill, W.B. Cushman, R. Unterreiner. 1990. "Visual Search in Air Combat". Naval Aerospace Medical Research Laboratory.

Steenblik, Jan W. 1988. "The Eyes Don't Have It". *Air Line Pilot.* October: 10-16, 57.

National Transportation Safety Board. 19 June 1968. Aircraft Accident Report: TransWorld Airlines, Inc., Douglas DC-9, Tann Company Beechcraft Baron B-55 In-Flight Collision, Near Urbana, Ohio, March 9, 1967. Washington, D.C.

Selected Statistics Concerning Pilot-Reported Near Midair Collisions (1984-1987). 1989. U.S. Department of Transportation. Federal Aviation Administration.

"Four Eyes Are Better Than Two—Or Are They?" September-October 1987. *FAA Aviation News*: 4-5.

How to Avoid a Mid-air Collision. September-October 1987: 7-9.

"Vision System Puts Eyesight in Blind Spots". 27 April 1991. *Science News:* 262.

2
The role of air traffic control

THE ROLE OF AIR TRAFFIC CONTROL (ATC) IS EASILY ONE OF THE MOST misunderstood and misinterpreted concepts in flying. Pilots are often confused as to the scope of ATC coverage and services, proper communication techniques, and correct phraseology. The ATC system as a whole is one of the more prominent and important resources we have for collision avoidance, yet it is sometimes disregarded or misused simply because pilots have never fully learned how it all works.

What you always wanted to know about ATC equipment

It's best to let the experts handle the nuts and bolts of ATC equipment. I will, however, touch on some relevant points concerning radar and radar coverage. Before getting into that, I'd like to address a more intangible side to air traffic control. You can always count on two very unpredictable variables in the system: pilots and controllers.

Days of the Great Waldo Pepper are gone

Taking off without telling anyone, doing a few aileron rolls off the end of the run-way, punchin' some holes through the white puffies. Those days are gone forever, at least the days of legally flying in this manner. However, the news seems not to have reached every pilot. True, these instances are few and far between, but flying in the wrong airspace, at the wrong altitudes, at the wrong headings, and without permission is not rare. Those mistakes were made before a new classification of airspace got un-derway, which could add to the confusion for some pilots.

Your very own (new) piece of the sky

As of 16 September 1993, a new definition of airspace classification went into ef-fect. No more of those familiar acronyms: PCA, TCA, ARSA, ATA. Even the terms of controlled and uncontrolled airspace no longer exist. They are now all letter-desig-nated, A through E and G.

(The letter F is used internationally but not in the United States.)

Examine Fig. 2-1. The FAA still hasn't mastered an "easy to read" airspace seg-ment diagram, but it is a bit less confusing than the previous system.

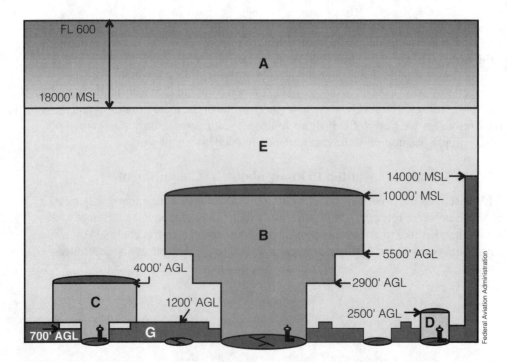

Fig. 2-1. *Airspace reclassification.*

A, B, C, D, E, AND G

The new classification of airspace conforms to the international definitions and certain changes from the previous classifications apply.

Class A airspace

Class A is the new name for the Positive Control Area (PCA). The airspace is still controlled from 18,000 MSL to FL 600 and includes the jet routes. Just like before, airspace entry is only through ATC clearance, you must be instrument-rated, file an IFR flight plan, and maintain two-way radio communication.

Class A airspace quick reference

Class A airspace	IFR	VFR
Operations permitted	Yes	No
Entry requirements	ATC clearance	n/a
Minimum pilot qualifications	Instrument rating	n/a
2-way radio communications	Yes	n/a
Aircraft separation	All	n/a
Changes from existing rules	No	n/a

Derived from *FAA Aviation News*—Reprint

Class B airspace

Class B is the new name for a Terminal Control Area (TCA). ATC clearance is required for airspace entry, and it's still available to both IFR and VFR traffic provided the pilot is at least instrument-rated when flying in IMC and holds at least a student pilot certificate when operating under VMC.

Traffic advisories and safety alerts are, of course, available from ATC. The minimum for VFR flight is still 3 statute miles, but the big difference is in the minimum distance from clouds. Under the new classification, when VFR in Class B airspace, you just need to be "clear of clouds." The old rule, under TCA airspace, was 500 feet below, 1000 feet above, and 2000 feet horizontal.

Class B airspace quick reference

Class B airspace	IFR	VFR
Operations permitted	Yes	Yes
Entry requirements	ATC clearance	ATC clearance
Minimum pilot qualifications	Instrument rating	Student
2-way radio communications	Yes	Yes
Aircraft separation	All	All
Traffic advisories	Yes	Yes**
Safety alerts	Yes	Yes
Minimum flight visibility	n/a	3 statute miles
Minimum distance from clouds	n/a	Clear of clouds

Changes from existing rules	No	Yes

**Workload permitting
Derived from *FAA Aviation News*—Reprint

Class C airspace

Class C airspace used to be known as Airport Radar Service Area (ARSA). Airspace entry for IFR traffic requires ATC clearance, whereas VFR traffic must provide radio contact. You still must be instrument-rated to fly IFR in Class C, and at least a student pilot to operate under VFR. Aircraft separation services are only between IFR-IFR and IFR-VFR traffic (no VFR-VFR).

And remember the speed restrictions: 250 KIAS below 10,000 feet MSL and 200 KIAS below 2500 feet AGL within 4 nm of the primary airport.

Class C airspace quick reference

Class C airspace	IFR	VFR
Operations permitted	Yes	Yes
Entry requirements	ATC clearance	Radio contact
Minimum pilot qualifications	Instrument rating	Student
2-way radio communication	Yes	Yes
Aircraft separation	All	IFR-VFR
Traffic advisories	Yes	Yes**
Safety alerts	Yes	Yes
Minimum flight visibility	n/a	3 sm*
Minimum distance from clouds	n/a	500' below 1000' above 2000' horizontal

*Statute miles
**Workload permitting
Derived from *FAA Aviation News—Reprint*

Class D airspace

The old classifications of Class D airspace were Airport Traffic Areas (ATA) and Control Zones (CZ). Entry requisites, minimum flight visibility, and minimum distance from the clouds have all remained the same. The big changes, however, pertain to the new ceilings in the Class D airspace. The upper limits of the Control Zone has been lowered from 14,500 feet MSL to 2500 feet AGL. The upper limits of the Airport Traffic Area has been lowered from 2999 feet AGL to 2500 AGL.

Class D Airspace Quick Review

Class D airspace	IFR	VFR
Operations permitted	Yes	Yes
Entry requirements	ATC clearance	Radio contact
Minimum pilot qualifications	Instrument rating	Student

Minimum flight visibility	n/a	3 sm*
Minimum distance from clouds	n/a	500' below
		1000' above
		2000' horizontal
Changes from existing rules	No	No

*Statute miles
Derived from *FAA Aviation News—Reprint*

Class E airspace

Class E airspace used to be known as Controlled Airspace—General. The primary requirements have remained the same, but the specifics of flight operations can still be a little confusing, so it is worth reviewing them.

- Minimum flight visibility: 3 statute miles below 10,000 feet MSL; 5 miles at or above 10,000 feet MSL.
- Minimum distance from clouds: 500 feet below, 1000 feet above, and 2000 feet horizontal below 10,000 feet MSL. 1000 feet below, 1000 feet above, and 1 statute mile horizontal at or above 10,000 feet MSL.

Class E airspace quick reference

Class E airspace	IFR	VFR
Operations permitted	Yes	Yes
Entry requirements	ATC clearance	None
Minimum pilot qualifications	Instrument rating	Student
2-way radio communications	Yes	No
Aircraft separation	IFR/SVFR*	n/a
Traffic advisories	**	**
Safety alerts	Yes	Yes
Minimum flight visibility	n/a	see preceding text
Minimum distance from clouds	n/a	see preceding text
Changes from existing rules	No	No

*Special VFR
**Workload permitting
Derived from *FAA Aviation News—Reprint*

Class G airspace

Class G airspace was once known as Uncontrolled Airspace. There are specific changes; however, it's important to note that there will continue to be airports in Class G airspace. At those airports with an instrument approach procedure, the floor of controlled airspace will generally be a Class E area extending upward from 700 feet AGL.

As with Class E airspace, there are very definite requirements pertaining to flight operations.

- Minimum flight visibility: Night operations below 10,000 feet MSL—3 statute miles. Day or night operations at or above 10,000 feet MSL—5 statute miles.
- Minimum distance from clouds: Operations above 1200 AGL, but less than 10,000 MSL—500 feet below, 1000 feet above, 2000 feet horizontal. Operations at or above 10,000 feet MSL—1000 feet below, 1000 feet above, 1 statute mile horizontal.

Class G airspace quick reference

Class G airspace	IFR	VFR
Operations permitted	Yes	Yes
Entry requirements	None	None
Minimum pilot qualifications	Instrument rating	Student
2-way radio communication	No	No
Aircraft separation	None	None
Traffic advisories	**	**
Safety alerts	Yes	Yes
Minimum flight visibility	n/a	1 sm*
Minimum distance from clouds	n/a	see preceding text
Changes existing rules	No	No

*Statute mile
**Workload permitting
Derived from *FAA Aviation News—Reprint*

You can't be a little illegal

We pilots aren't off the hook just yet. We have to live up to our end of the bargain, which means controllers can't always help us if we're violating established rules. Let's use the example of unauthorized airspace entry. Although some pilots make a habit of illegally sneaking through controlled airspace, it's more likely that pilots inadvertently cross these boundaries. Regardless, if the pilot doesn't understand the airplanes's position in relation to different segments of airspace or gets distracted and doesn't realize what has done, unauthorized airspace entry can be an extremely dangerous predicament to be in.

I've lost him on radar

The following report of a mid-air collision is a good illustration of how easy it can be for a pilot to unintentionally enter controlled airspace and the tragic consequences that can follow.

Background information

15 January 1987. Skywest Flight 1834, a Metro II turboprop, collided with a single-engine Mooney M20 near Salt Lake City, Utah, at 7000 feet.

Pilot experience: Skywest captain: 3885 total flight hours, 1863 hours in Metroliner series aircraft. Skywest first officer: 4555 total flight hours, 1205 hours in Metroliner series aircraft. Mooney flight instructor: 2548 total flight hours, 1332 as a flight instructor. Mooney pilot: 301 total flight hours.

Reported weather at time of accident: High scattered clouds. Visibility 10 to 20 miles. Ground was snow-covered.

Probable cause

The NTSB determined that the probable cause of this accident was the lack of navigational vigilance by the Mooney instructor-pilot, which led to the unauthorized intrusion into the Salt Lake City Airport Radar Service Area (ARSA). Contributing to the accident were the absence of a Mode-C transponder on the Mooney and the limitations of the air traffic control system to provide collision protection.

The accident

At 1250:28, Mountain Standard Time, Flight 1834 was in contact with the Salt Lake City International Airport final controller and had been cleared to descend to 7000 feet. For the next minute and a half the controller gave the Skywest crew a couple of heading changes and vectors around arriving traffic. Flight 1834 collided with the Mooney at 1251:58.

At approximately noon, the pilot of the Mooney performed touch-and-go landings at the Salt Lake Municipal 2 Airport (SLC 2). SLC 2 is located about 10 miles southwest of Salt Lake International. The Board could only speculate that the purpose of the flight was to give instrument instruction to the pilot.

By 1235 the Mooney had left the SLC 2 traffic pattern and had proceeded 25 miles to the southeast of Salt Lake International before turning towards the northwest. During the course of the investigation, the Board learned that general-aviation pilots often used "homemade" instrument approaches off a commercial radio station beacon. The observed ground track of the Mooney appeared to be heading straight towards that beacon, therefore, the Board determined that it was possible the pilots were using that procedure during instrument training.

According to the investigation, it was while the pilots of the Mooney appeared to be on course with the radio station beacon that they inadvertently entered the ARSA. About one minute later the Mooney collided with the Skywest.

The Board concluded that at the time of impact, the Mooney was in a level-flight, left bank of about 15 degrees, and the Metro II was in a left bank of about 30 degrees with a nose-up pitch attitude of 24 degrees.

The aftermath

The Board determined that the crew of Flight 1834 had made an evasive maneuver seconds before impact but too late to avoid the collision. The two pilots and six passengers aboard the Metro II and the two pilots aboard the Mooney were killed.

The investigation

The investigation centered on two key issues: First, the Board wanted to determine why the Mooney pilots unintentionally entered the ARSA. And second, they needed to learn why the final controller did not issue a traffic advisory to Flight 1834.

ARSA airspace

The vertical limits of the Salt Lake ARSA 5-mile circle extended from the surface to 8200 feet. The 10-mile outer circle vertical limits extended from 5400 feet to 8200 feet. The exception of those limits was a "keyhole" in the south quadrant of the 10-mile outer circle that accommodated traffic from the SLC 2 airport. It was also used as the localizer course for the ILS to Salt Lake International. The vertical limits for the "keyhole" area was from 5800 feet to 8200 feet.

Entering the ARSA

The NTSB looked at several theories as to why the pilots of the Mooney inadvertently entered the ARSA. One of the possible explanations was that both pilots were distracted while practicing instrument procedures and were unaware that they had overflown SLC 2 and had crossed into the ARSA. However, because of the lack of hard evidence, the Board was unable to indisputably determine that was the case. Regardless of the actual cause, however, the Board did conclude that the instructor pilot had the responsibility of remaining vigilant over the navigational status of the airplane, including its ground track and altitude.

According to the accident report, the inadvertent intrusion of the ARSA by the Mooney pilots was a causal factor because neither the Skywest crew nor the final controller was expecting an aircraft operating at 7000 feet within the ARSA without radio contact. The pilots in the Mooney had the responsibility to remain clear of the ARSA. Consequently, their failure to do so was causal to the mid-air collision.

A side note of interest

Here's what the FAA has to say about "homemade and makeshift" instrument approaches: FAA Bulletin 78-14 states that such approaches cannot be used for purposes of meeting the requirements of instrument training and certification. However, it is not uncommon for instructor pilots to use such procedures during instrument training and those practices are acceptable for basic training in instrument skills.

The controller's actions

The second issue the Board investigated was why there were no pertinent traffic advisories provided to either aircraft although both targets appeared on the final controller's radar scope. According to the report, the final controller's first priority was to separate Flight 1834 from other IFR traffic. Because the Mooney was not equipped with a Mode-C transponder, nor had contacted ATC for a discrete transponder code, the airplane appeared as an untracked VFR target.

The final controller testified that he and his colleagues at Salt Lake International were accustomed to observing non-Mode-C targets operating in and near the traffic pattern at SLC 2, presumably below the ARSA. They believed to have had an understandable expectation that such targets were not within the ARSA airspace if they were not in radio contact.

Shortly before the accident, the final controller was working an arriving Boeing 737 and had noted that the airliner's data block had overlapped the Mooney's target for 38 seconds. About 48 seconds before the mid-air, the two targets separated on the radar display and the controller noticed that the untracked target was nearly directly over the SLC 2 airport. At that time it was no longer a concern to the final controller.

According to the report, the final controller said he did not see any VFR targets in the vicinity of the Skywest before the collision, and he had no reason to believe that the target he had observed earlier was the airplane later involved in the accident. However, during the several seconds after the Mooney's target passed to the north of SLC 2, the final controller was busy providing traffic advisories to Flight 1834 concerning traffic other than the Mooney. The Board believed that because the Mooney was not in radio contact with the final controller, it was understandable that even if the controller had noticed the target in the seconds before the collision he might have subconsciously dismissed it as being in the traffic pattern at SLC 2 and below the ARSA, as it was expected to be.

Although the Board concluded that the final controller's failure to detect the traffic conflict and to provide safety advisories was an element in the events that led to the accident, it determined that the controller's performance was not considered a causal factor because of the circumstances of the conflict. The Mooney was untracked, not in radio contact, and assumed to be below the ARSA airspace.

PRACTICAL APPLICATIONS AND LESSONS LEARNED

1. Always know your exact position. You should be aware of your location especially when you're a "squawking 1200," untracked, VFR target. Think of it as maintaining navigational vigilance.

2. Maintain a thorough visual scan. A lot of activity occurs near airspace segment boundaries, so you must maintain a thorough visual scan.

3. Don't fly near airspace boundaries unless you have a legitimate reason. These areas can be dangerous. Don't practice your airwork around them. You might be legal, but it's just plain stupid. If you find yourself skirting the airspace between two segments, maintain visual and navigational vigilance.

4. Communication does not mean inconvenience. Many pilots would rather stay out of, or beneath, controlled airspace just to avoid using the radio. In this particular case, the pilots of the Mooney would most likely have been allowed to do exactly what they wanted to do, with little subsequent interference from ATC, if they had notified ATC. They would have gone about their business but with one important difference: They would have been a tracked target.

MORE RESPONSIBILITIES AND OBLIGATIONS

Pilots have responsibilities and obligations to themselves, to other traffic, and to the air traffic control system for the orderly and efficient flow of traffic as well as for safety.

Entering Class B airspace

Let's examine some of these responsibilities and obligations before entering Class B airspace. As an example, you've been talking with approach control and told them of your intentions. Most likely you want either to land at an airport within that airspace or to fly through it enroute to your destination. After receiving a new transponder code and squawking ident approach says, "Radar contact."

What does "radar contact" mean to you?

1. I'm not cleared into Class B airspace; ATC just has me on their radar.

2. Because approach knows of my intentions, "radar contact" automatically means that I'm cleared into Class B airspace. The correct answer is "1."

Many pilots have long misunderstood the phrase "radar contact" to mean that they have received ATC clearance into that airspace. It does not.

According to the Airman's Information Manual (AIM), the definition of "radar contact" has two parts. Most pilots don't get past the first section, but it's the second statement that gets pilots in some pretty hairy, and illegal, predicaments.

1. Controller-to-pilot. "Used by ATC to inform an aircraft that it is identified on the radar display and radar flight following will be provided until radar identification is terminated." When informed of "radar contact," a pilot automatically discontinues reporting over compulsory reporting points.

    Nowhere in the definition does it say ". . . proceed into controlled airspace . . .."

2. Controller-to-controller. ". . . to inform the controller that the aircraft is identified and approval is granted for the flight to enter the receiving controller's airspace."

    All this means is that your aircraft is identified on the radar scope, and that a handoff into the next controller's airspace is approved. Again, no additional sentence gives the pilot permission to enter Class B airspace.

So, the only way that you're allowed to enter B airspace is when you hear the words, "Cleared to enter (or 'into') B airspace." Until that happens you must remain outside of the controlled airspace. And while you wait, remember to still scan, scan, scan.

Radar following services

Before we move on, another term needs to be addressed. In the first part of the "radar contact" definition, there is a statement ". . . radar following will be provided . . .." Does this mean, "kick back and let ATC do the flying?" Absolutely not. Controllers weren't put on this earth to hold the hands of lazy pilots.

According to the AIM, the definition of "radar flight following" is: "The observation of the progress of radar-identified aircraft, whose primary navigation is being provided by the pilot . . .." Therefore, it's still up to the pilot to maintain the correct heading and altitude and always know the exact position. Basically, ATC still expects you to fly your airplane.

Staying VFR is still a pilot's responsibility

There's that "R" word again. By now, it should be obvious that even under the watchful eye of ATC, the safety of a flight is still the pilot's responsibility. The following are a few additional examples of responsibilities when operating under VFR.

1. If flying through Class B or Class C airspace, you might be advised to "remain VFR." What if there are clouds around? That's why it is so important to understand the legal requirements for the minimum distance from clouds (refer back to the Quick Reference guides). ATC is not going to do it for you.

2. Likewise, a controller could vector you too close to an area of clouds. It's up to you to advise the controller that you'll violate the VFR cloud separation minimums if you accept the vector.

3. Another common occurrence is ATC assigning a non-VFR altitude. That's fine, he put you there for a reason. But when you're told to "resume own navigation" or "maintain VFR altitude," that means to climb or descend to the appropriate VFR altitude and stay there.

VFR altitudes

While I'm on the subject of VFR altitudes, let's refresh your memory on what they are. When flying VFR, in level flight above 3000 feet AGL and below 18,000 feet, the rule is as follows:

Magnetic Course: 0–179 degrees, odd thousands MSL + 500 feet.
For example: 3500 feet, 5500 feet.
Magnetic Course: 180–359 degrees, even thousands MSL + 500 feet.
For example: 4500 feet, 6500 feet.

Setting the record straight

The intended purpose of ATC is to promote the safe and orderly separation of traffic. Sounds good. But there's a catch. According to FAA Order 7110.65E, "Controllers shall give priority to separating IFR aircraft . . . ." It further states that, ". . . traffic advisories are provided as an additional service . . . workload permitting and contingent upon higher priority duties."

In the wake of another mid-air, that between Wings West Flight 628 and a Rockwell Commander (see chapter 3), the FAA reemphasized, through a prepared statement, that:

. . . assigning of discrete transponder codes in this situation [under ATC supervision] could lead pilots into believing they are receiving a service that the controller might not be able to provide.

The FAA added:

". . . advisory services provided to VFR traffic are predicated on workload, frequency congestion, radar limitations, and traffic volume."

In a nutshell, VFR traffic will receive advisories only if ATC is not busy or if there is a potential safety conflict. Unfortunately, this regulation is sometimes misunderstood or misused by the pilot community.

AIR TRAFFIC CONTROL AND THE VFR PILOT

Let's put this in perspective by using a few examples.

1. "Well, I'm squawking a discrete transponder code, and I've been periodically talking with ATC. So it goes without saying that I'll be provided with traffic advisories."

   No, you won't. Even though you're "squawking and talking," remember, you're still VFR. Don't expect to automatically get traffic advisories. It's neither a regulation nor obligation for ATC to provide that service to you.

   However, you have a regulation to follow. It is that you: ". . . shall maintain vigilance to see and avoid other aircraft."

   A suggestion: After you've made your initial radio call and hear "radar contact," request traffic advisories. There's still no guarantee that you'll receive any, due to ATC workload at the time, but at least if the controller has a few extra minutes you could be at the top of the list to get one or two. On the other hand, the controller might not be busy at all so you might be lucky and end up receiving more advisories than you know what to do with. In the world of collision avoidance, you can never have too many traffic advisories.

2. "I'm not really sure where Class B airspace begins, but I'm sure approach will tell me if I accidentally fly into it."

   Don't count on it. First, an attitude like that is irresponsible. Second, it goes back to the reason controllers were put on this earth, and it wasn't to watch out for pilots who don't bother to figure out their positions. If you do get a response from ATC, you might get a call for a "violation notification" or to tell you that you've just been involved in a near-miss with a 727.

Another suggestion: Know your exact position and where you are in relation to other airspace, for two important reasons. One, you must be aware of the surrounding airspace boundaries. It's just too dangerous to be aimlessly buzzing around those areas. And two, when you supply ATC with a position report, they are probably vectoring traffic dependent on that information. If you're only guessing, or you think a ballpark estimate is good enough, it's not. Mid-airs and near-misses have directly resulted from erroneous position reports from pilots.

Diffusion of responsibility

The previous two scenarios are actual examples of a concept known as "diffusion of responsibility." The tendency is for pilots to relax attentiveness and vigilance when under radar control. It's safe to say that all of us have been guilty of this mistake from time to time. Remember, the little blinking amber light on the transponder in the cockpit does not mean "sit back and relax."

The National Aeronautics and Space Administration (NASA) conducted a study on near mid-air collisions and found a definite connection between those incidents and the state of vigilance, or lack of vigilance, of the pilot in a controlled environment. The researchers viewed this condition as a subconscious idea of shared responsibility between pilot and controller. The study states that many pilots, under ATC supervision, believe that they will be advised of traffic that represents a potential conflict. Therefore, they tend to relax their visual scan for other aircraft until warned of its presence.

Back when I didn't know any better, I remember the overwhelming sense of relief I experienced when I heard those calming words, "radar contact." I felt totally safe. "ATC's got me. They won't let anything bad happen to me." In that state of naiveté, I was actually, and unwittingly, handing over the keys of the airplane to the controller. Remember, when you're looking out the window more to sightsee than to watch for traffic, you have just demoted yourself from pilot-in-command to baggage.

A reduced state of vigilance

While we're on the subject of responsibility, yet another condition needs to be mentioned. A reduced state of vigilance can affect both pilots and controllers.

A pilot's perspective. Anytime a pilot shares his responsibilities with a controller, he is, in effect, also reducing his state of vigilance. No longer is the pilot being attentive to a visual search, navigation, systems checks, fuel checks, and just about anything else. "ATC will tell me when there's traffic or when I'm off course. And besides, I'm only 10 minutes from landing, I'm home free!"

In the next chapter you'll see how dangerous the problem really is. Whether the pilot is doing it consciously or not, it still has the same tragic results.

A controller's perspective. The NTSB conducted a study on a reduced state of vigilance after noticing a distinct pattern in the circumstances surrounding many controller mistakes. This situation, especially during light-to-moderate-traffic workloads, had contributed to five mid-air collisions between April 1988 and April 1989.

Results from this study show that controllers have a tendency to relax their level of alertness in a low-workload environment, which makes them susceptible to operational errors and omissions. In addition, because of their FAA training and experience levels, controllers tend to focus an inordinate amount of attention to targets that have been identified (tracked/IFR) as opposed to those that are unidentified (untracked /VFR).

Runway incursions: Kissin' cousins to mid-air collisions

ATC-related runway incursions—collisions between aircraft and vehicles while still on the ground—are very similar in nature to mid-air collisions. Whether airplanes are being moved on the ground or in the air, controllers still must remain alert and vigilant. Because ground incursions are not a particularly uncommon occurrence, the NTSB conducted a special investigation.

The study concluded, foremost, that heavy traffic and reduced visibility were rarely a factor. On the contrary, traffic was reported light or moderate at the time of most of the incursions where controller actions were involved. In some of the controller-induced runway incursions, the controllers were working as few as two aircraft.

Radar, what the heck is it?

Every basic flying book talks about radar, so I'm not going to spend much time on it. But just in case your old Jeppesen primer is stuffed in a box somewhere and you haven't read it in a while, here's a quick refresher on the subject. It is obviously a simplification of some outstanding technology. Because I don't want to get bogged down in too much radar theory, this discussion is limited to some topics typical of many ATC radars.

Radar can detect distant objects by means of transmitted and reflected radio waves. When electronically processed, these waves can be used to determine the distance and bearing of an object. Through the use of an antenna, high-frequency radio waves are transmitted. Frequently these antennae are directional and rotating, but they might be flat-plated and even electronically scanned, depending upon their function and when they were produced. The energy transmitted travels at the speed of light. If an object is within the range of these transmissions, the energy is reflected back from the object.

Generally, the antenna that transmits the pulse wave also receives the reflected signals. The radar receiver quickly computes the time it took the pulse of energy to travel out and return. Since the radio pulse travels at a constant speed, once the time is known the distance is easily computed. This distance is presented as the range of the radar contact on the scope. As you dozed off in your ninth-grade science class, you were unknowingly being taught the principle of radar. Distance = Rate × Time. Ring a bell?

When the direction from which the reflection hits the antenna is analyzed, it is compared against a known heading. The resultant bearing is translated into the azimuth on a scope. When the azimuth and range are presented together, the radar-scope operator now has a radar contact, or skin paint, of an aircraft that she or he can monitor.

Some radars can further process a signal and determine its Doppler shift and conclude a rate of range change. This rate can give a velocity component to the range and azimuth of the contact, and the radar operator can determine how fast the contact is moving and in what direction. Other radars can also determine a contact's altitude. They use an antenna that determines direction as a vertical component, or angle, and processes that information to deduce the actual altitude of a contact above a known reference, the ground, or MSL.

Although all this sounds quite complicated, the processor works like your brain while listening for thunder as a kid. Remember seeing lightning, then "counting potatoes" until hearing the thunder to determine how far the lighting bolt was when it hit (range)? And just looking out the window determined direction (azimuth). With radar, a transmitter sends that "lightning bolt" of radio energy out to hit something, then listens to the echo. Basically, any detection occurring as a consequence of a beam of energy bouncing off an aircraft, or ship, or thunderstorm, is called "passive detection." The object being detected is doing nothing to assist in the detection process. The spot on the radar scope produced by the passive reflection might also be called a primary radar return.

Active detection. Another type of detection used by air traffic controllers is called "active detection." This detection requires the assistance of special equipment in the object being acquired to help the detection process. The transponder is the link to complete an active-detection cycle. The ground transmitter sends an interrogation message with coded electromagnetic energy (radio waves). The transponder receives that message and responds to the interrogation with a code. That code is the four-digit Mode-3 code programmed into the transponder by the flier. With Mode-C activated, the transponder also sends altitude information to the ATC receiver, so a height-finder radar is not necessary to determine the altitude of the aircraft. These active transmissions are displayed as secondary radar returns and frequently referred to as beacon replies.

Radar units are divided into two categories: primary and secondary.

Primary radar. Airport surveillance radar (ASR) is a type of primary radar designed to provide relatively short-range coverage in the general vicinity of an airport. ASR is usually used by approach control, departure control, and tower controllers to provide vectors and aircraft separation within the immediate proximity of an airport.

Primary radar has several shortcomings, including being negatively affected by certain weather and atmospheric conditions. Precipitation and ground clutter, caused by reflections on the earth's surface, frequently impair the primary radar display. Furthermore, aircraft targets have a tendency to vary in size. Because primary radar returns do not verify specific aircraft, it's difficult for controllers to positively identify targets unless they have pilots execute a series of distinguishing maneuvers, such as turns.

Secondary surveillance radar. Secondary radar functions separately from primary radar. However, in normal traffic-control use, it is interconnected with either the long-range route surveillance radar (ARSR) or the ASR. The most notable difference between the two types of radar is that secondary radar is capable of interrogating an aircraft's transponder. With the pertinent flight information that is provided by a transponder and then displayed on the radar scope, a controller can positively identify a target without requiring any of the maneuvering that is necessary under primary radar. The remaining limitations of the primary radar are either eliminated or greatly reduced.

Radar coverage is not the see all, be all

The Associated Press reported in September 1993 that the 1989 ASR-9 improved ATC radar system, which is operating at 62 airports and cost $839 million to develop and implement, has numerous problems. Among these discrepancies are "phantom" blips, missing planes, and a vulnerability to system crashes. These problems are not inherent to just the ASR-9 but are common to many ground-based radar. Below are a few common or possible problems radars and radar operators might encounter.

Old and decrepit. One common problem is the age of returns. If it takes an antenna 20 seconds to sweep 360 degrees, then the position of a blip, or return, is 20 seconds old by the time its position is updated. At 300 knots TAS, an airplane has moved 1⅔ nm by the time the position of the primary radar return is updated.

Excuse me, but would you please move your building? Another limitation is that radars cannot see through everything. Buildings and mountains mask certain areas from the energy transmitted by the radar. While some radars have a moving target display where buildings and stationary objects are not displayed on the scope, the obstacles still block the beam and can conceivably hide planes in their shadow.

Flying in the shadows. Another limitation of many radars is the scan pattern. We have all heard that flying low can position a plane under radar coverage. It is actually a matter of flying in the shadow of various obstacles. When radar scan patterns from multiple transmitters are overlapped, the severity of this problem is reduced.

Raining cats and dogs. Heavy rain, as in a thunderstorm, can also create a shadowed area behind the phenomena. Radars can be circularly polarized to try and alleviate this problem, but very dense precipitation still reduces a radar's sensitivity to picking up skin paints.

Ghosts and goblins. Another radar concern is "ghosting." Ghosting is a situation that occurs when two or more targets are within an antenna beam of a system that employs FM (frequency modulation) ranging. When this occurs, the radar does not know where one target is with respect to the other. The blips could appear as one big blip. Advanced techniques of adjusting waves can reduce this problem.

Accuracy is a relative term. False or missing targets are not uncommon to many radar systems. Eastern Flight 401, before crashing in a swamp, was observed off altitude by a controller just prior to impact. Because the controller said that his system was frequently in error, he only queried the pilot instead of telling him to check altitude. Accuracy is always measured in terms of points below 100 percent. No system is perfectly accurate 100 percent of the time.

Strange but true. Finally, like any piece of technology, radar systems are limited by our ability to maintain them. They are powered by electricity, so when the volts are gone, so is the picture. And radios, phones, lights, etc., can all affect the radar and radar operator's capabilities.

It's all we've got. Although our ATC system might have bugs, professional controllers have been making the best of the situation for years. Try to arrange a tour of a local ATC facility and see the system our taxes are paying for. It gives any non-radar operator a great opportunity to ask questions and see who is working what type of equipment, as well as a chance to discuss capabilities and limitations.

It's not a perfect world

Besides the known limitations of people and machines, the ATC system has numerous other safety issues that directly affect a collision-avoidance environment.

Task saturation

Although studies have shown a marked increase in operational errors during low to moderate controller workloads, task saturation can be just as serious a safety hazard. At some point, the workload can increase so rapidly that it physiologically and psychologically overloads the controller, resulting in a tunneling of perception and attention.

Incident 1

1989. Trans World Airlines (TWA) Flight 806 and Continental Airlines Flight 122 came within 500 feet of each other near Houston, Texas, Intercontinental Airport.

Situation

The Continental jet made a descending right turn instead of a left turn as instructed by ATC. When the controller noticed the error, he confused the call signs by advising "Continental 806" to stop its descent. Neither aircraft acknowledged, so both continued on their intended flight paths. Two minutes after Continental 122 started its erroneous turn it passed approximately 480 feet behind and at the same altitude (3200 feet) as TWA 806.

The controller was monitoring 14 aircraft at the time of the near-miss.

Airspace saturation: the southern California connection

Airspace saturation in high-density areas is a continuous safety threat. The Los Angeles Basin, as one example, has an estimated .3 aircraft per square mile, the equivalent of 15 aircraft within a 4-mile radius, at all altitudes. Present-day ATC capabilities are simply not able to adequately handle these increased volumes of traffic.

In part, this airspace saturation is one of the reasons southern California is plagued by such a high number of ATC-related operational errors. Industry-wide, these kinds of mistakes are at less than 1 per 100,000 operations. However, operational errors at high-activity facilities are two to three times that rate. For instance, Palmdale Center, the largest ATC facility in the west, normally handles more than two million aircraft operations a year. At one time, the error rate at Palmdale was at an alarming 3.41 mistakes for every 100,000 operations.

Incident 2

1988. Two Boeing 747s came within 20 seconds of a head-on collision over southern California. According to the FAA report, the controller realized a collision was imminent and told one crew to turn right. That maneuver, however, placed the two aircraft even closer. Seconds later, the same crew saw the other jet and avoided the collision.

Coast TRACON

The NTSB conducted a study that specifically singled out problems with the Coast Terminal Radar Approach Control (TRACON) facility in southern California. The site provides approach control service to three military installations, El Toro Marine Corps Air Station (MCAS), MCAS Tustin, and Los Alamitos Army Airfield; and three civilian airports, John Wayne, Long Beach, and Fullerton.

In a 14-month period, nine violations of traffic separation occurred. In a 5-month period, eight operational errors occurred due to lack of controller experience and improper coordination between adjacent facilities. The safety report pointed out that the rate of operational errors at the Coast TRACON had been substantially higher than at other U.S. ATC radar facilities with similar traffic volume.

Incident 3

1987. An America West Airlines passenger jet, after takeoff at John Wayne, California, Airport, came within 500 feet of an army helicopter. According to the FAA incident report, the controller "temporarily forgot" that the helicopter was in the vicinity of the America West. The helicopter "dove in front of the aircraft and passed underneath it."

Incident 4

1988. A Western Airlines Boeing 737 and a Transtar McDonnell Douglas MD-80 came within 31 seconds of a head-on collision near Barstow, California. The controller was busy handling another airplane with a radio failure and forgot to clear the Transtar to a different heading. The conflict alert function on the ARTS III radar sounded, which prompted the controller to immediately clear the Western crew to climb over the Transtar.

MANPOWER SHORTAGES

The nation's ATC system has never fully recovered from the 1981 Professional Air Traffic Controllers' Organization (PATCO) strike, which forced ATC facilities to manage with only limited manpower. This situation has repeatedly deteriorated the level of safety at numerous locations and has been a factor in numerous near-misses.

U.S. TRANSPORTATION DEPARTMENT STUDY

In 1989, the U.S. Transportation Department (DOT) reviewed ATC operations at several busy Northeast corridor facilities. Each had a history of manpower shortages and high incidents of operational errors. Those sites included New York, Boston, Philadelphia, and Washington, DC.

The report concluded that the New York TRACON did not have enough fully qualified, or full-performance-level (FPL) controllers. Specifically, the New York TRACON's staff of FPL controllers decreased more than 12 percent in 1986, during a period when the number of aircraft handled fell only 5 percent. During that time, the TRACON facility was managing with 74 percent FPL controllers, while operational errors involving traffic separation violations jumped more than 150 percent.

The report determined that a combination of the controller shortage and inadequate management at the facilities often forced FPL controllers to work two radar sectors, each of which previously would have been handled by one controller. The report went on to say that the shortage also limited the training provided to newly assigned controllers. Because the overall level of expertise was low, additional FPLs had to man the scopes, reducing the number of instructors available to teach the new hires.

FEDERAL AVIATION ADMINISTRATION STUDY

In 1987 and 1989, the FAA studied other troubled facilities and found similar operational problems at every category of ATC site.

Los Angeles Tower. According to the 1987 FAA report on manpower shortages at the nation's third busiest tower facility, staffing was one of the toughest problems. Inspectors ". . . were appalled to find supervision of controllers severely limited because staffing shortages and other problems kept managers too busy to supervise."

Coast TRACON. The same FAA report noted that a plan to transfer airspace from Orange County and Long Beach, California, to the better-equipped Coast TRACON was postponed indefinitely because ". . . the facility would be unable to handle the increase of traffic due to critical staff shortages." Coast TRACON is authorized to have 63 controllers but had only 38.

Houston Intercontinental tower. As the 1989 FAA investigation revealed, manpower shortages still plagued the nation's high-density facilities. Houston Intercontinental was staffed with a large ratio of trainees: 219 FPL controllers to 94 developmental controllers. The report pointed out that 15 of the 18 controllers involved in mistakes had only one to three years of experience.

Houston Center. The FAA study showed that between 1986 and 1989, Houston Center had twice the number of operational errors as its counterparts, including those at the busier Fort Worth Center. In 1989 alone, Houston had 42 operational errors, which accounted for nearly one-third of all mistakes reported in the southwest region. Although a resectorization of airspace was viewed as a contributing factor, staffing deficiencies had also been considered to be a primary cause.

RADIO COMMUNICATION AND PHRASEOLOGY

Remember the last time you tried getting into the traffic pattern on a busy Saturday afternoon? I've flown on days when it looked and sounded like the "Flying Monkey Circus" was in town. You know how it goes. You tune in the tower frequency, pick up the mike, and before you can depress the button, you hear one very long string of screeching noises, inane babbling, and zoo-like sounds. You hear a split-second pause, and with lightning speed you move your finger again toward the button. Too late. You now are forced to listen to, "Ahhhhh, tower, ahh, this is Cessna, 'um, two four, ahhh, Fox, ahhhhh, over 'um the Kiowa VOR, ah, with, ahh, information, 'um, ah, Bravo." By the time you hear the fourth "ahh," you let out a scream of frustration and begin flying 360s. And maybe—just maybe—you'll be able to get on the radio before you run out of gas.

Radio communication? Not even close. Try radio miscommunication. In most collision-avoidance environments, effective radio communication combined with good scan techniques might be the only two available resources that you have. We already know about the physical limitations of see and avoid. Take away effective radio communication and you have just increased your chances of being involved in a mid-air collision.

Your radio voice

If you mumble in person, you most likely mumble over the radio. If you have a high-pitched voice in person, you probably sound like a "screaming Mimi" over the radio. If you're a fast talker in person, you might sound like a fast-talking, mumbling, "screaming Mimi" over the radio. A speech pattern that is understandable in a face-to-face conversation doesn't always come across that way over the radio.

Here are a few tips on effective radio communication:

1. Think before you talk. If you know what you're going to say before you depress the mike button, you will eliminate a lot of the "ahs" and "ums."

2. Speak clearly and slowly. Not only will you be more understandable, but you probably won't have to repeat yourself as often.

3. Lower your voice pitch slightly. Sometimes when you speak slowly your voice automatically sounds lower. But not always. It's especially true if you naturally have a high-pitched voice. If that's the case, and this goes for women in particular, make sure your radio voice sounds a little deeper than your normal conversational level.

4. Be direct and concise; short and to the point.

5. Avoid using unfamiliar acronyms and nonstandard phraseology. Effective radio communication means that you must first be understandable. If no one knows what you're talking about you're not understandable.

What you say is not always what you mean

Effective verbal communication is not just what you say but also how you say it. Ambiguous and indirect phraseology is quite common, especially when a pilot is in a critical phase of flight and is being inundated with other tasks. But in a departure or arrival stage of flight, that's exactly the wrong time to make poor radio calls. Remember, there's a much greater possibility for a mid-air to occur at those busy times.

Avoid ambiguous phraseology

The following excerpts are from selected NTSB accident reports. They should in no way portray the crews negatively. These are common communication errors that all of us have made at one time or another. It's important, though, to understand the relevance of these mistakes in a see and avoid environment and an emergency situation.

Mid-air collision between PSA Flight 182 and a Cessna 172. (Accident is discussed in greater detail in chapter 3.)

Approach: "PSA . . . traffic twelve o'clock, one mile, northbound."
PSA: "We're looking."
Approach: "PSA . . . additional traffic's . . . twelve o'clock, three miles just north of the field northeastbound, a Cessna one seventy-two climbing VFR, out of one thousand four hundred."
PSA: "Okay, we've got that other twelve."

Within 20 seconds, Flight 182 had received two traffic advisories pertaining to aircraft at their "twelve o'clock" position. Therefore, when Flight 182 said they had, ". . . that other twelve," which traffic advisory were they referring to? The controller assumed that they had the 172 in sight. Although that was the most likely conclusion, there was no way to tell for sure since other aircraft were in the vicinity.

Be clear and direct. Anytime you are given more than one traffic advisory in a short period of time, or when there is confusion over which aircraft you have in sight, you should always clarify your response. Instead of ". . . we've got that other twelve," what would've been a clearer and more direct reply?

PSA: "PSA one eighty-two has the northeastbound Cessna in sight. Still looking for north bound traffic."

Listen, understand, and remember. Oftentimes we don't hear all the information that is given in a traffic advisory. Heading, altitude, attitude, or aircraft type can easily be missed when you're busy with checklists and there's a lot of activity on the radio. This is why it's so important to pay attention and listen for your traffic advisories.

Just as common, and this doesn't happen exclusively to new pilots, is misunderstanding the heading of your traffic. Say you were given the same two traffic advisories that Flight 182 had received. The first was northbound at one mile, and the second was northeastbound at three miles. You detect only one aircraft, which seems to be flying in a northerly direction, so you report, "Northbound traffic in sight." Since you weren't really listening to either traffic advisory, but remember hearing something about northbound traffic, you assume the aircraft you're looking at is the northbound traffic, when actually it was the northeastbound traffic.

You can take two easy steps to help avoid this mistake:

1. Learn and memorize your compass headings and the reciprocals. That way, when you hear a traffic advisory that includes the aircraft's heading, you can immediately determine if it is flying away from you or toward you. Say you were flying in a northeasterly direction and your traffic is flying southwestbound. You

are then aware that an aircraft is coming in your direction. Likewise, if you're still northeastbound, and your traffic is heading west at your two o'clock position, you can be on the lookout for an aircraft that will be crossing your flight path from the right.

A simple rule to help with figuring out reciprocals:

—Add two to the first number, then subtract two from the second, or,

—Subtract two from the first number, then add two to the second.

For example: What is the recip of 3-6-0 degrees?

Answer: 3–2=1, 6+2=8, and 0 on the end: 1-8-0

Another example: What is the recip for 1-1-0 degrees?

Answer: 1+2=3, 1–2=–1, and a zero on the end: 2-9-0

2. Know what view of the threat aircraft will be visible from your position. Visualizing your traffic's position in relation to your own enables you to understand what view of the aircraft you'll be looking for, front view, belly view, rear-quarter view, etc.

Nondirective phraseology

Mid-air collision of PSA Flight 182 and a Cessna 172.

Approach: "PSA . . . traffic's at twelve o'clock, three miles out of one thousand seven hundred."

PSA: "Traffic in sight."

Approach: ". . . maintain visual separation, contact Lindbergh tower . . . ."

PSA: "Okay."

PSA: "Lindbergh PSA . . . downwind."

Tower: "PSA . . . traffic twelve o'clock, one mile, a Cessna."

PSA: "Okay, we had it there a minute ago."

Tower: ". . . roger."

PSA: "I think he's pass(ed) off to our right."

Tower: "Yeah."

Cockpit: "He was right over here a minute ago." "Yeah."

Notify ATC as soon as you've lost sight of your traffic. "We had it there a minute ago," and "I think he's passed off to our right," are not examples of directive communication. Be clear, direct, and concise. "PSA 182 has lost the traffic, request advisories," is a more directive, no-nonsense message.

Controllers, don't be part of the problem. The tower controller made only two comments after the PSA's transmissions. "Roger" and "Yeah." Noncommittal, nondirective, and no help. Don't wait to hear the magic words, "traffic no longer in sight," before you speak up and take charge of the situation. Remember, this is a team effort. When the pilot fumbles the ball, pick it up.

Galaxy Airlines Flight 203, a Lockheed Electra, crashed shortly after takeoff from the Reno, Nevada, International Airport. The NTSB determined that the probable cause of this accident was the crew's failure to monitor the flight path and airspeed of the aircraft following an unexpected vibration.

Captain (Intra-cockpit): "Tell 'em we need to make a left downwind to get outta here, get it back on the ground."
F/O: "Galaxy . . . like to make a left downwind, we gotta get back on the ground."
Tower: "Galaxy, say again."
Captain (Intra-cockpit): "Tell 'em we have a heavy vibration."
F/O: "Ah, sir, we'd like to make a left downwind. We've gotta heavy vibration in the aircraft."
Tower: "Galaxy . . . roger . . . maintain VFR . . . left downwind . . . do you need equipment?"
F/O: "Affirmative."

Nine seconds later, the aircraft hit the ground. Be clear, direct, and concise. In such a situation, declare an emergency, give the controller any special requests, and get off the radio. It is not the time to be long-winded.

Be understandable. Because the pilot was not clear, direct, and concise with his transmission to ATC, the controller had to reply, "say again." In turn, the pilot had to repeat his message instead of flying the airplane.

A side note of interest

The vibration was caused by the air start access door opening in flight. According to the Safety Board, the aircraft could have returned for a successful landing but the crew failed to monitor the flight path and airspeed. As you can see from the above transcripts, they spent a considerable amount of time—time they didn't have to waste—with ATC communications.

Words to live by—literally

Following the theme of the latter part of this chapter, I'm keeping this conclusion short and to the point. Remember: Work on your radio voice. Be clear, direct, and concise. Avoid any words or phraseology that might not be understandable to others.

CHAPTER 2 REVIEW

- Airspace reclassification
- A airspace (formerly Positive Control Area)
- B airspace (formerly Terminal Control Area)
- C airspace (formerly Airport Radar Service Area)
- D airspace (formerly Airport Traffic Areas and Control Zones)
- E airspace (formerly Controlled Airspace—General)
- G airspace (formerly Uncontrolled Airspace)

Mid-air collision
Mid-air collision of Skywest Flight 1834 and a Mooney M20. Causal factor was the unauthorized and inadvertent entry into an ARSA by the Mooney pilot.

- Always know your position.
- Maintain a thorough visual scan.
- Airspace boundaries
- Communication

ATC services
- "Radar contact" does not mean a pilot is automatically cleared into controlled airspace.
- Radar following services can be beneficial to VFR pilots.

VFR altitudes
- Level flight, above 3000 feet:
  —0–179 degrees, odd thousands MSL + 500 feet.
  —180–359 degrees, even thousands MSL + 500 feet.

Purpose of ATC
- Promote safe and orderly separation of traffic
- Priority to IFR traffic
- Additional services to VFR traffic on a workload-permitting basis

ATC and the VFR pilot
- Pilots still have responsibilities and obligations even when under ATC supervision.
- Ask for additional services.

Diffusion of responsibility
- A belief of shared responsibility when under ATC supervision
- A reduced state of vigilance
- Lack of attention and situational awareness
- Shared responsibility
- Boredom
- Complacency

Runway incursions
- ATC-related factors similar to mid-air collisions

Radar
- Detect distant objects by means of transmitted and reflected radio waves
- Distance = Rate × Time
- Passive detection occurring as a consequence of a beam of energy bouncing off of an aircraft

- Active detection relies on transponder interrogation
- Primary radar provides short range coverage
- Can be negatively affected by precipitation and ground clutter
- Secondary surveillance radar is interconnected with either the long-range route surveillance radar or the short-range radar.
- Capable of interrogating aircraft transponders
- Not as limited as primary radar

Radar limitations
Inherent or common problems:

- "Phantom" blips
- Age of returns
- Obstructions
- Scan pattern
- Heavy rain
- Ghosting
- Maintenance

ATC and human factors
- Task saturation
- Airspace saturation
- Manpower shortages

Radio communication
- Speak with a radio voice
- Be clear, direct, and concise

Phraseology
- Avoid ambiguous phraseology
- Avoid indirect phraseology
- Avoid unfamiliar acronyms
- Be understandable

Chapter 2 references

Andrews, J.W. 1991. *Air-to-Air Visual Acquisition Handbook*. Lincoln Laboratory. Massachusetts Institute of Technology.

Cardosi, Kim, Pamela Boole. 1991. *Analysis of Pilot Response Time to Time-Critical Air Traffic Control Calls*. U.S. Department of Transportation. Federal Aviation Administration.

Humes, Edward. 30 May 1988. "Mistakes at LAX Jumped 57% Last Year." *Orange County Register:* A4-5.

Hopkin, V. David. 1988. "Air Traffic Control." *Human Factors in Aviation.* Ed. Wiener, Earl L. and David C. Nagel. San Diego: Academic Press: 639-663.

Keesling, Otto. 7 August 1991. Federal Aviation Administration Air Traffic Representative. Personal interview.

Lednovich, Michael. 22 January 1987. "Controllers Cite Flaws at Area's Main Radar Site." *Orange County Register:* B8-9.

McKenna, James T. 1 April 1991. "ATC System Upgrade Hampered by Delays, But New FAA Attitude Encourages Industry." *Aviation Week and Space Technology:* 49-50.

Stein, Earl. 1992. *Air Traffic Control Visual Scanning.* U.S. Department of Transportation. Federal Aviation Administration.

"Air Traffic Radar Full of Bugs." 19 September 1993. *Las Vegas Review-Journal:* 1A.

"Dangers on Rise in Southern California Skies." 29 May 1988. *Orange County Register:* A6-8.

"NTSB Report Says Safety Diminished at Coast TRACON." 29 May 1989. *Aviation Week and Space Technology:* 42.

National Transportation Safety Board. 4 February 1986. Aircraft Accident Report: Galaxy Airlines, Inc., Lockheed Electra-L-188C, N5532, Reno, Nevada, January 21, 1985. Washington, DC.

National Transportation Safety Board. 15 March 1988. Aircraft Accident Report: Midair Collision of Skywest Airlines Swearingen Metro II, N163SW, and Mooney M20, N6485U, Kearns, Utah, January 15, 1987. Washington, DC.

National Transportation Safety Board. Special Investigation Report. Runway Incursions at Controlled Airports in the United States. Washington, DC. 1986.

3
Mid-air collisions:
Flying by the myth,
dying by the reality

IN THE PREVIOUS CHAPTERS I DISCUSSED THE LIMITATIONS OF OUR PRIMARY resources—ourselves and ATC. But sometimes the lessons don't really hit home until we study the events leading to a mid-air, and all accidents for that matter, and come to the harsh conclusion that we are oftentimes flying by the myth and dying by the reality.

The following mid-airs all have a common thread: the pilot-controller connection. I've chosen these particular examples because they all began as very routine and typical flights. Although they represent a wide range of aircraft types and pilot experience, the scenarios are common to all pilots. A key point to remember is that at times flying is flying is flying, no matter if you have 100, 1000, or 10,000 hours. Mid-airs are not a low-time pilot or inexperienced-controller problem.

To get the most out of accident studies, don't be a passive observer-reader. While reading a report or article, you criticize every word that was spoken in the cockpit, while declaring, "How could they miss that?" Or better yet, "I'm too good of a pilot to let that happen to me." So before you proudly give yourself a gold star on the forehead for being such a safe pilot, just remember, mid-airs can happen anytime, in any weather, and to any pilot. We need to learn from other people's situations, and plan accordingly.

As you read each case study, pay particular attention to the length of time between events. You have to realize how much can happen in an extremely short period of time.

CASE 1: CLEAR SKIES AND RADAR CONTACT

24 August 1984: Wings West Airlines Flight 628, a twin turboprop Beech 99, collided with a single-engine Rockwell Commander near San Luis Obispo, California.

Pilot experience: Wings West captain: 4110 hours, 873 in Beech 99. Wings West first officer: 6194 hours, 62 in Beech 99. Rockwell Commander instructor: 4857 hours, 4395 in single-engine aircraft. Rockwell Commander pilot: 2450 hours, all in military aircraft.

Reported weather at time of mid-air collision: 15,000 feet scattered. Visibility 15 miles. Temperature 71F. Winds calm.

Probable cause

The NTSB determined that the probable cause of this accident was the failure of the pilots in both aircraft to follow the recommended communications and traffic advisory practices for uncontrolled airports. Other factors included the physiological limitations of human vision and reaction time and the short time available to the controller to detect the conflict in order to issue a safety advisory. A contributing cause was the Wings West Airlines policy that required its pilots to tune one radio to the company frequency at all times.

Clear skies

Yes, you can have a mid-air collision in clear skies. And yes, you can have a mid-air collision while under radar contact. It has, unfortunately, occurred more times than any of us would like to think about, which is all the more reason to thoroughly discuss the events that commonly lead to these disasters. The mid-air between this commuter and a general-aviation aircraft is one such accident that is a clear reminder of how the combination of physiological limitations, a breakdown in communications, and a misunderstanding of uncontrolled airport traffic procedures can result in tragedy.

The accident

Shortly after 1100 Pacific Daylight Time, Wings West Flight 628 departed San Luis Obispo County Airport (UNICOM) enroute to San Francisco International. At 1116, as Flight 628 climbed on a westbound heading, the flight crew contacted the Los Angeles Air Route Traffic Control Center (ARTCC) and requested their IFR clearance to San Francisco. The controller assigned a discrete transponder code to the flight and added, ". . . radar contact six [miles] northwest of San Luis Obispo Airport, say altitude." Flight 628 answered, "Three thousand one hundred [feet], climbing." Los Angeles ARTCC then cleared the flight to San Francisco, as filed, and to climb and maintain 7000 feet. The crew promptly read back the clearance. According to the controller, he lost radar contact with Flight 628 within seconds of their last transmission. The crew never responded to the controller's subsequent radio calls.

The Rockwell Commander, with two pilots aboard, departed Paso Robles Airport (FSS) at 1052 for a routine check-out flight. They were flying in the vicinity of the San Luis Obispo Airport, possibly preparing to practice instrument approaches, when the two aircraft collided 8 nm northwest of the airport at 3400 feet.

The investigation

Cockpit visibility study. As part of the investigation the NTSB conducted a cockpit visibility study to determine how detectable the airplanes were to each pilot.

Figure 3-1 illustrates the visibility as seen from the Wings West captain's windshield. For nearly 20 seconds the Rockwell remained in the design eye reference point of the captain. The target remained relatively stationary because both aircraft were in a head-on encounter.

Beechcraft model 99
Camera attitude - normal
Pilot's eye position
  41 1/2 inches above floor
  5 inches aft rear most column movement

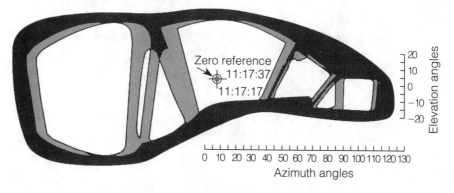

Captain

Fig. 3-1. *Cockpit visibility study. Wings West Flight 628 Captain position.* NTSB

Figure 3-2 illustrates the visibility as seen from the Wings West first officer's windshield. For nearly 20 seconds the Rockwell remained in the design eye reference point of the first officer. The target remained relatively stationary because both aircraft were in a head-on encounter.

Figure 3-3 illustrates the visibility as seen from the Rockwell instructor-pilot's windshield. During the last 20 seconds before impact, Flight 628 appeared slightly below and to the right of the design eye reference points of both pilots. The target remained relatively stationary for the entire 20 seconds because both aircraft were in a head-on encounter.

Figure 3-4 illustrates the visibility as seen from the Rockwell pilot's windshield. During the last 20 seconds before impact, Flight 628 appeared slightly below and to the

Beechcraft model 99
Camera attitude - normal
Copilot's eye position
  41 1/2 inches above floor
  5 inches aft rearmost column movement

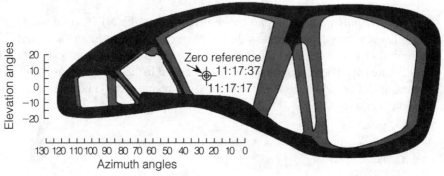

First officer

Fig. 3-2. *Cockpit visibility study. Wings West Flight 628 First Officer position.* NTSB

Rockwell commander 112/114
Copilot's eye position
  42 1/2 inches above floor
  2 inches aft rearmost column movement
Note: Copilot's visor removed

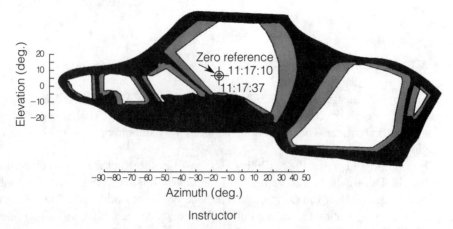

Instructor

Fig. 3-3. *Cockpit visibility study. Rockwell Commander instructor pilot position.* NTSB

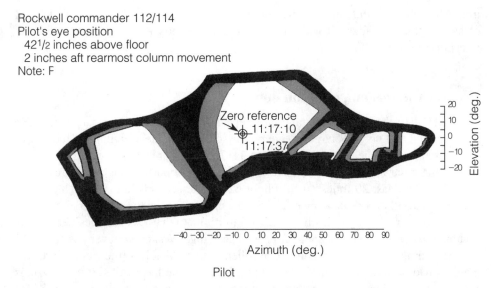

Rockwell commander 112/114
Pilot's eye position
 42½ inches above floor
 2 inches aft rearmost column movement
Note: F

Fig. 3-4. *Cockpit visibility study. Rockwell Commander pilot position.* NTSB

right of the design eye reference points of both pilots. The target remained relatively stationary for the entire 20 seconds because both aircraft were in a head-on encounter.

The ATC connection

The radar. A significant portion of the accident investigation centered on the ATC operations at the Los Angeles ARTCC (Los Angeles Center), specifically low altitude sector 15 (R-15). The radar computer had a conflict alert (CA) program designed to indicate potential mid-airs. A limitation of the program, however, is that the program functions only if the airplanes involved are equipped with altitude-encoding transponders (Mode-C) and each has been identified with a given track. At the time of the accident the radar scope had been set at the 60-nm range, and at that setting, 1 inch on the scope equals 5.45 nm. The scope had also been configured to display all 1200 (VFR) transponder codes up to an altitude of 24,200 feet.

The controllers. A developmental controller and a full performance level (FPL) controller were monitoring R-15 sector, with two other FPLs periodically checking the developmental controller's progress. Although the developmental controller was a qualified ATC specialist, he was undergoing a certification check on the R-15 sector.

Traffic was considered moderate at 1116, when the Wings West crew made its initial call to the R-15 developmental controller. The controller was in the process of sequencing a commuter and an airliner for landing at Santa Barbara, which were displayed on the scope at the opposite corner from San Luis Obispo. Because of two additional aircraft in the Santa Barbara area, it took him nearly 40 seconds to coordinate the traffic and turn over the two landing aircraft to Santa Barbara Approach Control. After a bit of confusion on the controller's part as to which Wings West flight called, he finally realized it was Flight 628 and promptly assigned them a discrete transponder code.

Now you see 'em, now you don't

At 1117:16 the developmental controller had Flight 628 under radar contact. He later testified that no VFR targets were on his scope in the near vicinity of the Wings West aircraft when he made that call. At 1117:23 the controller once again looked around the radar scope for any possible conflicts. He reported that the nearest VFR traffic was "at least 20 miles" from Flight 628. Nine seconds later, the Wings West crew read back their IFR clearance. The R-15 controller spoke to two other aircraft and at 1118:40 he tried to contact Flight 628 to inform them that Los Angeles Center was no longer receiving their transponder code. The Wings West crew never answered.

According to the developmental controller, "I know that if it [the Rockwell Commander] had been there [on his radar scope], I sure would have called it to the Wings West aircraft . . . I cannot understand why it would not have been on my scope." The FPL controller administrating the R-15 checkout to the developmental controller also testified that the only VFR traffic he saw were the targets ". . . 20 nautical miles away . . . in the Santa Barbara area." The other two FPLs were not looking at the R-15 scope at the time of the mid-air.

The radar ground-track plot later revealed that at 1116:22 the airplanes were about 6.9 nm apart, and the Rockwell was almost directly in front of Flight 628. Between 1116:22 and the collision, the aircraft closed on each other at about 544 fps. Except for the Rockwell's slight-right turn, they remained on a head-on course. The plot had also produced a collision point time at 1117:38 at an altitude of 3400 feet. Since the crew of Flight 628 began to read their IFR clearance at 1117:32, it is apparent that the mid-air occurred only one or two seconds after they finished their transmission.

Two controllers and four pilots

What happened in a mere seven minutes of flying time that left 17 people dead? The NTSB conducted a series of studies in order to answer that disturbing question. After the Board made a thorough analysis of the radar equipment and found it to have been functioning properly, the investigation probed other related factors. The results of those studies and analyses were a clear reminder that no one element of collision avoidance guarantees a safe flight. Rather, it is a combination of understanding the limitations and related factors that are inherent to a see and avoid environment and effectively using all available resources. The Board also found evidence to prove that the Rockwell's radar return (1200 transponder code) was within one inch of Flight 628's radar return. The Board then determined that while the developmental controller was preoccupied with the Santa Barbara traffic, he most likely acquired a "tunneling of his mental and visual attention." The FPL, too, had been distracted with various controller duties and most likely had focused, or "tunneled," his attention elsewhere.

Tunneling of the mind and eye

Here's a practical and real-life instance when the eye-brain connection (discussed in chapter 1) proves to be a significant factor in mid-air collisions. Given the right—or wrong, depending on how you look at it—set of circumstances, everyone is prone to a tunneling effect of the eye and brain. It's actually a combination of the eye's natural blind spots and an intense concentration level to a particular task.

An eye-opening study

In 1991 scientists and psychologists joined Vilayanur Ramachandran from the University of California-San Diego and Richard Gregory of the University of Bristol in England to research the visual phenomenon of natural blind spots. It has long been noted that, although we do not experience black spots or clouded vision, each eye possesses a blind spot in the retina corresponding to the head of the optic nerve. The way in which the brain compensates for these natural holes in our field of vision was the basis for this study.

In the past, theories suggested that the brain simply ignores visual blind spots, and operates as if they do not exist. The results of this latest study, however, proposes that the brain's visual system might create a physiological representation of visual information surrounding blind spots, one that automatically paints a coherent scene by filling in the optical void.

The team of Ramachandran and Gregory created a series of experiments employing computer-generated designs with deleted sections serving as artificial blind spots. In one test, the researchers directed four volunteers to watch a computer screen with a background of twinkling dots in different shades of gray. Each viewer focused just to the right or left of a small, blank, gray square near a corner of the screen. On 10 consecutive trials, all reported that within an average of five seconds the square vanished and the twinkling dots took its place.

In yet another experiment, the computer displayed a pink background with twinkling black dots and a small gray square with black dots moving horizontally across it. When the same volunteers focused just to the right or left of the square, they reported this gray patch also faded in a matter of seconds, but in two stages. First, the gray region in the square vanished and the surrounding pink seeped in; then the moving dots disappeared and a few seconds later the twinkling dots took their place.

Further tests indicated a marked increase in the fading and filling-in process, in addition to the movement of the objects on the computer screen. During one trial, the researchers waited until the filling-in of the gray square occurred, then wiped the image off of the screen and replaced it with a smaller replica in the same location. Participants noted they saw the new square pop into view, fade and fill-in with black dots a few seconds later. Using the same computer-generated arrangement, the researchers waited until the volunteers reported that the gray square had faded completely, then switched off the image and replaced it with an identical square that had been shifted slightly to the left or right. Participants then described how the squares appeared to move in position, rather than instantly materialize in the correct location. Ramachandran and

Gregory believe this is the result of the brain stimulating an unconscious illusion of motion.

These tests have shown a remarkable similarity to the tunneling phenomenon mentioned by the Safety Board during its Wings West investigation. As in the case of the study's participants, the computer-generated squares, much like a data block on a radar scope, faded and eventually disappeared when stared at for even relatively short periods of time. When the squares were reduced in size, the volunteers saw the new square pop into view, fade and fill in within a few seconds. Lastly, when the researchers eliminated the square, then brought it back in a slightly different location, the participants saw the square move into place, even though the image remained stationary on the computer screen.

The brain actually fools the eye into thinking it sees an object it had viewed just seconds earlier. When an identical image reappears, the brain remembers it in a certain location and sends a message to the eye. The eye then interprets the image the way the brain has remembered it, whereby providing a sometimes false or skewed perception.

The mid-air connection

With the study's results, it is possible to examine a likely scenario that occurred moments before this mid-air. As stated earlier, the developmental controller was preoccupied with other traffic and duty responsibilities and admitted he never saw the Rockwell's radar return even though it was within one inch of Flight 628's data block. The controller had directed his vision and mental concentration to one area of the radar scope—for the Santa Barbara traffic—then shifted his eyes several inches to another part of the scope to search for the Wings West data block. His eyes then had to refocus onto a moving, known image [Flight 628]. The controller's brain had already remembered that there were no threats to the Wings West aircraft, therefore he was not expecting to find a conflict.

As the study's observations further suggest, when a person stares at a moving, colored square, filled with twinkling dots, similar to a moving, colored data block that is filled with flickering symbols, the dimmer color (gray) is overtaken by the stronger color (pink); while the moving dots vanish and the twinkling dots take their place. Although the radar returns of Flight 628 and the Rockwell were within one inch apart, the developmental controller did not expect to see any other VFR traffic within 20 miles of the Wings West aircraft. He had also just spent the previous several minutes at a high-concentration level while working a moderate flow of traffic in the Santa Barbara area. It is, therefore, reasonable to speculate that the developmental controller's eyes might have faded one or both radar returns.

Through the results of the Safety Board's investigation, and this more recent independent study, it is easier to understand how visual phenomena can sometimes work against controllers in a collision-avoidance environment.

Proper communication could have been the key

The Safety Board also examined the evidence to determine whether the accident might have been avoided if the pilots of either or both airplanes had followed the recommended communication and traffic advisory practices described in the Airman's Information Manual (AIM). Since the radar data showed that the Rockwell had approached the San Luis Obispo County Airport from the northwest and was virtually aligned with the localizer approach course as it neared the airport, the Board concluded that the instructor pilot was most likely shooting a practice instrument approach. At 1116 an unidentified radio call, "Inbound approaching Dobra [intersection]," was received on the San Luis Obispo UNICOM frequency. Since the Rockwell was the only airplane in the vicinity that was inbound, the Board reasoned that the transmission must have come from it. The Rockwell pilots made no other radio call to the UNICOM or to the Los Angeles ARTCC.

Communication at uncontrolled airports

According to the AIM, "At airports without a tower, pilots wishing to make practice instrument approaches should notify the facility having control jurisdiction of the desired approach." In this instance it was Los Angeles ARTCC, specifically R-15 sector. The AIM further recommends, ". . . pilots approaching an uncontrolled airport . . . call on the common traffic advisory frequency (San Luis Obispo UNICOM) and announce their position and intentions."

The accident also might have been avoided if the flight crew of Flight 628 had complied with the same recommended traffic advisory and departure procedures. According to the AIM, ". . . pilots departing an uncontrolled airport . . . monitor the airport's common traffic advisory frequency (San Luis Obispo UNICOM) until 10 miles from the airport . . .." Although Flight 628 had two functional communication radios, a Wings West operational procedure required one radio be kept on the company frequency at all times. Thus, the flight crew transferred the other radio from the UNICOM frequency to that of the Los Angeles ARTCC when they were only five miles from the field. Therefore, Flight 628 had already switched off the UNICOM frequency when the Rockwell made the call, "inbound approaching Dobra."

A costly lack of communication

The Safety Board strongly believed that if the Rockwell pilots had informed Los Angeles Center of their intentions to conduct practice instrument approaches, the R-15 developmental controller would have known of their presence before he began to handle Flight 628. According to the Board, had the controller been aware of the Rockwell's location, he would have had about 28 seconds to issue a traffic conflict advisory to the Wings West crew. In the Safety Board's opinion: "Had this been done . . . the accident probably would not have happened."

Little chance for the pilots

Although the analyses of the ground tracks and closure rate of the two aircraft indicated that there might have been sufficient time for the pilots of each airplane to have detected an object, it was improbable that the pilots could have recognized that it was an airplane and reacted in time to avoid a collision.

Numerous factors were against the pilots that day. Besides the obvious physiological limitations of the human eye, the rapid head-on closure rate and lack of relative motion of the airplanes to each other complicated matters. Additionally, each airplane was painted predominantly white, which made detection exceedingly difficult on such a bright and sunny morning.

The Safety Board speaks out

From the evidence obtained throughout this investigation, the Safety Board concluded that the Wings West and Rockwell pilots' ability to see and avoid each other was "quite marginal" under the circumstances that were present. The Board also confirmed that there are, ". . . occasions when the [external] factors of a traffic conflict will exceed the physiological capabilities of the pilot to see and avoid an oncoming airplane."

PRACTICAL APPLICATIONS AND LESSONS LEARNED

1. Be specific when you transmit your location. "Inbound approaching Dobra" tells other pilots absolutely nothing. At what altitude are you approaching? At what distance? "Approaching" can mean anything from five miles, two miles, or for some, over the point.

2. Include your aircraft type in a transmission. It's very helpful to know what type of aircraft your traffic is. "Cessna 42 Mike . . ." at least tips other pilots into looking for a Cessna. Likewise, "Piper 54 Fox . . ." notifies other pilots that a low-wing aircraft is their traffic. And if you're flying a twin-engine, be sure and add, "Twin Cessna . . .." Pilots will not only be aware of what shape to look for, but they will also know that their traffic most likely does not have a ground speed of 80 knots. The time frame for detection is, therefore, greatly shortened.

3. Including all the necessary information can help with visual search and detection. "Rockwell two Sierra Mike, five miles northwest of Dobra, 3000 feet, inbound for San Luis Obispo." A pilot hearing this transmission would know the vicinity in which to start looking for the aircraft and immediately know if the traffic was a potential threat.

4. Maintain vigilance over and around all airports. A 10-mile radius of any airport, especially one that is uncontrolled, is an extremely hectic and potentially dangerous area. Proper communication and visual scanning is a must. Stay alert.

5. Take full advantage of dual radios. Many aircraft have dual radios. Always keep one radio tuned to your departure or arrival airport for at least a 10-nm radius. Do the same when flying near airports while enroute on a cross-country.

6. Company radios should be a secondary priority. Nothing that is said on a company frequency could be more important than hearing your traffic. Safety, not convenience, should drive policy.

7. Do not abdicate responsibility. Radar contact does not relinquish traffic detection responsibility to ATC. When they provide separation, it is from known aircraft.

8. Read the Airman's Information Manual. The AIM is a very important and practical guide that should be applied to your flying routine. Always keep a current copy handy.

CASE 2: MODE-C—A FALSE SENSE OF SECURITY

20 January 1987: A twin-engine Piper Navajo (N60SE), operated by the Sachs Electric Company, collided with a twin-engine U.S. Army Beech U-21A (Army 18061) over Lake City Army Ammunition Plant, Independence, Missouri.

Pilot experience: Navajo pilot: 7418 hours, 4751 in multiengine aircraft. U-21 pilot: 5983 hours, 217 in U-21. U-21 copilot: 6266 hours, 1528 in U-21.

Reported weather at time of mid-air collision: 25,000 feet thin scattered. Visibility 20 miles. Temperature 26F.

Probable cause

The Safety Board determined that the probable cause was the failure of the radar controllers to detect the conflict and to issue traffic advisories or a safety alert to the flight crew of the U-21. The deficiencies of the see and avoid concept as a primary means of collision avoidance were also causal factors.

The flight of N60SE

At 1221 Central Standard Time the Navajo, with a pilot and two passengers on board, departed the Kansas City Downtown Airport enroute to their home base of St. Louis. The aircraft had an operating Mode-C transponder, which was squawking the 1200 VFR code.

The pilot advised the local controller that he would make a left turn to the east after departure. The pilot's acknowledgment of the controller's approval of the left turn was the last known radio transmission from the Navajo.

The flight track of N60SE was reconstructed from Kansas City International Airport Terminal Radar Approach Control (TRACON) and Kansas City ARTCC recorded secondary (transponder) radar data. According to this evidence, the Navajo turned to an easterly heading after departing Kansas City but remained beneath the 5000 foot base of the TCA. Its Mode-C target was detected by the TRACON at 1222:48 when the airplane was still near the Downtown Airport and at 1600 feet. The target was tracked eastbound at a constant rate of climb until the radar return was lost at 1227:58 and 7000 feet.

The flight of Army 18061

At 0944, Army 18061 departed Calhoun County Airport (Anniston, Alabama) enroute to Sherman Army Airfield (Fort Leavenworth, Kansas), with two pilots and one passenger on board. The aircraft was equipped with an operating Mode-C transponder. The IFR-filed flight was uneventful and progressed routinely at 8000 feet. At 1218, Kansas City ARTCC cleared Army 18061 to descend to 7000 feet. The U-21 was level at that altitude when, at 1221, the ARTCC handed off the flight to the Kansas City TRACON-east radar controller. The crew was advised to expect a visual approach and was given the weather as, ". . . sky clear, visibility 10, wind from 260 at 7 knots . . ." At 1225, Army 18061 was notified of a traffic advisory, ". . . twin Cessna . . . 12 o'clock position, five miles distant, at 8000 feet, IFR, and southwest bound." Seconds later the crew reported, "Traffic in sight." Radar contact with the flight was lost about 1228.

Examination of the radar data confirmed that the traffic advisory to Army 18061 did not pertain to the Navajo, and the U-21 was well clear of the reported traffic when the two aircraft collided. The data further proves that Army 18061 did not alter its heading after its last clearance, and the airplane maintained 7000 feet until radar contact was lost.

Nose to nose

Figure 3-5 shows the angle of impact between the U-21 and the Navajo. The illustration is a dramatic reminder of the limitations of see and avoid.

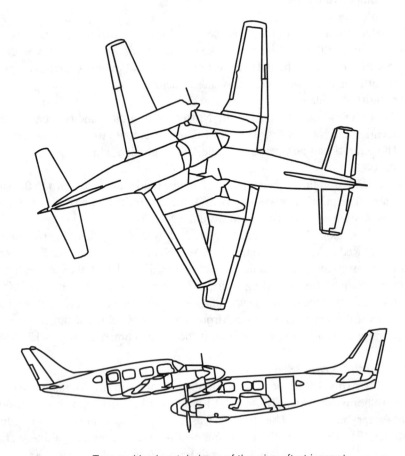

Top and horizontal views of the aircraft at impact

Fig. 3-5. *Angle of impact: Mid-air collision of U.S. Army U-21 and Piper Navajo.* NTSB

The ATC factor

At the time of the accident, the east radar position at the Kansas City TRACON was staffed by an area supervisor and a developmental ATC specialist. The supervisor had been monitoring Army 18061 for only seven minutes but had provided the crew with the traffic advisory regarding the twin Cessna. The developmental controller had just sat down at the position, so had observed the radar screen for about one minute before the accident. Both controllers later reported not seeing any primary or secondary radar information pertaining to the Navajo.

The day after the accident, a flight inspection of the radar system and associated TRACON radio frequencies was conducted by the FAA. No discrepancies were found. The Safety Board requested the FAA play back the relevant recorded Kansas City TRACON radar data, using their Retrack Program Computer.

The Retrack Program can, through the use of recorded data from the TRACON, display ARTS III alphanumeric symbology like that shown on the east radar controller's scope. Although it cannot replicate the entire radar portrayal, it duplicates the alphanumerics generated by the ARTS III program and its associated logic.

An aircraft operating under an IFR flight plan is tracked on the radar scope by a full data block (FDB). An FDB includes aircraft location, identification, altitude, ground speed, and flight-plan data. A limited data block (LDB) appears on the scope to represent an untracked-VFR target. The aircraft's transponder code and altitude readout, if Mode-C is operating, is the only data available to the controller.

The FDB of Army 18061 appeared on the scope at 1221:40 and remained on the display until the collision. Likewise, the LDB of N60SE came into view about 1222:45 and also remained on the scope until the collision. On the last presentation that showed both airplanes, the position-tracking symbols were nearly overlapped and at the same altitude.

ARTS III safety features

The ARTS III has an automatic offset feature designed exactly for these scenarios. To eliminate the possibility for data-block information being unidentifiable, the computer shifts [offsets] each block that is in danger of overlapping. According to the retrack presentation, the FDB of Army 18061 and the LDB of N60SE shifted the appropriate distance, which should have given the controllers an unobscured view of the data blocks.

In addition, controllers using this system cannot suppress 1200 (VFR) transponder codes. They are depicted automatically on the radar scope with a computer-generated triangle over the primary and secondary targets for non-Mode-C targets. Mode-C transponder targets are shown by a computer-generated square over the primary and secondary targets. The system also displays the altitude in a three-digit code attached to the square by a ¼" leader line.

Conflict alert

The aural and visual alerts associated with the conflict-alert system are based on projected position and velocity data for tracked Mode-C targets. A controller would not be alerted by the system if either of the involved aircraft was not tracked, even if it was equipped with an operating Mode-C transponder. Communication with a controller, or even operating a Mode-C transponder during a VFR flight, would help provide collision-avoidance protection to a pilot. However, a pilot receiving VFR flight-following services would result in the radar controller tagging the target and automatically initiating the track needed by the conflict-alert system.

The conflict-alert system and collision avoidance

During this investigation, the Safety Board chose to evaluate the usefulness of the conflict-alert system with regards to potential collisions between tracked and untracked Mode-C radar targets. The Board manually tagged the LDB associated with N60SE, which automatically changed it to an FDB-tracked target. This simulated FDB remained on the radar scope until it merged with Army 18061's FDB, and ultimately vanished at the moment of collision.

The Board also noted that the conflict-alert visual and aural alarms activated more than 40 seconds before the actual collision, and continued until the radar targets disappeared. This time would have been ample for a controller to issue a traffic or safety advisory.

Cockpit visibility study

A cockpit visibility study was conducted to determine the location of each airplane with respect to the field of vision of the pilot(s) in the other airplane. A binocular camera was used to photograph the cockpits of two airplanes with structurally identical cockpit visibility to the accident airplanes. The camera rotated about a vertical axis that is normally 3.5 inches from the lenses, approximating the distance between the front of the eye and the pivot point about which the head rotates. The resulting photographs showed the outline of the cockpit windows as seen by a crewmember rotating his head from side to side. Monocular obstructions within the window, such as the windshield or door posts, were also defined by the photographs.

Results of the cockpit visibility study

The results of the study showed that the Navajo was visible through the windshields of both U-21 pilots. The aircraft would have appeared 13 degrees left and 2 degrees below the U-21 pilot eye reference points. Since the army aircraft was in level flight, the eye reference point was the horizon. Neither pilot's view would have been obstructed by the windshield, door posts, windshield wipers, or any other airplane equipment.

The U-21 would have appeared 18 degrees to the right and 3 degrees below the Navajo pilot's eye-reference point. Because the center windshield post of the Navajo partially obstructed the pilot's view of the U-21, his view would have temporarily been restricted to only his left eye. The copilot's view, however, was never obstructed.

The probability of visual detection

Prior to the accident, an air-to-air visual acquisition study had been conducted by Lincoln Laboratory at the Massachusetts Institute of Technology. Because the circumstances surrounding the U-21 and Navajo flights closely coincided with the model produced from this study, the NTSB used the analyses to determine the probability of visual acquisition between the army and Navajo pilots shortly before the collision. The data given were the speeds of both airplanes, headings, the area profile at the presentation angle, the number of pilots in each airplane engaged in the traffic search, and the visual range. The outcome indicated that the probability of target acquisition would not have been high until the last few seconds before the collision. It was determined that the Navajo pilot only had a 27 percent chance of seeing the U-21 at 12 seconds before impact. Similarly, the army pilots had only a 33 percent probability of seeing the Navajo at 12 seconds before the collision. These results, however, assumed a relatively low pilot workload and unobstructed view of the opposing aircraft. If any of the three pilots had become distracted with workload, or there were obstructions to a clear view of the other airplane, which the Navajo pilot experienced, these probabilities would have been much less.

Could this mid-air have been prevented?

According to the NTSB, the answer is " yes." Remember the outcome of the conflict alert-retrack test the Board conducted? If the Navajo pilot had requested flight-following services, he would have been assigned a discrete transponder code, giving him tracked status. If this had been the real-life scenario, the conflict-alert feature of the ARTS III system would have alerted the controllers of the potential conflict 40 seconds before impact. An aural alarm would have been activated and the two data blocks would have flashed.

The Board believes that most likely the east radar controllers were distracted from monitoring traffic in the moments before the collision because of their position-relief briefing and associated duties. Their workload was considered light, which also might have contributed to a reduced state of vigilance on the part of both controllers. Therefore, the Board feels that if the Navajo had also been tracked, the warning systems would have alerted the controllers in plenty of time to divert the accident.

PRACTICAL APPLICATIONS AND LESSONS LEARNED

1. Contact ATC when flying in a radar-controlled environment. Because the Navajo pilot was not in communication with Kansas City TRACON, there was no opportunity for ATC to provide traffic advisories to him.

2. When VFR, ask for flight-following services. Even when you're operating under Mode-C, the controller still sees only a 1200 VFR code. Yours could be just one of many, particularly on a busy day. Report in and ask for a discrete transponder code. Remember, since you're VFR, ATC will still provide traffic advisories only work-permitting, but at least they are aware of your presence and call sign.

3. Don't assume anything. The Board suggested that since ATC had already notified the army pilots of traffic, and because the army pilots heard few radio calls, perhaps leading to a belief that the controllers were not busy, the U-21 pilots might have assumed that they would be alerted to any additional traffic.

CASE 3: LOST IN THE HANDOFF

1 May 1987: A twin-engine Cessna 340 collided with a single-engine North American SNJ-4 (T-6) approximately 12 miles northwest of the Orlando, Florida, International Airport.

Pilot experience: The Cessna 340 pilot: 2335 hours, 344 in the 340. The T-6 pilot: 7118 hours, 296 in the T-6.

Reported weather at time of mid-air collision: Clear skies with 4000 feet scattered. Visibility 7 miles.

Probable cause

The NTSB determined that the probable cause of this accident was the failure of the Orlando-west controller to coordinate the handoff of traffic to the Orlando-north controller and the failure of the north controller to maintain radar target identification. Contributing to this accident was the limitation of the see and avoid principle, in the circumstances of this mid-air, to serve as a means of collision avoidance.

The flight of the Cessna 340

The Cessna pilot and his family were about to complete a cross-country that had originated in Iowa earlier that same day. At 1538 Eastern Daylight Time, the pilot contacted Orlando approach control north sector and reported he was level at 5000 feet. The aircraft was operating under Mode-C. Moments later he was cleared to ". . . descend and maintain three thousand." At 1545 the flight was handed off to the final controller, and the pilot reported, ". . . with you three thousand." That controller advised the Cessna pilot to ". . . present heading . . . maintain three thousand . . . straight into one eight right." The call was acknowledged, which was the last transmission of the Cessna pilot. The flight had been in the Orlando area only eight minutes before the collision with the T-6.

The flight of the T-6

Earlier that afternoon, the pilot of the T-6 departed Orlando Executive Airport, approximately seven miles north of Orlando International, for a skywriting flight over Disney World and Sea World. Although the aircraft had a transponder, it did not have Mode-C capability. At 1542, the pilot contacted Orlando International west sector controller and requested, ". . . like to descend [from 10,500] out to the west . . . back into Exec." The controller then cleared him to ". . . descend and maintain six thousand . . . two seven zero heading." As the pilot descended through 7700 feet the controller vectored him to 340 degrees for traffic separation.

The west controller attempted to coordinate a lower altitude for the T-6 by calling the north-sector controller, who was busy talking to other aircraft. The west controller eventually got through to the final controller, who gave the approval for the T-6 to descend to 2500 feet. The T-6's traffic was a Boeing 727 arriving from the northwest and landing at Orlando International. The T-6 pilot responded, ". . . has the traffic . . ." as the 727 passed on his right side going the opposite direction.

Seconds later, the west controller advised the pilot to ". . . maintain visual separation . . . seven twenty seven . . . direct to the VOR. Continue descent . . . to four thousand . . . contact approach . . ." The T-6 pilot then contacted the north controller and reported ". . . with you six thousand."

He was cleared to ". . . descend . . . one thousand five hundred." The transmission was acknowledged, followed by ". . . proceed to the airport anytime." At 1547 the T-6 pilot "rogered" the last clearance, and seconds later collided with the Cessna.

The anatomy of the collision—look out below

Figure 3-6 illustrates three views of the angle of impact. The mid-air occurred at 3000 feet as the C-340 was southeastbound in level flight, while the T-6, after completing a right turn with a bank angle of 45 degrees, was southeastbound descending wings level to 1500 feet. Allowing for a descent from 6000 feet to 3000 feet, the minimum average rate of descent of the T-6 was 2000 fpm. The ground speed of each aircraft was approximately 175 kts.

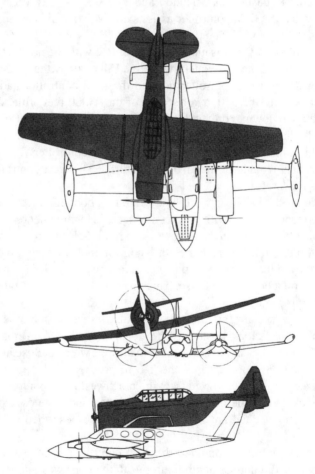

Fig. 3-6. *Angle of impact: Mid-air collision of Cessna 340 and North American T-6.* NTSB

Prior to the T-6 pilot making the right turn, he was flying straight at the Cessna at a distance of a little more than three miles and 3000 feet vertical. At that point, however, he would have been watching the 727 traffic as directed by ATC and the 340 would have been below his nose. Even during the turn and after the rollout, the 340 would still have remained well below his field of view.

At the angle and altitude in which the T-6 was positioned to the 340, the Cessna pilot would have had to lean over and look up as much as 30 degrees in order to catch a glimpse of the T-6. Once the T-6 pilot had made his final turn, there was obviously no chance for the 340 pilot to see him because the T-6 was then directly behind him.

Miscoordinations, distractions, and assumptions

Each Orlando airport is assigned a specific letter that is entered in the data tag of individual aircraft. "T" designates Orlando Executive, and "M" represents Orlando International. Provided the final controller assigns an "M," this also means that the aircraft is at or descending to 3000 feet.

When the west controller was unable to coordinate with the north controller for a lower altitude for the T-6, he subsequently received an okay by the final controller for 2500 feet. Because the west controller noticed the final controller had assigned an "M" tag associated with the 340, and because of the "3000 feet" rule, the west controller cleared the T-6 down to only 4000 feet. Although the west controller had never gotten through to the north controller for a coordinated handoff, and because he had since diverted his attention to another aircraft, the west controller ". . . assumed that the [north controller] would see the [T-6] in the turn." The west controller described his workload as moderate.

The north controller had been working the 340 for about 20 miles when the T-6 pilot came on his frequency: ". . . with you six thousand." He remembered seeing the "T" and a "V" (representing VFR) in the data block of the T-6. He then transferred the 340 to the final controller. Moments later the north controller cleared the T-6 down to 1500 feet, since he believed the aircraft was on a northwest heading. The T-6 was actually in his right turn, not on a northwest course. This proved to be a key operational error on the part of the north controller.

By this time, the two aircraft were about two miles from each other and the 340 was at the T-6's two o'clock position. The north controller then noticed the data block of the T-6 go into coast, but since the two aircraft were so close he was not surprised or concerned. He soon cleared the T-6 to proceed to the airport "anytime" based on a primary target he observed tracking northwest in the vicinity of the coasting T-6 data block. When the pilot "rogered" the clearance, the controller diverted his attention to another quadrant in his sector. He also described his workload as moderate.

When the final controller approved the west controller's request to descend the T-6, he stated that he did not see another aircraft to the northwest, nor was the 340 in handoff status to him. The final controller reported that his workload was light.

ATC and the mid-air connection

Several key ATC factors, in the Board's opinion, either caused or contributed to this mid-air collision. First, the north controller failed to notice that the T-6 was in a steep bank, passing through a northwest—340 degree—heading. Instead, the controller had misinterpreted the aircraft's position as being on a northwest course. The T-6 was in this turn for two minutes—ample time for the controller to verify its track.

The Board determined that the T-6's data tag began to coast because his antenna, which is on the bottom of the airplane, was shielded from the ARTS IIIA antenna during the aircraft's turn just before the collision. In addition, because the two aircraft were so close to one another, the system could not discriminate between each beacon code. Even the 340's data tag was intermittently coasting.

It was later discovered that the coasting data tag the north controller was tracking was not that of the T-6. Because the primary target was heading northwest, and since he thought the T-6 was on a northwest course and not in a turn, he assumed incorrectly. This primary target ranged from 2½ miles to 5 miles away from the T-6's position. According to the Board, the north controller should have been able to recognize that this was not the T-6.

The Board has its say

The data tag of the T-6 was continuously coasting for 46 seconds. The Board, therefore, believes that the lack of proper radar identification techniques, a failure to maintain target identification, and an over-reliance on automation on the part of controllers were causal factors to this mid-air collision.

The Board referred to the FAA Air Traffic Control Handbook, which defines certain guidelines and responsibilities for controllers. The handbook states that the controller must use more than one method of identification when the target goes either into coast status or there is doubt as to the proximity or position of targets. The handbook goes on to say that the ". . . use of ARTS equipment does not relieve the controller of the responsibility of ensuring proper identification, maintenance of the identity, handoff of the correct target associated with the alphanumeric data, and separation of aircraft." Also, the handbook was supplemented by an Orlando International order that directs controllers: "Do not coordinate with another controller when he/she is obviously too busy to handle the distraction."

PRACTICAL APPLICATIONS AND LESSONS LEARNED

1. Say what you really mean. The T-6 pilot reported to the north controller ". . . with you at six thousand." What he actually told the controller was that he was level at 6000 feet. He was not. The T-6 pilot was descending through 6000 feet. The phraseology should have been: ". . . passing through six thousand for four thousand."

2. Don't assume anything. The west controller "assumed the north controller would see the T-6 in the turn." Instead of realizing the aircraft was in a turn, the north controller thought it was on a northwest course. How you perceive a situation doesn't mean that someone else will interpret it the same way.

CASE 4: ARE WE CLEAR OF THAT CESSNA?

25 September 1978: Pacific Southwest Airlines (PSA) Flight 182, a Boeing 727, collided with a Cessna 172 three nautical miles northeast of Lindbergh Field, San Diego, California, at 2600 feet mean sea level (MSL).

Pilot experience: PSA captain: 14,382 hours, 10,482 in the Boeing 727. PSA first officer: 10,049 hours, 5800 in the Boeing 727. PSA second officer: 10,800 hours, 6587 in the Boeing 727. Cessna instructor pilot: 5137 hours. Cessna pilot: 407 hours.

Weather at time of mid-air collision: Clear. Visibility 10 miles. Winds calm.

Probable cause

The NTSB determined the probable cause of the accident was the failure of the flight crew of Flight 182 to comply with the provisions of a maintain-visual-separation clearance, including the requirement to inform the controller when visual contact was lost. Contributing to the accident was the failure of the controller to advise Flight 182 of the direction of movement of the Cessna, the failure of the Cessna pilot to maintain his assigned heading, and the improper resolution of the conflict alert by the controller.

The accident

Around 0816 Pacific Standard Time, an instructor pilot and his instrument student departed Montgomery Field (San Diego) in a Cessna 172. They proceeded to Lindbergh Field to practice ILS approaches. About 45 minutes later, after completing their second approach, the Lindbergh tower local controller cleared them to maintain VFR and contact San Diego approach control. When the 172 pilot called San Diego approach he reported that he was at 1500 feet and northeastbound. The controller verified that he was under radar contact. He was then told to maintain VFR at or below 3500 feet and to fly a heading of 070 degrees. The Cessna pilot acknowledged and repeated the controller's instruction.

At 0853:19 Flight 182 radioed San Diego approach and reported being at 11,000 feet. They were cleared to descend to 7000 feet. Moments later, when the PSA pilot notified the controller that "... airport's in sight," he was cleared for a visual approach. The call was acknowledged.

Shortly before 0900, the approach controller advised Flight 182 that there was "... traffic [at] twelve o'clock, one mile, northbound." Five seconds later (0859:33) the pilot answered, "We're looking." Again, in a matter of seconds (0859:39), the controller told Flight 182, "Additional traffic's twelve o'clock, three miles, just north of the field, northeast bound." The first officer responded, "Okay, we've got that other twelve."

Still yet another report came, this time only 25 seconds later, "... traffic's at twelve o'clock, three miles, out of one thousand seven hundred." This advisory was believed to have been referring to the 172. The first officer replied, "Got 'em," quickly followed by the captain informing ATC "Traffic in sight."

Flight 182 was then cleared, at 0900:23, to ". . . maintain visual separation . . ." and to contact Lindbergh tower. The call was acknowledged. Immediately thereafter, the controller advised the Cessna pilot that there was, ". . . traffic at six o'clock, two miles, eastbound. A PSA jet inbound to Lindbergh, out of three thousand two hundred. Has you in sight." The pilot "rogered" the call.

At 0900:34, Flight 182 reported to Lindbergh tower that they were on the downwind leg for landing. The controller replied, ". . . traffic, twelve o'clock, one mile, a Cessna." Six seconds later, the captain asked the first officer, "Is that the one [we're] looking at?" The first officer answered, "Yeah, but I don't see him now." At 0900:44, the crew informed the controller, "Okay, we had it there a minute ago." Followed shortly by, "I think he's passed off to our right." The controller acknowledged the call with a "Yeah."

The crew continued to discuss the location of the traffic, and at 0900:52 the captain said, "He was right over there a minute ago." The first officer answered with a "Yeah." Eighteen seconds later the captain told the controller they were going to extend their downwind leg three to four miles.

From the number of traffic advisories in a relatively short period of time, it was obvious the skies near Lindbergh Field were very busy that morning. The PSA crew had been pretty successful in detecting their traffic, but there was one aircraft that kept eluding them.

At 0901:11, the first officer asked that chilling question, "Are we clear of that Cessna?" The second officer replied, "Supposed to be," followed by the captain's remark, "I guess." A deadheading PSA pilot who was riding in the jumpseat answered, "I hope." Ten seconds later, the captain remembered, "Oh yeah, before we turned downwind, I saw him about one o'clock, probably behind us now." A few seconds later the first officer said, "There's one underneath." He then added, "I was looking at that inbound there."

At 0901:47, the approach controller advised the Cessna pilot of ". . . traffic in your vicinity, a PSA jet has you in sight. He's descending for Lindbergh." The sound of the mid-air collision was heard on Flight 182's cockpit voice recorder at exactly 0901:47. Twenty-one seconds later, the jet hit the ground.

The ATC connection

At 0901:28, 20 seconds before the controller notified the Cessna of the traffic advisory, the data blocks of Flight 182 and the 172 began to merge, triggering a conflict alert at San Diego Approach Control. Within a few seconds, the data blocks were overlapping and the controller was unable to distinguish either aircraft's altitude readout. After discussing the situation with his supervisor, both controllers elected not to manually offset the data blocks. The approach controller concluded that because Flight 182 said they had the "traffic in sight," and they confirmed the controller's request to maintain visual separation, he did not believe any further action needed to be taken. As the conflict alert progressed, however, he did advise the Cessna ". . . traffic in your vicinity . . . ," albeit too late. Flight 182 was no longer on his frequency.

PRACTICAL APPLICATIONS AND LESSONS LEARNED

1. Clear and concise communication. Avoid ambiguous ("We've got that other twelve.") and nondirective ("He was right over there a minute ago.") phraseology.

2. Immediately notify ATC when you've lost sight of your traffic. Precious seconds tick away as you hopelessly look for your traffic. Ask for help.

3. Redirect the communication. Controllers, if you don't get a clear and decisive response from a pilot, be directive. Reissue the advisory if there is any possibility the pilot has either misunderstood or has lost the traffic. Don't be part of the problem.

Chapter 3 references

Andrews, J.W. 1991. *Air-to-Air Visual Acquisition Handbook.* Lincoln Laboratory. Massachusetts Institute of Technology.

National Transportation Safety Board. 16 February 1988. Aircraft Accident Report: Midair Collision of Cessna 340A, N8716K, and North American SNJ-4N, N71SQ, Orlando, Florida, May 1, 1987. Washington, DC.

National Transportation Safety Board. 3 February 1988. Aircraft Accident Report: Midair Collision of U.S. Army U-21A, Army 18061, and Sachs Electric Company Piper PA-31-350 N60SE, Independence, Missouri, January 20, 1987. Washington, DC.

National Transportation Safety Board. 29 August 1985. Aircraft Accident Report: Midair Collision of Wings West Airlines Beech C-99 (N6399U) and Aesthetec, Inc., Rockwell Commander 112TC, N112SM, near San Luis Obispo, California, August 24, 1984. Washington, DC.

National Transportation Safety Board. 20 April 1979. Aircraft Accident Report: Pacific Southwest Airlines, Inc., B-727, and a Gibbs Flite Center, Inc., Cessna 172, N7711G, San Diego, California, September 25, 1978. Washington, DC.

4
Crew resource management: It's not just for the big boys

THE ESSENCE OF CREW RESOURCE MANAGEMENT (CRM) IS THE APPLICATION of managerial techniques to the field of aviation, a blending of a pilot's technical skills with that of his or her leadership abilities. A person flying as the only pilot on board might consider that there is nothing to manage. However, there is. Remember, this total mid-air collision-avoidance concept is based on effectively using all of your available resources: yourself, your airplane, air traffic control, maintenance, dispatchers, weather folks, maps, charts, approach plates, checklists, and weight and balance forms. Even if you fly 172s every other weekend, you still must manage your resources. You are still the pilot-in-command.

A LESSON IN HUMAN FACTORS

For purpose of this discussion, I will focus on ways of managing your most influential resource—yourself. We are the first link to an error chain. Whatever insight and information we can gather on ourselves gives us the opportunity of not advancing to that next link.

Why is it that every action, or inaction, we do in the air seems to have a domino effect and that the cause can sometimes even be traced back to something we did, or didn't do, before we ever left the ground? This is one of those universal questions that every pilot has wondered after one of those of flights when everything seemed to go wrong. The answer is actually a scientific one.

In human factors terms, a SHEL model (Fig. 4-1) represents the interrelationships between three kinds of resources and their environment. Every resource previously mentioned actually falls into one of three categories: hardware, software, or liveware. Hardware is the aircraft itself and its systems. Software includes all the regulations and Standard Operating Procedures, manuals, checklists, maps, charts, tables, and graphs. Human factors experts differ on exactly where to incorporate these particular items; however, for this exercise I'll include them as software. Liveware includes you and all the people you deal with on the ground and in the air. All three of these elements are then encompassed in a flight environment. This pertains solely to the actual physical environment and weather in which the aircraft operates. We obviously have no control over the environment, but we do have some control over the other factors.

HUMAN FACTORS AND THE COLLISION-AVOIDANCE CONNECTION

No resource is totally isolated from the others. If one element is inferior, it has a negative impact on all the others. Let's run through an ugly scenario to see how one little problem on the ground can snowball to bigger troubles in the air.

Liveware. No matter how often you fly, or how second-nature flying has become, you should always do some mental housekeeping even before you get within eyeshot of the airplane. Ask yourself, "Am I in top form for today's flight?" You take a big yawn and shrug, "I guess so." You have just started the domino effect into motion.

Although you've gotten plenty of sleep, you're still a bit tired. Maybe you're preoccupied with things going on in your life and just don't feel like flying today. Whatever the case, you arrive at the airport to meet your student. You feel confident with the student's ability because he's about a month away from a check ride. This is good, because you're not in the mood for one of those unpredictable, hair-on-fire, nail-biting, heart-pounding, gut-wrenching flights associated with a pre-solo student. Before you can slide over to the coffee maker, your student greets you at the door and informs you that the pre-flight has already been completed. Great. You grab some java, and the two of you move into the weather room to find that the rest of the morning will be good enough for the airwork you want to do, but by noon things might get a little soupy.

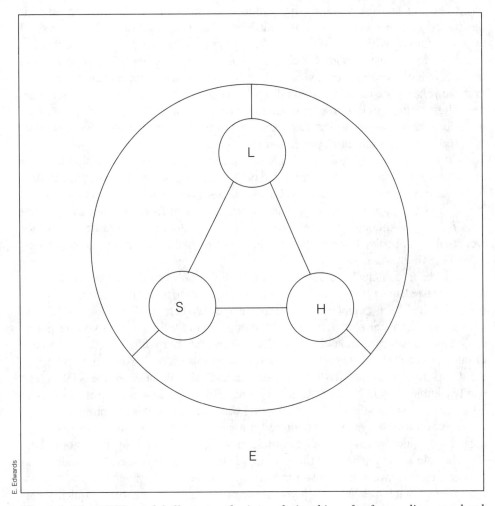

E. Edwards

Fig. 4-1. *The SHEL model illustrates the interrelationships of software, liveware, hardware, and environment.*

After chatting about today's lesson and sipping the last of your coffee, you drag your weary bones out to the plane, a good six feet behind your very enthusiastic student. You perform a cursory checklist cross-check and off you go toward the active. You gaze upward to see the clouds and haze rolling in; so much for that forecast. Oh well, this'll be good experience for the kid.

Because of traffic in the pattern, your clearance is to maintain runway heading for two miles, turn left and proceed to the practice area. On climbout, the haze has become more like fog and the visibility has dropped considerably. Your bright-eyed-and-bushy-tailed student has been transformed into the cowardly lion with saucer-sized eyes communing with the instruments. You, of course, are not yet aware of this because you're too busy looking for clear openings through the fog bank. Suddenly, out of the corner of the windshield, you catch a glimpse of a dark spot coming at you. You grab the yoke to turn left away from this unknown target, but the plane turns right. Fortunately, the other aircraft dives and you don't hear a thump, so you must have missed it. Immediately, you're on the radio telling tower of your problem. By this time, marginal has turned into thick patches of IMC.

Let's get everything straight: You have a plane that flies in the opposite direction of its control movements, you just missed colliding with another aircraft, your student is catatonic, you're now officially IFR, and you discover an inoperable VOR.

Thanks to a fast-thinking controller, traffic is cleared from the area and you are vectored home. Although you could barely use the rudder pedals because your knees were shaking so badly, the unpredictable, hair-on-fire, nail-biting, heart-pounding, gut-wrenching flight was over.

Maintenance, including the supervisor that you've only heard about but never really thought existed, meets you at the ramp, aircraft logs stuffed under their arms. An annual inspection had been completed on the plane the day before. Somehow, the aileron wiring had been incorrectly reinstalled. Although you're fully aware of your responsibilities as an instructor, you not so casually look over at your withering student and ask through clenched teeth, "Didn't you do a flight controls check?" You then turn back to the droop-shouldered, sweaty-lipped mechanic and ask, "What about the VOR?" The barely audible reply is, "We're waiting for a part, so the plane was to be flown only in VFR. Didn't you read the logs?" "Well, um, I was a little tired this morning."

This is a true story. I've embellished it a wee bit, but the main events really did happen. The pilot was an otherwise conscientious and clear-thinking 1000-hour CFI.

This tale accomplished one thing. It proved the relevance of the SHEL model and the connection between human factors and collision avoidance. Every action, or inaction, is closely interrelated. When you allow one part to fail, the others quickly collapse.

Liveware-liveware interface. You (liveware) were complacent, fatigued, preoccupied, and provided little in the way of communication. You showed poor judgment and decision-making skills by not canceling the flight when the weather turned nasty. You and your student (liveware) were busy with other matters and were not looking for traffic, even though you had poor visibility and were in an airport traffic area. Your student's past ability and enthusiasm tricked you into thinking the student had everything under control. You and your student also contacted someone (liveware) from the weather service. Although the forecast was a bust, the interaction with the forecaster provided the clues to derive a correct idea of the actual weather and the hints that the environment was rapidly changing.

Liveware-hardware interface. The airplane (hardware) was broken. You (liveware) didn't catch it because you weren't paying attention. Your student (liveware) didn't catch it because of lack of experience and knowledge. Maintenance (liveware) didn't catch it, either.

Liveware-software interface. Let's start with the airplane's schedule (software). Did someone (liveware) at the flight school make a notation about the VOR? Or did that information slip through the cracks? Was the checklist (software) used during the pre-flight inspection? Did the student (liveware) complete the checklist? We already know that you didn't have much to say during the checklist cross-check. Did either of you look at the maintenance logs (software) for previous write-ups?

Liveware-environment interface. You encountered unexpected bad weather (environment). Although the presence of weather is uncontrollable, what we (liveware) do near and in the weather is totally up to us. Poor judgment—"It doesn't look that bad"—and faulty decision-making—"It'll be good for the kid"—can have disastrous results.

Hardware-environment interface. You had a broken VOR (hardware) in weather (environment) that was marginal VFR rapidly deteriorating to IFR.

Software-environment interface. Did you check the appropriate regs (software) for marginal VFR, VFR, partial panel, and VFR clearance in IMC?

OTHER FACTORS TO CONSIDER IN COLLISION AVOIDANCE

Each person involved with a particular flight has a personal SHEL model. Therefore, a pilot or controller does not have just an individual L-H, L-S, and L-E interface to think about. Rather, they might conceivably have to deal with every possible SHEL model combination. For instance, there are the L-L (pilot-pilot, pilot-controller, controller-controller, pilot-passenger; H-H (ATC equipment, onboard equipment, TCAS II-TCAS II), and E-E (economic issues-political factors-social concerns) interactions to consider.

The moral of the story

Even if you're the pilot-in-command of a general-aviation aircraft, you must continuously manage and monitor a host of factors and situations. As the previous flight scenario illustrated, in a collision-avoidance environment, poorly managed resources can quickly lead to an otherwise avoidable near-miss. Just as we've already learned how to compensate for our visual limitations, so, too, can we learn how to recognize the variables associated with human factors and collision avoidance.

THE GOALS OF CREW RESOURCE MANAGEMENT

This concept has proven so successful that many of the world's airlines have at least some form of CRM training. To better understand the benefits of CRM, and how general-aviation pilots can incorporate it into their flying regimes, it is best to learn from those professionals that use it every day.

The core of CRM is to create teamwork. A common misconception is that this concept is just a fancy way of describing crew coordination. Not true. CRM is far more encompassing and broad-based than just teaching crews to "get along." The various CRM techniques are designed to enhance management skills, which includes learning how to effectively manage all of your available resources, improve effective communication with others, and provide an overall productive-work environment. It also develops an insight into a person's behavior pattern during normal and emergency situations. Lastly, CRM methods emphasize crew decision-making and judgment training.

Is there a real need for CRM?

The following incident is one kind of crew resource management that should serve as a horrible example. It was front-page news in November 1993. A small charter airline flight was delayed nearly two hours leaving Las Vegas, Nevada, for Palm Springs, California, because a fist fight between the pilot and copilot erupted after the two argued over a $5 bet. When the fray ended, one pilot had two black eyes and the other had a finger bitten through to the bone.

The question: Did these pilots follow basic CRM principles? I guess you could say that they were working as a team towards a common goal—each wanted to kill the other. Did they use all of their available resources? Probably. They used what they had, at least: their fists and their teeth. I suppose if they had a baseball bat and some chains handy they would've use those resources too.

Although that incident was an extreme case, the end result—the total disregard of teamwork—is very common. As I had stated in the beginning of the chapter, CRM can be applied to general-aviation flying and can significantly enhance your collision-avoidance skills, but it's important to first understand what CRM can offer to a more traditional crew setting.

As early as 1976, researchers at NASA's Ames Research Center studied the value of total crew involvement and teamwork. Scientists conducted a study involving 18 experienced Boeing 747 pilots. During a simulator test, which involved a progressive emergency coupled with bad weather, flight attendants were asked to interrupt the cockpit conversation with unimportant requests. Several flight engineers abandoned their critical fuel-burn calculations to oblige the cabin crew, resulting in gross operational errors, including one miscalculation of 100,000 pounds of fuel. Some captains played an active managerial role and set priorities that called for postponement of these requests. Still others either never heard what the flight attendant asked for or did nothing to stop the flight engineer from discontinuing his duties.

It was noted that when a smooth flow of resource management ceased to exist, a distinct breakdown in crew involvement occurred. There was no longer a work environment with a cohesive team effort, but rather one of individuals doing their own things. When this breakdown occurred, eyes tended to remain inside the cockpit rather than outside, scanning for traffic. Altitude and heading errors became more common, allowing the airplane to be positioned where it wasn't expected to be.

Teamwork is everybody's concern, no matter what you fly or how much you get paid for doing it. Keep in mind that all pilots must view each flight as a team effort. Pilot-pilot. Pilot-controller. Pilot-maintenance. Pilot-forecaster. Pilot-lineman. Whether you're flying solo and don't fully cooperate with ATC clearances or are sitting in the left seat of a three-holer taking command with a "single-seat" mind set, the end result is the same: a breakdown in the managing of your available resources and a deterioration of your collision-avoidance environment.

According to a Flight Safety Foundation study, Human Performance Factors in Accident Investigation, the flight crew was identified as a causal factor in nearly 65 percent of all air-carrier accidents. The comparable factor for commuter airlines was close to 75 percent. The NTSB conducted its own study, using more than 17,000 factors associated with all aircraft accidents. The NTSB study concluded that, in part, pilot error was a cause in 86 percent of all accidents and 90 percent of the fatal accidents researched.

We can talk statistics all day, but the message doesn't really hit home until those numbers are attached to a person, a fellow pilot. For this discussion, I chose to highlight three airline accidents. When I was a student and low-time pilot, I was under the erroneous assumption that general-aviation accidents occurred because the pilot was inexperienced and, therefore, did something stupid. I also thought that when airline accidents happened there must have been some unforeseen, earth-shattering, and irreversible circumstance that suddenly struck the crew. After all, airline pilots were among the best and most-experienced fliers around, so the same things that happened to that 200-hour general-aviation pilot couldn't possibly have happened to the 10,000-hour professional. However, once I started studying accident reports, I quickly found that quite often the final link that causes a Cessna to crash is the identical final link that causes a Boeing to go down. That revelation—if it can happen to a seasoned captain, it can certainly happen to me—continues to make a lasting impression on me. As you study these next few accidents, think of the similarities between those events and the situations you've been in. It could surprise you.

Although the circumstances of each accident are different, the commonality between all of them is that a series of breakdowns in CRM occurred for a certain period of time prior to the accident. It was those unconstructive behavioral patterns that intensified to the point at which there was no turning back and the accident became inevitable.

Note: The following accounts and transcript excerpts are from the NTSB accident investigation reports. They should in no way be construed to portray the crews of Air Florida Flight 90, Midwest Express Flight 105, and United Flight 173 negatively. Whether certain proposed scenarios actually took place or not are of little consequence. What is important, however, is learning from past events so the same mistakes are never repeated.

CASE 1: AIR FLORIDA FLIGHT 90 SINKS IN THE POTOMAC

Over the years, much has been said about this accident. So much in fact, that by now many pilots have either forgotten the causes or flippantly say, "Tell me something new, I've heard it before." Unfortunately, even professional aviation safety experts have grown weary of Flight 90, and any discussion about the accident usually falls on deaf and disinterested ears.

However, the numerous lessons that we can learn from this accident are timeless. If we've heard it all before, why do the same mistakes keep reappearing in accident reports? Read carefully, for the practical applications that we can use, no matter what type of airplane we fly, makes this accident one of the most significant in terms of making us safer and more-aware pilots.

13 January 1982: Air Florida Flight 90 took off from Washington National Airport during a snowstorm, struck the 14th Street Bridge, and plunged into the Potomac River. Of the 74 passengers on board, 70 were killed, four of the five crew also died, along with four motorists.

Pilot experience: Captain: 8300 total flight hours, 1100 as 737 captain. First officer: 3353 total flight hours, 992 in the 737. Of his total flight hours, 669 were in F-15 fighter jets.

Reported weather at time of accident: A SIGMET (Significant Meteorology) was issued that was valid from 1340 to 1740 EST that included the District of Columbia and Virginia. Moderate occasional severe rime or mixed icing in the clouds were reported by aircraft throughout the mid-Atlantic region, and the freezing level was from the surface to 6000 feet.

Probable cause

The NTSB determined that the probable cause was the flight crew's failure to use engine anti-ice during ground operation and takeoff; the crew's decision to take off with snow and ice on the airfoil surfaces of the aircraft; and the captain's failure to reject the takeoff during the early stages when his attention was called to anomalous engine instrument readings.

Narrative of the accident

Flight 90 arrived at National, in heavy snow, at 1329. The length of time between certain events is very important to remember. Conditions at the airport included moderate to heavy snowfall from 1240 to 1616, forcing National to close from 1338 to 1453. The scheduled departure of Flight 90 had already been delayed one hour and 45 minutes. At 1450, 70 minutes before takeoff, the captain requested the jet be de-iced. Twenty minutes later, they were loaded and ready for pushback. However, because of the combination of ice, snow, and glycol on the ramp, the tug became stuck and could not budge the jet. Snow was still falling heavily when the crew decided to push themselves back by using their thrust reversers. While operating their reversers for an estimated 30 to 90 seconds, much of the snow and slush on the ground blew back onto the aircraft surfaces. The attempt was unsuccessful and they called in a second tug. Finally, Flight 90 was pushed back without further difficulty.

Although the combination of weather and thrust reversers might have contributed to the disaster, what was allowed to occur during the last several minutes of Flight 90 is the most disturbing of all. While taxiing, the crew began the after-start checklist. When the first officer called, "anti-ice," the captain replied, "off." According to the 737 manual, ". . . engine inlet anti-ice system shall be on when icing conditions exist . . .." The Board eventually sent the tape to the FBI voice lab for analysis, where their suspicions were confirmed. The report states that the crew's checklist response seemed to be without hesitation, and there was no discussion regarding the existing weather conditions. Therefore, the Board concluded that there was no evidence the crew ever considered the use of engine anti-ice during the snowstorm.

As they approached a second de-icing area, the crew intentionally parked close behind another jet. The purpose was to use that airplane's exhaust to help in their own de-icing. Although both pilots had previously commented on the severity of the weather, they placed little importance on this last de-icing. The captain was concerned about having his windshield de-iced but remarked, ". . . don't know about my wings." The first officer then replied, ". . . all we need is the inside of the wings [presumably the leading edge devices] . . . the wingtips are gonna speed up on eighty [knots during takeoff roll] . . . they'll shuck all that other stuff ." A minute later they discussed the condition of the wings as they were being de-iced. The captain noted, "I got a little on mine." While the first officer responded, ". . . this one's got about a quarter to half an inch on it all the way." The Board believed that they were talking about ice or snow accumulation.

Seconds later, the first officer asked the captain: "See this difference in that left engine and right one?" The captain responded with a "yeah" and no further comment. Meanwhile, the first officer continued to question the problem: "I don't know why that's different . . . 'less it's hot air going into that right one, that must be it . . . from his exhaust . . . it was doing that at the chocks awhile ago . . . ." The captain completely ignored the first officer's comments and even changed the subject. One minute later, the first officer again expressed concern over the same discrepancy by saying, "This thing's settled down a little bit, might'a been his hot air going over it."

The instrument to which the first officer was referring was the Engine Pressure Ratio (EPR), which is the primary gauge to set and monitor thrust on JT8D engines. The EPR is equal to the ratio of the pressure measured at the engine discharge (Pt7) to the pressure measured at the compressor inlet (Pt2). The EPR target value for takeoff thrust is a predetermined setting dependent on existing conditions. Therefore, if the airflow is disrupted going through the Pt2 probe, the EPR readout will be erroneous.

As Flight 90 left the second de-icing area, the Pt2 probe had already iced-over, which was a direct result of the crew's failure to turn on the anti-ice. The situation was further compromised when, at the gate, slush was blown back onto the surface of the jet, including the intakes. In addition, the exhaust blast from the other airplane in the de-icing area caused some of the ice that had already formed in the Pt2 probe to melt. When the jet then taxied away from Flight 90, the probe refroze into a solid block of ice.

I hope you caught the telltale remark the first officer made while trying to determine the reason for the EPR fluctuation. Although he eventually convinced himself the problem was due to the "hot air going into the right one," he revealed, "it was doing that at the chocks." Obviously, Flight 90 didn't have exhaust blowing in the intakes while at the gate, in the chocks. Unfortunately, neither crewmember picked up on that observation, nor did they discuss the discrepancy any further. They allowed the flight to continue.

As the crew taxied towards the active runway, weather conditions at the airport were updated to indefinite ceiling, 200 feet obscured, visibility ½ mile, moderate snow, temperature and dew point 24 degrees F and wind 010 degrees at 11 kts. Only eight minutes later the crew verified the predetermined EPR setting of 2.04. (I discuss the significance of that setting and the impact it had on the accident a little later.) Flight 90 was then hurriedly ". . . cleared for takeoff . . . no delay on departure . . . traffic's [an Eastern 727] two and a half out for the runway."

Almost immediately after Flight 90 started its takeoff roll, the first officer, who was flying, called, "God, look at that thing, that don't seem right, does it?" Followed by, ". . . that's not right . . .," to which the captain responded, "Yes it is, there's eighty." The first officer reiterated, "Naw, I don't think that's right . . . maybe it is . . . I don't know." Two seconds after the captain called V2 (climb speed), the stickshaker sounded, followed by the captain yelling, "Forward, forward." At 1601, the aircraft struck the heavily congested northbound span of the 14th Street Bridge and plunged into the frozen Potomac River.

The aftermath

This accident did not have to happen. As late as 18 seconds before V2, the crew could have safely rejected the takeoff. Why didn't they? There are many reasons, some that are obvious and others so subtle that they usually go undetected. Either way, they all became links to a deadly chain of events, and no one factor should be dismissed as insignificant.

PRACTICAL APPLICATIONS AND LESSONS LEARNED

Note: This section is divided into two areas of concentration: technical skills and human factors.

1. Know your airplane's operations manual. In the case of Flight 90, the 737 manual clearly states:

   . . . the Pt2 probe will ice up in icing conditions if anti-ice is not used; and an erratic EPR readout could be an indication of engine icing.

   The manual further explains that when the Pt2 probe becomes solidly blocked, EPR fluctuations will cease. Flight 90 experienced both scenarios. Another factor overlooked from the manual was the known abrupt pitch-up characteristics the 737 has with wing leading edge contamination. The advisory to pilots states: "If leading edge roughness is observed or suspected for any reason, care should be exercised to avoid fast/over rotation." The NTSB has since recommended: ". . . prohibition of takeoff if leading edge contamination is observed or suspected."

A thought: When was the last time you read your ops manual or aircraft bulletins? Besides just reading them, think of possible emergencies you might encounter, even unlikely ones. Then, "chair-fly" your decisions at home. This way, you have the time to think carefully through your reactions and mentally prepare yourself before the emergency.

Collision avoidance connection: Understanding the mechanics and aerodynamics of your airplane helps to keep you ahead of it and in control of a developing situation. The less time you spend with your head in the cockpit groping for clues and solutions to your latest dilemma, the more time you have to actually fly your aircraft and maintain scanning vigilance.

2. How's your airmanship? Flight 90 went into a stall shortly after rotation. Because the crew believed that thrust was already at the takeoff limit (from the EPR setting), the pilots chose to concentrate their efforts on pitch attitude. It should have been apparent from the continuation of the stickshaker and the steady decrease in airspeed that the jet was not recovering. Therefore, the Board believes the crew should have responded immediately with a thrust increase, regardless of their assumption that EPR limits would be exceeded.

A thought: As the old saying goes: "There's nothing more useless than altitude above you, runway behind you, and fuel you've already burned!" If you can, climb with your throttles, not with the stick. For specific aircraft procedures, read your ops manual.

Collision-avoidance connection: It goes back to the principle of flying the airplane. When you're allowing it to fly you, your attention has been diverted away from all the other crucial elements of flying, including control of your altitude and heading, and scanning for traffic.

3. Know what you're looking for during your instrument cross-check. Multiengine pilots might frequently get into a habit of just glancing at *matched needles* instead of actually reading the indications. Flight 90 had matched needles. They were just all the wrong readout. The EPR was set at 2.04, but the N1 (low pressure) was 80 percent, Exhaust Gas Temperature (EGT) read 4000 degrees centigrade, N2 (high pressure) was 85 percent and the fuel flow was at 5500 lbs/hr. However, the instruments should have read: N1: 92 percent; EGT: 4500 degrees centigrade; N2: 90 percent, and fuel flow: 8000 lbs/hr. These indications, in turn, determined the EPR was actually at 1.70—not 2.04.

A thought: Matched needles don't automatically mean that everything's okay. First, understand what you're looking for, then read the instruments.

Collision-avoidance connection: Misinterpreting your instruments because you were looking at them instead of reading them can cause you to be cruising at the wrong altitude or heading, where a busy controller doesn't expect you to be. Likewise, misreading the engine instruments is just setting yourself up for an otherwise avoidable emergency. Neither is conducive for effective collision avoidance.

4. Watch out for your fellow pilots. Flight crews who saw Flight 90 before and during takeoff observed unusually heavy accumulation of snow and ice on the jet. Even more disturbing was the airline crew which, when taxiing past Flight 90, saw ". . . almost the entire length of the fuselage with snow and ice . . . including the top and upper side of the fuselage above the passenger cabin windows." They never called Air Florida with this information.

A thought: One can only wonder what would have happened if that crew had alerted Flight 90 by simply saying, "Air Florida, you're covered with snow and ice . . .."

Collision-avoidance connection: I'm sure you're wondering what all this has to do with collision avoidance, but there is a connection. It goes back to the L-L element of the SHEL model. Collision avoidance is a team effort, a specific mind-set. A pilot who is looking out only for himself is not likely to give other pilots the benefit of a position report as he's approaching an uncontrolled airport or navaid. If they're not willing to tell a fellow pilot of an obvious safety hazard, then airborne communication is probably not high on their priority list.

5. Concise and direct communication is vital for a safe flight. None of us can argue with that, but why don't we do it as a standard part of our flying regime? The cockpit transcript of Flight 90 is filled with choppy and incomplete sentences, half-developed ideas, and discussion not essential to flight. The NTSB suggested that the captain never truly listened to the first officer, nor did he sense the urgency in his voice. The first officer never effectively communicated his distress; there were many "maybes" and "I don't knows."

A thought: Listen not only to what is said, but also how it's said. This idea applies during your interaction with controllers, weather folks, maintenance personnel, and anyone else you come in contact with during your flight. It doesn't matter if you fly 172s or 747s, effective communication is a sound foundation for a safe flight.

Collision-avoidance connection: Clear, direct, and concise communication is vital to collision avoidance. Re-read chapter 3 if you're still hazy on the consequences you face when speaking gibberish.

6. Assertiveness. Why wasn't the first officer more assertive when telling the captain his concerns? Was it fear of stepping on the captain's toes? Perhaps he was just taking his cue from the captain, who was the more-experienced airline pilot.

A thought: The first officer's previous flying experience included being a single-seat F-15 check and instructor pilot. This individual obviously was used to calling his own shots in a very aggressive environment, yet he did not speak up on that fateful day. If this situation can happen to a qualified flier like that, it can happen to anyone. The next time things aren't right, or the hair stands up on the back of your neck, or you have a funny feeling, take action.

Collision-avoidance connection: The cockpit is not the place to be timid. Misunderstood an ATC clearance? Confused where your traffic should to be? Are you lost? Things just don't feel right? Then assert yourself to ask questions. Take command of the situation. Don't let some silly little oversight escalate into an avoidable mid-air.

7. Indecisiveness: Both pilots fell into this trap at a critical time, during takeoff. According to the Air Florida Training Manual: "Any crewmember will call out any indication of engine problems affecting flight safety." However, "The captain ALONE makes the decision to reject a takeoff." It appears that the first officer was waiting for that decision from the captain, but it never came.

    A thought: Even if you only suspect a problem—make a decision! Who's going to argue with you when you tell them your reason was for safety?

    Collision-avoidance connection: Decision-making is part of being in command of a situation. Waiting for ATC to give you traffic advisories or not being able to make up your mind about which course of action to take just wastes precious time that you might not have to spare.

8. Complacency. Researchers have obtained valuable insight about human behavior after studying videotapes of numerous crews' interaction during simulated flights. Over-familiarity and complacency are common problems for crews who are accustomed to working together or are well-acquainted with the airplane. Neglected and ignored checklist items are not that rare.

    A thought: Take time to read your checklist and listen to the answer. Also very helpful is touching the switch or light after the callout, before proceeding to the next checklist item.

    Collision-avoidance connection: Over-familiarity of an airplane, a route, an airport, and those with whom you fly creates a tendency for pilots to let down their guards. In this case that means their situational awareness, visual scanning, and altitude and heading clearances.

9. Intimidation. Most pilots don't think of being intimidated by ATC, but it happens. Flight 90 had not even taxied onto the runway when the tower told them: ". . . no delay . . . in departure." Because of the limited visibility, the local controller could not see Flight 90 at the end of the taxiway, nor could he see it on the takeoff roll. As it turned out, ATC had violated traffic separation regulations and were bringing jets in so close that Flight 90 wasn't even off the runway when the 727 behind it landed.

    A thought: Nobody wants to be the jerk that screwed up departures and arrivals on a busy day. However, when you're feeling rushed, or know the inbound traffic is too close, hold short. Remember who is pilot-in-command. Takeoff clearance is a clearance, not an order.

    Collision-avoidance connection: Not just the inexperienced pilots or those that fly infrequently can be intimidated by ATC, especially on a busy day. Sometimes it comes from a simple desire to accommodate everybody. "Sure,

I'll take off immediately even though I haven't finished my checklist," "I don't see my traffic, but the controller's so swamped I better not bother him," "What!? Was that clearance for me? The controller was curt with me the last time I asked him to repeat something, so I think I'll just let this one go." Effectively manage your available resources, in this case ATC, and always remain in control of the collision-avoidance environment.

CASE 2: MIDWEST EXPRESS FLIGHT 105—
ENGINE FAILURE ON TAKEOFF

6 September 1985: Midwest Express Airlines Flight 105, a McDonnell Douglas DC-9, crashed shortly after takeoff at Mitchell Field, Milwaukee, Wisconsin, after it encountered a catastrophic engine failure.

Pilot experience: Captain: 4600 total flight hours, 1100 in the DC-9. First officer: 5197 total flight hours, 1640 in the DC-9, including 1140 as a DC-9 captain.

Probable cause

The NTSB determined that the probable cause of this accident was the flight crew's improper use of flight controls in response to the catastrophic failure of the right engine during a critical phase of flight. This improper use led to an accelerated stall and loss of control of the airplane. Contributing to the loss of control was a lack of crew coordination in response to the emergency.

How the accident happened

During the initial climb, at about 450 feet AGL, there was a loud noise and a loss of power associated with an uncontained failure of the 9th and 10th stage high pressure compressor spacer of the right engine. According to witnesses, Flight 105 continued to climb to about 700 feet AGL, and then rolled to the right until the wings were in a near vertical, approximately 90-degree banked turn. During the roll, the crew entered an accelerated stall, lost control of the airplane, and crashed. The crew of four and the 27 passengers were fatally injured.

The silent cockpit

The following is an excerpt of Flight 105's cockpit voice recorder (CVR) tape, as reported by the NTSB. Notice that there was virtually no communication between the pilots during the final seconds of the flight.

15:21:26.4 Sound of loud clunk.
15:21:26.7 Sound similar to engine spooling down.
Captain: What . . . was that?
Captain: What . . . we got here . . .?
Captain: Here.
F/O: (call to tower) Midex . . . we've got an emergency here.
15:21:36.0 Sound similar to stickshaker starts and continues until end of tape.

Captain: Oh . . .

F/A: (First flight attendant over PA) Heads down.

15:21:41.7 (Ground proximity warning system) Whoo— (Sound of the beginning of first "whoop" of the GPWS.)

15:21:41.9 End of recording.

Silence is not golden in the cockpit. During the investigation, the NTSB learned that Midwest Express pilots sometimes practiced an unwritten, non-FAA-approved "silent cockpit" philosophy. The principle was not to make any unnecessary callouts or to even verbalize the nature of an emergency until after reaching 100 knots and at least 800 feet on takeoff. Although the Board could not determine if the pilots remained relatively quiet because of this philosophy, they do believe that it influenced their actions. Nevertheless, the Board concluded that a more likely reason for the lack of cockpit communication between the pilots was because of their sense of confusion and being overwhelmed by the emergency.

According to the investigation, the sound of uncertainty in the voice of the captain when he said, "What . . . was that?" and, "What . . . we got here . . .?" suggested that he was asking for assistance from the first officer rather than making a rhetorical remark. The Board also believed that because the first officer failed to respond, his silence added to the overall confusion of the crew. Surprisingly enough, only seconds later, the first officer "broke his silence" and notified the tower controller of their emergency. The Board further believed that time would have been better spent going through emergency checklists or at least coordinating a course of action with the captain.

PRACTICAL APPLICATIONS AND LESSONS LEARNED

1. Use your common sense. If you find yourself being required, or strongly encouraged, to practice an obviously unsafe procedure, don't follow the crowd. Speak up. Use your common sense and knowledge of procedures.

   Collision-avoidance connection: Watch out for unsafe or impractical procedures that, among other things, can take your attention away from visual scanning.

2. Aviate. Although the crew had never experienced this type of emergency, either actual or in the simulator, they still could have prevented the stall and subsequent loss of control. Know your airplane's limitations and capabilities—it could mean survival in catastrophic emergencies.

   A thought: Aviate, navigate, and communicate is a good rule of thumb, and acting in that order of priority makes sense.

   Collision-avoidance connection: Emergencies have a tendency to cause head-lock in the cockpit. Don't fall into that trap. Remember to aviate, navigate, and communicate.

3. Be clear, direct, and concise. Be a helpful, intelligent, and active participant when communicating during an emergency. Speaking in disjointed sentences, yelling a string of expletives, or becoming mute has no redeeming qualities in an emergency, or even normal, situation.

Collision-avoidance connection: Clear, direct, and concise communication is crucial in a collision-avoidance environment. Reread chapter 3.

CASE 3: UNITED FLIGHT 173—ENGINES FLAMING OUT

This accident is discussed in greater detail in chapter 6. The events which led to the crash of United Flight 173 revealed a clear breakdown of CRM. Therefore the analysis of the accident warrants inclusion in this chapter.

28 December 1978: United Airlines Flight 173, a McDonnell Douglas DC-8, crashed into a wooded area near Portland, Oregon, after the aircraft experienced total fuel exhaustion.

Pilot experience: Captain had 27,638 total flight hours, 5517 as captain in the DC-8. First officer had 8209 total flight hours, 247 as first officer in the DC-8. Second officer had 3895 total flight hours as a second officer, 2263 in the DC-8.

Probable cause

The NTSB determined that the probable cause of the accident was the failure of the captain to properly monitor and respond to the aircraft's fuel state. He also failed to respond to the crewmembers' advisories regarding the fuel situation. Contributing to the accident was the failure of the two other crewmembers to either fully comprehend the criticality of the fuel state or to successfully communicate their concerns to the captain.

The accident

The crew of Flight 173 flew a low-altitude holding pattern for more than one hour while they dealt with a landing gear malfunction. The captain subsequently became so preoccupied with the task of preparing the flight attendants for a possible emergency landing that he no longer monitored the rate of fuel burn. Although the first and second officers made repeated attempts to tell the captain of the deteriorating fuel situation, the comments were not appropriately addressed.

Communication is a two- or three-way street

The following are portions of the intracockpit conversation that occurred during the final 27 minutes of Flight 173, as discussed in the NTSB accident report. Pay particular attention to the specific interaction between the crewmembers. As you read the transcripts, apply a little math and you'll be able to calculate their actual fuel state. Hint: Flight 173's fuel burn was 13,209 pounds per hour, or 220 pounds per minute.

1746:52
F/O: How much fuel we got . . ?
S/O: Five thousand [pounds].
F/O: Okay.
1748:54
F/O: . . . what's the fuel show now . . ?

Captain: Five [thousand pounds].
F/O: Five [thousand pounds].
Captain: That's about right. The fuel pumps are starting to blink.
1750:16
Captain: Give us a current [weight] . . . another fifteen minutes.
S/O: Fifteen minutes?
Captain: . . . give us three or four thousand pounds on top of zero fuel weight.
S/O: Not enough.
S/O: Fifteen minutes is gonna . . . really run us low on fuel. Right?
1756:53
F/O: How much fuel you got now?
S/O: Four . . . thousand . . .
F/O: Okay.

Captain tells second officer to leave the cockpit and check on the cabin preparations. Second officer returns approximately four minutes later.

1806:40
?: I think you just lost number four . . .
F/O: Better get some crossfeeds open . . .
S/O: Okay.
F/O: We're goin' to lose an engine . . .
Captain: Why?
F/O: We're losing an engine.
Captain: Why?
F/O: Fuel.
1807:06
F/O: It's flamed out.
S/O: We're going to lose number three in a minute . . .
1813:21
S/O: We've lost two engines . . .
Captain: They're all going.
1814:55
Sound of impact.

A breakdown of CRM

At the conclusion of this investigation, the Board stated that it believed this accident exemplifies a recurring problem: a breakdown in cockpit management and teamwork during a situation involving malfunctions of aircraft systems in flight.

Follow the leader

For years, the standing airliner joke has been: "Rule number 1. The captain is always right. Rule number 2. See rule number 1." Even today that belief can be found in some cockpit environments.

During the Board's investigation of Flight 173, members agreed that because a captain is a crew's leader, and usually the more experienced airline pilot, the person in that position is more likely to dictate and manipulate the objectives and priorities of a flight. Additional studies on leadership have also noted that standard operating procedures would sometimes not be followed at both regional and major airlines because the captain "has done it his way for years."

At one regional airline, it was brought to the attention of its chief pilot that many first officers routinely carried little notebooks with remarks concerning which captains do what. At the same airline, it was reported that some captains chose to do all of the cockpit duties themselves, including duties of the first officer.

John Nance, airline pilot and safety expert, has also spoken candidly on this subject:

For decades there has been little support for copilots and flight engineers who questioned a captain's judgment, and the problems cut across the industry. After all, if you offend the captain you're paired with for the next four weeks, it's going to be a difficult month. Being diplomatic gets in the way of being responsible, especially when your airline refuses to encourage assertiveness.

The Safety Board also found that a captain can just as easily lead his crew by applying subtle pressure. The captain can, therefore, set the tone of "It's best if we think the same." The rest of the crew might not want to rock the boat and would be content to just have a trouble-free, three-day trip.

Whether a captain uses the strong-arm method or a more subtle approach, it can still hinder interaction and might even force another crewmember to yield the right to express an opinion.

In the case of Flight 173, the captain became preoccupied with the emergency landing preparation, thereby directing a great deal of the cockpit conversation to that subject. According to the investigation report, the first officer did not speak in a positive or direct tone when commenting on the fuel situation. Not until the number four engine flamed out did he vocalize a direct message, "Get this . . . on the ground." Likewise, the second officer never told the captain in an assertive manner that the fuel situation was becoming critical. Although he did inform the captain that "fifteen minutes is really gonna run us low on fuel," he did not take the issue any further.

PRACTICAL APPLICATIONS AND LESSONS LEARNED

1. Be an effective communicator. Remember the rule: Be clear, direct, and concise.

   Collision-avoidance connection: Effective communication in the cockpit and on the radio is an integral part of collision avoidance.

2. Don't be intimidated. Gray hair, bifocals, and a thick logbook do not guarantee that every decision the pilot makes will be the correct one. You're also in the cockpit because of your knowledge, skill, and experience. Don't allow an unsafe situation to continue just because you're too intimidated to speak up.

Collision-avoidance connection: This rule is also true for commercial and instrument students when they fly with their CFIs. More ratings and a few hundred extra hours does not automatically make CFIs, or anyone else for that matter, safer pilots than their advanced students. Expect to someday fly with a CFI who doesn't regard see and avoid that big of a deal. Remember not to get intimidated into not applying what you've already learned about collision avoidance. The student might just be able to teach the teacher a thing or two.

3. Three pilots: one team. This lesson is the culmination of lesson numbers one and two. Gather the necessary information from your own knowledge base, speak up in a clear, direct, and concise manner, and don't let a negative environment in the cockpit intimidate you from correcting an unsafe situation.

Collision-avoidance connection: This lesson applies to general-aviation pilots as well. How you approach flying—knowledge, airmanship, communication skills, assertiveness, decision-making—and how you manage your available resources—fellow pilots, ATC, maintenance, forecasters—all play a part in the total mid-air collision-avoidance concept.

A personal thought

Anyone who has been flying for awhile will sooner or later have to deal with an accident on a personal level. When you get that dreaded phone call late at night, it can really make you stop and think about those proverbial links to the deadly chain of events. The lessons that we can all learn from Flight 90, Flight 105, and Flight 173 are very powerful and thought-provoking. Good aviators have died. Well-trained aviators have died. But you can break those links. Whether it's through your ability to communicate, your decision-making and judgment skills, systems knowledge, experience, assertiveness, common sense, or gut-feeling, if you're aware of a potentially dangerous situation, don't allow it to continue.

CRM and overall safety

It is important to note that the lack of CRM causes more than accidents. Researchers have also found that the relationship between poor communication and crew coordination contribute to even the simplest of operating errors. Remember how important the clear, direct, and concise rule in collision avoidance is. Incidents associated with the mishandling of engine settings, hydraulics, and fuel systems, and the misreading or missetting of instruments, resulting in altitude and heading busts, are higher among crews that do not practice CRM techniques.

Through NASA's Aviation Safety Reporting System (ASRS), pilots involved in accidents or incidents report their opinions on why those events occurred. Interestingly enough, 35 percent mentioned weak crew coordination; 16 percent named a relaxed cockpit environment with too much extraneous conversation; 15 percent spoke of misunderstanding other crewmembers; 10 percent specified complacency; and 5 percent cited a lack of confidence in subordinates, which in turn, caused them to do other crewmembers' duties.

THE CRM CONCEPT IN AIR-CARRIER OPERATIONS

In the wake of United Flight 173, the airline's upper-level management decided that drastic measures had to be taken to prevent another such crash. United Airlines' professional reputation was, indeed, on the line. The airline had never before had an accident caused by such gross negligence in the cockpit. Therefore, the company developed a special task force to study this situation and make recommendations.

In 1979, the task force received substantial support from NASA, which was also examining the problem. Independently, NASA had drawn up a report pointing out that of the 50 most recent commercial airline accidents, 30 could have been prevented by better communication among crewmembers. This report underlined the difference between individual pilot error and mistakes in management, judgment, and leadership; a subtle but significant distinction. Soon after, the experts determined that Flight 173 had not been undone by inadequate training or a technical failure, but by an inability to communicate. Never before had a major airline made such a radical conclusion. Not only did United forego the usual airline solution—develop a new checklist to fix a problem—but it contradicted the tradition that the captain was always right. The task force emphasized that in-depth instruction in management, communication, and human behavior was paramount in the safe operation of its aircraft. As you can see, this same philosophy is also the core of the total mid-air collision avoidance concept.

CRM integration in air-carrier operations

United Airlines, with the assistance of NASA's human factors division, pioneered one of the most respected CRM programs in the world. Although other airlines have outstanding CRM training in their organizations, this chapter focuses primarily on the CRM concepts that United has formally recognized.

One CRM perspective: United's program begins with an intensive three-and-a-half day seminar at a suburban Denver hotel. The airline purposely wanted the participants to be in a location far removed from the surroundings of a flight-training center. Each seminar is limited to 24 participants who are assigned to four six-person teams. The groups are equally mixed with captains, first officers, and second officers. Oddly enough, the airline has since found that putting together teams of people who probably disagree on some matters, like nonsmokers and smokers, works best. Once the teams are set, they stay that way for the duration of the seminar. When crews must eat together, work together, and socialize together, the necessary bonding needed to form a cohesive group is then able to take place.

The seminars have very little structure and are conducted by airline pilots that do not instruct, but rather manage and guide the participants in the right direction. This environment has been conducive to the learning process that is so critical to the CRM goals.

Awareness, practice and feedback, and continuous reinforcement

A specialized team of psychologists, researchers, and pilots determined that effective CRM training must incorporate three distinctive phases: awareness, practice and feedback, and continued reinforcement. Each phase is made of several key elements that, when applied, enhance the crew's overall work performance.

Awareness phase

The awareness phase focuses on the functioning of crews as teams, not just a collection of technically competent individuals. This stage also helps pilots learn how to best use their own personal leadership style while understanding their own behavioral traits during routine and emergency situations.

Prior to attending the seminar, pilots receive eight booklets that describe a series of nontechnical in-flight situations (i.e., weather-related scenarios). The questions that follow ask what the pilot would do if in that position. Responses are graded and an individual score is given to the pilot later. While attending the CRM seminar, the pilots take a similar questionnaire, only this time they must answer as a team. Surprisingly enough, most crews try and work on these problems individually. Only when time is running out do these crews start working together; and they soon realize that if they had worked as a team from the start, they would have completed the assignment.

Each exercise presents a series of questions designed to measure leadership and behavioral attitudes in five separate areas:

- Inquiry—whether the person takes an active or passive role in compiling facts
- Advocacy—whether feelings are stated aggressively
- Conflict resolution—how the pilot typically tries to find a solution when working with others
- Critique—how well the participant is able to evaluate personal performance and that of others
- Decision-making—assertiveness of the pilot

In each area, five choices are given and the participant is asked to circle the one believed a best personal description. In conflict resolution, for instance, the choices are:

A. When conflict arises, I try to remain neutral or stay out of it.
B. I try to avoid generating conflict, but when it does appear, I try to soothe feelings and to keep my crewmembers together.
C. I try to find a position that is acceptable.
D. I try to cut off conflict or win my position.
E. I seek out reasons for it in order to resolve underlying causes.

The pilots are also asked in other sections to score their preferences for particular actions or resolutions to problems.

The results of this phase show how decisions made individually are much poorer than those made collectively. And most importantly, crewmembers are able to analyze how they react to various leadership styles in the cockpit and how their own behavior can affect operational outcomes.

Practice and feedback stage

This phase exposes pilots to actual team-building as they go through problem-solving exercises. The focus is split between simulated flight decisions and scenarios that have nothing to do with flying. It puts the pilots into a situation in which they must solve problems but cannot draw on their experience. Once again the motive is to show the crews the importance of communicating and sticking together as a team.

The first part of this phase, which usually takes place on the second day of the seminar, is called line-oriented flight training (LOFT). The six-person teams are split into three-person crews—captain, first officer, and second officer—to begin the flight-simulator portion. While the crews are being videotaped, scenarios from actual accident reports are used to introduce a wide spectrum of in-flight problems, including windshear and other weather phenomena, mechanical failures, crewmember incapacitation, and sick passengers. It is important that the LOFT scenario itself does not overload the crew, but present believable and relevant situations. After two simulated flights, the tape is played back only to that specific crew and a CRM seminar guide; the tape is later erased. For the first time, these individuals see themselves functioning from a third-person perspective. This perspective in itself is the most powerful stimulus for attitude and behavior change.

LOFT studies

Researchers have obtained valuable insight concerning human interaction from these tapes, and several findings of significant importance have resulted from the more than 10 years of LOFT data.

First, any level of stress can produce a narrowing of perceptual attention. Accordingly, a less-than-peak-performance environment is created when the captain flies and directs crewmember activities while attempting to make final decisions regarding emergency actions to be taken. When LOFT experiments involved high workloads and multiple aircraft emergencies, immediate benefits were derived when captains transferred aircraft control to the first officers while concentrating on effective decision-making and problem resolution. In these cases, the captain had more time to analyze problems and develop effective plans.

This arrangement also provided other crewmembers with a greater sense of responsibility and promoted a high degree of vigilance and participation. Very simply, if a crewmember is treated and accepted as a valuable part of the team, then that person is going to respond accordingly.

The second finding is a problem with over-familiarity of standing operating procedures and checklists. Pilots who have flown the same airplane or route for years have a tendency to hear and see what they've come to expect. Even familiarity between crewmembers can have the same results.

And lastly, LOFT data has proven the need for CRM to include the coordination of the cabin crew's activities. It has been found to be highly effective for the captain to involve the flight attendants during the initial pre-flight brief. Discussing with the entire crew what procedure will be taken for a particular emergency enhances the overall safety of the flight. In addition, by setting the stage for open communication with the cabin crew, potentially serious malfunctions in the aircraft, such as pressurization, electrical, air conditioning problems, have been detected and corrected early.

The culmination of the LOFT segment of the seminar is a dramatic videotaped reenactment of the last hour of United Flight 173. Once pilots have been exposed to the concepts of CRM and have viewed the tape, as many as 70 situations were observed in which the crew of Flight 173 could have reacted more effectively.

Continuous reinforcement phase

This stage is to be carried out of the seminar and into the actual cockpit environment. After each phase of CRM training, a poll is taken to determine how many pilots in the course believe they already use CRM principles in the cockpit. At the beginning, typically 95 percent of the participants feel they fall into that category. By the second day, that figure has dropped to 75 percent; and at the end of the program, it has dropped even further, to only 15 percent. The reinforcement phase, therefore, is the most critical for the ongoing success of CRM training.

This phase is where the true test of CRM takes place. The feeling among many seminar graduates is that because every United pilot has gone through CRM, they all know what is expected from each other. As soon as a pilot notices another falling into the old way of conducting cockpit business, immediate action should take place. Some pilots say that even being as blunt as saying "You're being a jerk, let's practice some CRM" has been known to have a great impact. The philosophy at the airline is that the issue is too serious to overlook a potentially dangerous-cockpit environment.

Therefore, peer pressure is viewed as a key element during the reinforcement phase. But encouraging crewmembers to stick together as a team is just as important. After all, no one wants to be known as the weak link of a crew.

CRM: views beyond the seminar

Since 1978, great progress has been made to incorporate CRM techniques in the daily routine of airline pilots. A recent survey revealed that nearly 97 percent of all pilots who have completed the United seminar feel that CRM has definitely contributed to better relationships and management in the cockpit. A less-tense work environment rates at the top of their list. More effective communication ranks a close second.

Since CRM's conception, however, a small minority of older pilots has been the most critical of the program. They are concerned that CRM cuts too deeply into a captain's authority. In making inflight decisions, they feel experience must weigh very heavily, and the commander of the aircraft should not feel obligated to explain or discuss his actions with junior crewmembers. The captains fear that too much discussion will turn the cockpit into a debating forum, and the crewmembers close to promotion or seeking a way to establish their own authority will challenge the captain's decisions.

It has long been documented that the majority of all pilots are more task-oriented than people-oriented. Therefore, change, especially a seemingly forced change, is extremely difficult for those pilots that have been trained and indoctrinated to only one way of thinking. These pilots have seen themselves as leaders, not managers. To them, managers are people who sit behind desks. This is the challenge that faces pro-CRM crewmembers. Fortunately, however, with the application of solid reinforcement techniques, these incidents of resistance have not increased and, at some airlines, have even decreased.

CRM and airline management

Aviation safety and accident prevention most definitely has a dollar figure attached to it. The seriousness of that fact becomes evident when the upper-level management of an airline is skeptical as to the need for a CRM program. However, it has been noted that the most successful examples of CRM training are at airlines where the CEOs were convinced of the value of such training. United and Delta are two such airlines whose ambitious CRM programs resulted from a corporate commitment at the top.

Historically there have been two ways of convincing management to implement CRM training. Unfortunately, the first course is when an airline has experienced a series of accidents. United Flight 173, several Delta mishaps and incidents in 1987, and others have, over the years, forced upper-level management to deal with this issue. The second means has been through the strong advocacy of the line pilots themselves. Hawaiian Airlines, for example, has one of the best safety records in the industry. The airline obtained this record even without a CRM program. However, pilots convinced management this training would be valuable in helping prevent accidents in the future. Based on their own pilots' recommendations, Hawaiian's management enthusiastically adopted a CRM program because they were not satisfied to rest on their laurels.

CRM and air-carrier safety

Since United began its CRM training program, its accident rate went from one hull loss per one million operations to one hull loss per 4.8 million operations. The average for all U.S. carriers is still one hull loss per one million operations. But the progress of these managerial concepts and techniques, however, can be measured only during the aftermath of an incident or accident. That is the true test of CRM's success.

CASE 4: WINDSHEAR ON TAKEOFF

1984. United Airlines Flight 663, a Boeing 727, encountered windshear while departing Denver's Stapleton Airport.

The incident

The jet struck a localizer shack, but the crew managed to return safely, only to discover a 15-foot gash in the belly of the airplane. According to the NTSB report:

> United's cockpit resource management training played a positive role in preventing a more serious accident from occurring in Denver.

The Safety Board also found that the flight crew reacted in an exemplary manner because crewmembers had agreed, during their pre-flight briefing, to make a full-power takeoff as a precaution against reported windshear in the area. Each pilot was allowed to freely enter into this discussion. Moreover, the captain had included the cabin crew in this pre-takeoff briefing; therefore, there was no second guessing from any crewmember as to what to expect during an emergency.

Collision-avoidance connection: Excellent planning and thoughtful preparation had set the foundation for a safe flight. The crew prevented miscommunication, chaos, and head-lock at the most critical phase of the flight.

CASE 5: CRM IN ACTION

1989. United Airlines Flight 232, a McDonnell Douglas DC-10, was enroute from Denver to Chicago when it experienced a catastrophic emergency when parts of the number two engine disintegrated and exploded, which subsequently severed the hydraulic lines.

The wide-body jet, carrying 296 passengers, was over Iowa at 37,000 feet when the captain radioed Minneapolis Center and informed them that the aircraft had "almost no controllability, little elevator, and almost no aileron." A check pilot happened to be riding the jumpseat at the time and was quickly drafted as a fourth crewman. He knelt between the captain and first officer and manipulated the throttles at the crew's direction.

The captain credited the CRM program for enabling the crew to work as a team and solve the serious control problems. Because of the unlikely nature of the emergency, no checklist or training had ever been done on this situation. Therefore, according to the captain, "Before any decision was made, everyone had an input. We made it up as we went along."

Although passengers died, this emergency was still one of CRM's finest hours. A catastrophic emergency, 40 minutes to the nearest major airport, and an unofficial crewmember on his knees helping to fly the airplane—this response is the epitome of CRM.

Collision-avoidance connection: Here is an excellent example of effectively using all of your available resources. The crew maintained clear, direct, and concise communication among themselves as well as to ATC. The controllers were informed of the seriousness of the emergency and were able to separate traffic appropriately. No one was kept out of the decision-making loop. This type of mind-set produces a tremendous level of situational awareness and is an excellent way to approach a collision-avoidance environment.

CRM FOR GENERAL AVIATION

Let's review the idea that each flight is a team effort. You know the old saying, "No man is an island." Well, no pilot flies in a protective bubble. It has been well documented that how we interact with every person we come in contact with before and during a flight can significantly affect the outcome of that flight. Therefore, learning how to handle yourself and those around you is one of the keys to being a safer pilot. When those resources are managed effectively in a collision-avoidance environment, you tend to stay ahead of the airplane, complete necessary tasks more accurately, communicate clearly, and maintain situational awareness and scanning vigilance.

Pilot-pilot

Two issues are actually connected with this factor. One: Are you operating the aircraft as a crew? And two: Is your nonflying passenger also a licensed pilot?

If you fall into the first category, ask yourself the following questions:

1. Do I have a personal (nonprofessional) problem with this pilot?
   If "Yes," then make the decision to leave it at home.
2. Do I think this person is an incompetent pilot?
   If "Yes," then monitor and cross-check or take a bus.
3. Am I overly familiar with this person's flying techniques and habits?
   If "Yes," then monitor and cross-check. Don't expect or assume anything. Make absolutely sure that checklists, ATC clearances, frequency changes, etc., have been completed correctly.
4. Is my communication clear, direct, and concise?
   If "No," then make sure to think before you talk. Speak up. Say exactly what you mean. And watch extraneous chit-chat that could cloud the real message.
5. Do I get easily intimidated by this person?
   If "Yes," then be confident with your knowledge and skills. More flight time and a few gray hairs don't automatically make that person a better pilot. But if you are a bit shaky in certain areas, then crack open a book. Flying is a constant learning process.
6. Does this other pilot have a tendency to get us into a lot of unsafe situations?
   If "Yes," then speak up. I guarantee that suffering through a few dirty looks is better than dying.

What if you're the pilot and your passenger is one too?

1. My friend always wants to help out, but I'd rather fly and keep him as the passenger.
   First of all, a passenger who is also a pilot can be useful, especially if you insist that he help look for traffic. But you are still pilot-in-command. Therefore, fly whatever way makes you most comfortable. Remember, one pilot who has his head on straight is better than one-and-a-half pilots, any day.
2. Do I communicate in a clear, direct, and concise manner?
   If "No," and if you want your pilot friend to help, then you must tell him exactly what his limits are, in a clear, direct, and concise manner. If you want him to stop touching the radios, tell him in a clear, direct, and concise manner. Just remember to set the limits before you're shooting a night ILS approach in rain and fog.

3. Do I let my friend talk me into things that I know are either unsafe or beyond my ability?

   If "Yes," remember: You are pilot-in-command. Good advice should always be well received. That's part of good judgment. But don't allow the talking to continue if you know the information is wrong or you get that uneasy feeling in the pit of your stomach. You are the pilot-in-command.

Keep thinking. I'm sure you can think of plenty more examples, but this is a good start. Now take a few moments and ask yourself, "What would I do if . . . ?"

Pilot-controller

Remember, ATC can be one of your best resources, especially for collision avoidance. So use your friendly, neighborhood controller wisely.

1. Am I clear, direct, and concise when I talk to ATC?

   If "No," then speak up. Remember to use your "radio voice." Think before you talk. Know exactly what you're going to say before you pick up the microphone. Be short and to the point.
2. I'm the pilot-in-command, controllers work for me.

   Pilots and controllers make up a very unique team. Each sees things that the other can't. Without a coordinated effort between pilot and controller, all that could be lying between a safe flight and one that ends up as a smoking hole in the ground is a simple radio call.
3. Do I ask ATC for flight following services, even when I'm flying VFR?

   If "Yes," then you're catching on.

That's right, CRM is not just for the big boys

Still believe you have nothing to manage if you fly only bug-smashers on the weekends? Ah, I thought you'd change your mind. Now your error chain has stopped adding links. And that's a giant step towards becoming a safer pilot.

CHAPTER 4 REVIEW

- Crew resource management (CRM) is the concept of blending a pilot's technical skills with his or her leadership abilities.
- The SHEL Model represents the interrelationships of software, hardware, liveware, and the environment.
- The goals of CRM are to create teamwork, enhance management skills, improve effective communication skills, and provide a productive work environment. All of these are conducive to better situational awareness in all phases of flight, especially in a collision avoidance environment.
- Pilots of all experience levels can apply CRM.

The statistics
- Flight Safety Foundation research data shows that flight crews are a causal factor in 65 percent of all air-carrier accidents. Crews on commuter aircraft are a causal factor 75 percent of all commuter airline accidents.
- NTSB research data show that pilot error was a causal factor in 86 percent of all accidents and 90 percent of fatal accidents.

Learning from the accidents
The lessons learned from the crash of Air Florida Flight 90 are:

- Know your airplane's manual
- Enhance your airmanship skills
- Have a good instrument cross-check
- Watch out for your fellow aviators
- Communicate clearly, directly, and concisely
- Be assertive
- Be decisive
- Don't become complacent
- Don't be intimidated

The lessons learned from the crash of Midwest Express Flight 105 are:

- Use common sense
- Aviate
- Communicate clearly, directly, and concisely

The lessons learned from the crash of United Flight 173 are:

- Communicate clearly, directly, and concisely
- Speak up
- Don't allow an unsafe situation to continue
- Don't be intimidated

A personal thought
- Be aware of potentially dangerous situations
- Don't allow unsafe situations to continue

A breakdown of CRM
The lack of CRM can cause:

- Poor communication
- Poor crew coordination
- Mishandling of engine and systems' settings
- Misreading instruments

CRM and overall safety

Pilots involved in accident or incident report the following as causal factors:

- Weak crew coordination
- Too relaxed of a cockpit environment
- Misunderstanding crewmembers
- Complacency
- Lack of confidence in other crewmembers

CRM concept in air-carrier operations

- Airline CRM training programs are often developed after an accident or a series of incidents
- United Airlines developed its CRM program in the wake of United Flight 173
- Awareness, practice and feedback, and continuous reinforcement

There are three primary methods of CRM:

- Awareness phase
- Practice and feedback phase
- Continuous reinforcement phase
- Awareness phase deals with a pilot's personal leadership style and behavioral traits

Leadership and behavioral attitudes can be measured by the following:

- Inquiry
- Advocacy
- Conflict resolution
- Critique
- Decision-making

Practice and feedback phase focuses on team-building and problem-solving exercises through:

- Line-oriented flight training (LOFT)
- Continuous reinforcement phase is applied on the job

Other views on CRM
- Some pilots are concerned that CRM will hinder the captain's authority.

Airline management
- The most ambitious CRM programs result from a corporate commitment at the top.

Air-carrier safety
- Industry average: one hull loss per one million operations. United Airlines average since CRM: one hull loss per 4.8 million operations.

Flying the line with CRM
The lessons learned from the incident involving United Flight 663 are:

- Cockpit crew coordinated emergency procedures before they left the ground
- Captain included cabin crew in pre-takeoff briefing

The lessons learned from the crash of United Flight 232 are:

- Crew worked as a team
- Each pilot was encouraged to have an input in decision-making process
- Captain used all of his available resources

CRM for general aviation
Pilot-pilot:

- Personal problems
- Professional concerns
- Technical skills
- Communication skills
- Intimidation
- Pilot-in-command

Pilot-controller:

- Communication skills
- Knowledge of regulations and obligations

- Intimidation
- Pilot-in-command

Chapter 4 references

Baron, Sheldon. 1988. "Pilot Control." *Human Factors in Aviation.* Ed. Wiener, Earl L. and David C. Nagel. San Diego: Academic Press: 347-385.

Burrows, William E. 1982. "Cockpit Encounters." *Psychology Today.* November: 43-7.

Degani, Asaf, Earl L. Wiener. 1990. "Human Factors of Flight-Deck Checklists: The Normal Checklist". NASA.

Driskeal, James, Richard Adams. 1992. *Crew Resource Management: An Introductory Handbook.* U.S. Department of Transportation. Federal Aviation Administration.

Edwards, Elwyn. 1988. "Introductory Overview." *Human Factors in Aviation.* Ed. Wiener, Earl L. and David C. Nagel. San Diego: Academic Press: 3-25.

Englade, Kenneth F. June 1988. "Better Managers in the Friendly Skies." *Across the Board*: 36-45.

Foushee, H. Clayton and Robert L. Helmreich. 1988. "Group Interaction and Flight Crew Performance." *Human Factors in Aviation.* Ed. Wiener, Earl L. and David C. Nagel. San Diego: Academic Press: 189-227.

Foushee, H. Clayton, John K. Lauber, Michael M. Baetge, and Dorothea B. Acomb. 1986. "Crew Factors in Flight Operations: III. The Operational Significance of Exposure to Short-Haul Air Transport Operations." NASA.

Haynes, Alfred C. October 1991. "United 232: Coping With the Loss of All Flight Controls: Part I." *Air Line Pilot*: 10-4, 54.

Helmreich, Robert L., Ph.D. May 1991. "Does CRM Training Work?" *Air Line Pilot:* 17-20.

Jensen, Richard. 1989. *Aeronautical Decision Making Cockpit Resource Management.* U.S. Department of Transportation. Federal Aviation Administration.

Kantowitz, Barry H. and Patricia A. Casper. 1988. "Human Workload in Aviation." *Human Factors in Aviation.* Ed. Wiener, Earl L. and David C. Nagel. San Diego: Academic Press: 157-187.

Kapustin, Rudy. 20 April 1988. Former National Transportation Safety Board Chief Investigator.

Miller, C.O. 1988: "System Safety." *Human Factors in Aviation.* Ed. Wiener, Earl L. and David C. Nagel. San Diego: Academic Press: 53-80.

Nagel, David C. 1988. "Human Error in Aviation Operations." *Human Factors in Aviation.* Ed. Wiener, Earl L. and David C. Nagel. San Diego: Academic Press: 263-301.

Nance, John. 1986. "Blind Trust." New York: Quill.

National Transportation Safety Board. 10 August 1982. Aircraft Accident Report: Air Florida, Inc., Boeing 737-222, N62AF. Collision with 14th Street Bridge, Near

Washington National Airport, Washington, DC., January 13, 1982. Washington, DC.

Negrette, Arthur J. February 1987. "Cockpit Communication Could Save Your Life." *Rotor and Wing International*: 22-23.

Ott, James. 21 July 1989."Probe Focuses on Failure of Fan Disk in DC-10 Crash." *Aviation Week and Space Technology:* 30-1.

"Personality in the Cockpit." May 1988. *Air Transport*: 14-16.

Steenblik, Jan W. August 1988, "Two Pilots, One Team—Part One." *Air Line Pilot:* 10-5.

Steenblik, Jan W. September 1988. "Two Pilots, One Team—Part Two." *Air Line Pilot*: 10-4, 49.

Stone, Richard B. and Gary L. Babcock. 1988. "Airline Pilots' Perspective." *Human Factors in Aviation.* Ed. Wiener, Earl L. and David C. Nagel. San Diego: Academic Press: 529-560.

Viets, Jack. 15 January 1986. "Cockpit Resource Management and Airline Safety." *San Francisco Chronicle:* A9.

5
Pilot judgment and decision-making

D O YOU EVER YEARN TO BE DESCRIBED IN THESE TERMS? "HE'S A NATURAL pilot." "He has great instincts." Instead, do you find yourself settling for "In time, he'll be a good pilot?" You are not born a natural pilot, and when people say someone has great instincts, they are actually referring to a pilot's judgment and decision-making abilities. The good news is that those abilities are learned, not bred.

I THOUGHT JUDGMENT AND DECISION-MAKING WERE THE SAME

It's important to understand that there is a difference between having good judgment and making a good decision. The terms are not interchangeable. According to the dictionary, the definition of judgment is "The mental ability to perceive and distinguish alternatives. The capacity to make reasonable decisions. Wisdom." The definition of a decision is: "The act of reaching a conclusion or making up one's mind."

Good judgment comes from the ability to perceive a situation (become aware, observe, detect, achieve understanding) and be able to distinguish (recognize, set apart, understand differences) between correct and incorrect alternatives to a solution. The last part of the definition is wisdom, which in itself means good judgment. Notice that the same key words keep popping up throughout this book: awareness, observation, detection, understanding. Are you beginning to see a connection between good judgment and decision-making skills in a collision-avoidance environment?

Making the right decision is actually the end result of having good judgment. It's about using your ability to make reasonable decisions, processing the information, then acting on these decisions and the information.

Good pilot judgment can be learned

Just as you learn the mechanics of flight, so, too, can you learn good judgment. Remember, the core of the definition is to perceive and distinguish between correct and incorrect solutions. But sometimes pilots can't always accomplish that, even when they come equipped with a head full of facts and tons of experience. This is one reason why 20,000-hour pilots can get into a jam just as easily as a 200-hour pilot. Why is that, you ask? Because the foundation for good judgment is formed by each person's thought patterns.

Although countless ideas and opinions shape an individual's mental process, for the purpose of this discussion I'll focus on just five. But mix any of these five thought patterns while in a flight and collision-avoidance environment, and you'll find yourself making serious mistakes and poor decisions time and time again. Hazardous thought patterns exist, but fortunately, it is possible to prevent them from interfering with our judgment abilities; we just have to first be aware of their presence.

The five hazardous thought patterns

This exercise works best if you don't sneak a peek at what the five hazardous thought patterns are. At the end of the exercise, each will be revealed and discussed in detail.

The sole purpose of the following questionnaire is to help you evaluate your own thought patterns and attitudes as they might affect your judgment abilities. Answer the questions as honestly as possible. There are no right or wrong answers.

Instructions

1. Read over each of the five situations and the five choices. Decide which one is the most likely reason why you might make the choice that is described. Place a numeral 1 in the space provided on the answer sheet.

2. Continue by placing a 2 by the next most probable reason, and so on, until you have filled in all five blanks with 1, 2, 3, 4, and 5.

3. Do all 10 situations and fill in each blank, even though you might disagree with all of the choices listed. There are no correct, or best, answers.
   Example:

5 a. (your least likely response)

3 b.

1 c. (your most likely response)

2 d.

4 e.

Attitude inventory
Situation 1:

Nearing the end of a long flight, your destination airport is reporting a ceiling of 600 feet and ½ mile visibility, fog and haze. You have just heard another aircraft miss the approach (ILS minimums are 200 and ½). You decide to attempt the ILS approach. Why do you make the attempt?

3 a. Ceiling and visibility estimates are often not accurate.

5 b. You are a better pilot than the one who just missed the approach.

2 c. You might as well try—you can't change the weather.

4 d. You are tired and just want to land.

1 e. You've always been able to complete approaches under these circumstances in the past.

Situation 2:

You plan an important business flight under instrument conditions in an aircraft with no de-icing equipment. You'll be flying through an area in which "light to moderate rime or mixed icing in clouds, and precipitation above the freezing level" has been forecast. You decide to make the trip, thinking:

1 a. You believe that your altitudes enroute can be adjusted to avoid ice accumulation.

4 b. You've been in this situation many times and nothing has happened.

5 c. You must get to the business meeting in two hours and can't wait.

3 d. You do not allow an icing forecast to stop you; weather briefers are usually overly cautious.

2 e. There's nothing you can do about atmospheric conditions.

Situation 3:

You arrive at the airport for a flight with a friend and plan to meet his other friend who is arriving on a commercial airplane at your destination. The airplane you scheduled has been grounded for avionics repairs. You are offered another airplane equipped with unfamiliar avionics. You depart on an instrument flight without a briefing on the unfamiliar equipment. Why?

2 a. If the avionics are so difficult to operate, the FBO would not have offered the plane as a substitute.

5 b. You are in a hurry to make the scheduled arrival.

1 c. Avionics checkouts are not usually necessary.

3 d. You do not want to admit that you are not familiar with the avionics.

4 e. You probably won't need to use those radios anyway.

Situation 4:

You arrive at your destination airport to pick up a passenger after the fuel pumps have closed. Your calculations before departing determined that there would be enough fuel to complete the trip with the required reserves. The winds on the trip were stronger than anticipated, and you are not certain of the exact fuel consumption. You decide to return home without refueling since:

_5_ a. You can't remain overnight because you and your passenger have to be at the office in the morning.

_2_ b. The required fuel reserves are overly conservative.

_1_ c. The winds will probably diminish for the return trip.

_3_ d. You don't want to admit to your lack of planning in front of anyone else.

_4_ e. It's not your fault the airport services are not available; you will just have to try to make it home.

Situation 5:

You have been cleared for the approach on an IFR practice flight with a friend acting as safety pilot. At the outer marker, ATC informs you of a low-level windshear reported for your intended runway. Why do you continue the approach?

_3_ a. You have to demonstrate to your friend that you can make this approach in spite of the wind.

_1_ b. It has been a perfect approach so far; nothing is likely to go wrong.

_2_ c. These alerts are for less-experienced pilots.

_5_ d. You need two more approaches to be current and want to get this one completed.

_4_ e.   The tower cleared you for the approach, so it must be safe.

Situation 6:

You are about to fly some business associates in a multiengine aircraft. You notice a vibration during run-up of the left engine. Leaning the mixture does not reduce the vibration. You take off without further diagnosis of the problem. Why?

_5_ a. You need to be at your destination by five o'clock and are behind schedule. The aircraft can be checked there.

_1_ b. You have encountered the vibration before without any problem.

_4_ c. You don't want your business associates to think you can't handle the aircraft.

_2_ d. The requirement for two perfectly smooth running engines is overly conservative.

_3_ e. The shop just checked this plane yesterday. The mechanics would not have released it if there were a problem.

Situation 7:

You are in IMC and are receiving conflicting information from the two VOR receivers. You determine that the radios are out-of-tolerance and cannot determine your position. You believe ATC will soon suggest that you are off course and request a correction. You are thinking:

_2_ a. Try to determine your position so ATC won't find out that you are lost.

_3_ b. You will continue to navigate on the newer VOR receiver. It should work just fine.

5 c. You will get out of this jam somehow; you always do.

4 d. If ATC calls, you can be noncommittal. If they knew all, they would only make things worse.

1 e. Inform ATC immediately that you are lost and wait impatiently for a response.

Situation 8:

During an instrument approach, ATC calls and asks how much fuel you have remaining. You have only two minutes before reaching the missed approach point, and wonder why they have inquired as to your fuel status. You are concerned about severe thunderstorm activity nearby and assume that you could be required to hold. You believe that:

2 a. Your fuel status is fine, but you want to land as soon as possible before the thunderstorm arrives.

5 b. You are in line with the runway and believe that you can land, even in any crosswind that might come up.

4 c. You will have to complete this approach; the weather won't improve.

3 d. You won't allow ATC to make you hold in potentially severe weather—it's not their neck.

1 e. The pilot who landed ahead of you completed the approach without any problems.

Situation 9:

You are a newly rated instrument pilot conducting an instrument flight of only 20 miles. The turn coordinator in your airplane is malfunctioning. The visibility is deteriorating, nearing approach minimums at your destination. You continue this trip, thinking:

1 a. You've never had a need to use the turn coordinator.

2 b. You recently passed the instrument flight test and believe you can handle this weather.

5 c. Why worry about it—ATC will get you out of a bad situation.

3 d. You had better get going now before you get stuck here.

4 e. Back up systems are not needed for such a short trip.

Situation 10:

You encounter clear-air turbulence. You are not wearing a shoulder harness and do not put it on. Why not?

2 a. Putting on a shoulder harness might give the appearance that you are afraid—you don't want to alarm your passengers.

4 b. Shoulder harness regulations are unnecessary for enroute operations.

5 c. You haven't been hurt thus far by not wearing your shoulder harness.

3 d. What's the use in putting on a shoulder harness—if it's your time, it's your time.

1 e. You need to maintain aircraft control—there's no time for shoulder harnesses.

Interpreting your attitude inventory

Transfer the numbers from your questionnaire onto the Attitude Inventory Scoring Key (Table 5-1). The higher scores indicate the thought patterns and attitudes that you are susceptible to expressing. Remember, they do not indicate how your attitudes compare with anyone else, and it in no way represents a personality test.

Table 5-1. *The attitude inventory scoring key*

Situation	Scale I	Scale II	Scale III	Scale IV	Scale V	Total
1.	a. 3	d. 4	e. 1	b. 5	c. 2	15
2.	d. 3	c. 5	b. 4	a. 1	e. 2	15
3.	c. 1	b. 5	e. 4	d. 3	a. 2	15
4.	b. 2	a. 5	c. 1	d. 3	e. 4	15
5.	c. 2	d. 5	b. 1	a. 3	e. 4	15
6.	d. 2	a. 5	b. 1	c. 4	e. 3	15
7.	d. 4	e. 1	c. 5	a. 2	b. 3	15
8.	d. 3	e. 1	c. 4	a. 2	b. 5	15
9.	e. 4	d. 3	a. 1	b. 2	c. 5	15
10.	b. 4	e. 1	c. 5	a. 2	d. 3	15
Total	28	35	27	27	33	150

The sum of your scores across should be 15 for each situation. If it is not, go back and make sure that you transferred the scores correctly and check your addition. The grand total should be 150.

Adapted from the Jensen FAA/DOT Study: Aeronautical Decision Making—Cockpit Resource Management, January 1989.

Although you might easily recognize yourself fitting certain patterns, the results prove to be most beneficial when they take you completely by surprise. The first time I completed one of these exercises, I interpreted the results of my scores to mean I was some kind of hair-on-fire, macho buffoon. But just as I was about to can my score sheet and declare the last 20 minutes as a complete waste of time, I read the instructions. I had jumped in and started writing down numbers without paying attention to the purpose of the exercise. Once I calmed down and realized that the results meant that I was just vulnerable to that thought pattern, I could see the advantage of knowing that tidbit of information before I yelled, "Clear prop!" I think you will, too.

The five hazardous thought patterns

Scale I: Anti-authority
This attitude is found in pilots who resent any external control over their actions. They have a tendency to disregard rules and procedures. "The regulations and SOPs are not for me."

Scale II: Impulsivity
This attitude is found in pilots who act too quickly. They tend to do the first thing that pops in their head. "I must act now; there's no time to waste."

Scale III: Invulnerability
This attitude is found in pilots who act as though nothing bad can happen to them. Many pilots feel that accidents happen to others but never to them. Those who think this way are more likely to take chances and run unwise risks. "It won't happen to me." Famous last words.

Scale IV: Macho

This attitude is found in pilots who continually try to prove themselves better than others. They tend to act with overconfidence and attempt difficult tasks for the admiration it gains them. "I'll show you. I can do it."

Scale V: Resignation

This attitude is found in pilots who feel that they have little or no control over their circumstances. They might feel, "What's the use?" These pilots might also deny that a problem is as it appears and believe, "It's not as bad as they say." It's unlikely that they would take charge of a situation, and they might even go along with unreasonable requests just to be a nice guy. Another common feeling is, "They're counting on me, I can't let them down."

Countering hazardous thought patterns and attitudes

Granted, we all have bits and pieces of these nasty thought patterns and attitudes; that's what, in part, makes up our individual personalities. But the degree to which we display these patterns, especially in the cockpit, is where the real problem lies. This is how the attitude inventory fits in. One of the best ways to begin eliminating, or at least alleviating, these patterns is by simply recognizing what thought pattern and attitude you are most vulnerable to.

Hazardous thought patterns and collision avoidance

Let's see what effect our hazardous thought patterns can have in a collision-avoidance environment.

Anti-authority. "The regulations are for someone else."

No, FAR 91.67 is for everyone. Although there are physical limitations that we must consider, ". . . maintain vigilance to see and avoid other aircraft . . ." is still a regulation.

Impulsivity. "I must act now, there's no time to waste."

A hurried and haphazard visual scan does absolutely nothing to help prevent a mid-air collision. Don't think of see and avoid as a waste of time.

Invulnerability. "It won't happen to me."

No matter what your experience level, or what type of airplane you fly, you still could have a mid-air collision. Yes, it can even happen to you.

Macho. "I'll show you. I can do it."

You're so busy showing off or being a "sky god" that you forget basic safety habits. An effective visual search should never be disregarded or done only when there's nothing better to do.

Resignation. "What's the use?"

You are not helpless. That's what it means to use all of your available resources. If you can't do a task, either through a genuine lack of knowledge or skill, or because you have only two hands, it's not a crime. Be open to suggestions, guidance, and help from ATC and fellow pilots. Simply because we all experience physical limitations doesn't automatically mean target detection is hopeless.

The hazardous thought patterns exercise

Now that you have a better understanding of the five hazardous thought patterns, try this exercise to test your ability to spot each specific pattern. As we discussed earlier, being able to recognize these attitudes in yourself and others is half the battle. This exercise is also an excellent guide in helping you develop and enhance good judgment abilities. Remember, sound judgment leads to correct decisions.

The anti-authority hazardous thought pattern

From the five choices following each situation, pick the ONE choice that is the best example of an anti-authority hazardous thought pattern. Check your answers before you continue to the next situation. If you don't choose the correct answer, select another until you choose the correct one.

Situation 1:

You do not conduct a thorough preflight. On takeoff you notice that the airspeed indicator is not working; nevertheless, you continue the takeoff roll. Your passenger feels strongly that you should discontinue the flight and return to the airport. You then become upset with your friend. Which of the following options best illustrates the ANTI-AUTHORITY reaction?

mac a. You tell your passenger to "cool it" for butting in.

imp b. You start banging on the airspeed indicator to get it working.

an c. You think that the preflight check is something thought up by bureaucrats just to waste a pilot's time.

inv d. You tell the passenger that nothing dangerous will happen on the flight.

res e. Your passenger continues to become more upset, but you do nothing because you feel there is no use trying to calm the guy down.

Response options:

a. Macho. By acting in a superior way, you are being macho. "I can do it." Go back to situation 1 and select another option.

b. Impulsive. By becoming upset and banging on the airspeed indicator, and by not thinking about the situation, you are being impulsive. "Quick! Do something!" Go back to situation 1 and select another option.

c. Anti-authority. You selected the correct response. Looking at rules and procedures as just a waste of time, instead of taking them seriously, is an indication of an anti-authority attitude. Go on to situation 2.

d. Invulnerable. Thinking that nothing will happen to you shows an invulnerable tendency. Go back to situation 1 and select another option.

e. Resignation. By assuming that what you do has no effect on the passenger, the pilot is illustrating a tendency towards resignation. Go back to situation 1 and select another option.

Situation 2:

You have been cleared for an approach to a poorly lighted airport. You are not sure if this is the airfield where you want to land. The surrounding buildings do not look familiar, but it has been more than a year since your last visit. A much larger, more familiar airport is 15 miles away. Which of the following options best illustrates the ANTI-AUTHORITY reaction?

a. You decide to land anyway, thinking, "Of course I can handle this situation."

b. Rather than confuse yourself by thinking about options, you decide to land and get the flight over with.

c. You feel nothing will happen since you have gotten out of similar jams before.

d. You decide to land since the controller cleared you.

e. You decide to land because the regulations do not really apply in this situation.

Response options:

a. Macho. Thinking that you can handle the situation even when there is reason to be concerned is an example of a macho attitude. Go back to situation 2 and select another option.

b. Impulsive. "Quick! Do something! Anything!" Go back to situation 2 and select another option.

c. Invulnerable. Thinking that nothing will happen to you, even in a problem situation, is illustrating a tendency towards invulnerability. Go back to situation 2 and select another option.

d. Resignation. A pilot with the belief that "the controller is watching over me" has just relieved himself of duty as pilot-in-command. He has given in to the resigning thought of "What's the use?" Go back to situation 2 and select another option.

e. Anti-authority. Well done. You chose the correct response. Go on to situation 3.

Situation 3:

As you are preparing to give a first ride in an airplane to a friend, you announce that you do not believe in wearing shoulder harnesses. Rather than explaining the regulations and the potential dangers involved, you simply take off. Which of the following options best illustrates the ANTI-AUTHORITY reaction?

a. You know that, as a good pilot, you could handle any emergency long enough to buckle up.

b. It's just a local flight on a beautiful day so nothing could go wrong.

c. You feel that "seat belt" bureaucrats have invented yet another unnecessary regulation.

d. You feel that if you're going to crash, the harnesses won't save you.

e. You just want to get going.

Response options:

a. Macho. Thinking that you are good enough to handle any situation shows a degree of overconfidence, which is associated with the "I can do it" macho attitude. Go back to situation 3 and select another option.

b. Invulnerable. Sometimes even local flights result in mishaps. "It won't happen to me" is a clear indication of a invulnerable thought pattern.

   c. Anti-authority. You chose wisely. Go to the next hazardous thought exercise.

   d. Resignation. "What's the use?" Go back to situation 3 and select another option.

   e. Impulsive. The unreasoning desire to "just get going" is indicative of an impulsive attitude. Go back to situation 3 and select another option.

The impulsivity hazardous thought pattern

From the five choices following each situation, select the ONE option that is the best example of an impulsivity hazardous thought pattern. Check your answers from the response list and keep selecting until you have made the correct choice.

Situation 1:

As you enter the pattern, you normally lower the flaps. The tower suddenly changes the active runway. Distracted, you forget to use the before-landing checklist. On short final you find yourself dangerously low with a high sink rate. Glancing back, you realize that you forgot to extend the flaps. Which of the following options best illustrates the IMPULSIVITY reaction?

   a. You feel that nothing is going to happen because you've made intentional no-flap landings before.

   b. You laugh and think, "Boy, this low approach will impress people on the ground."

   c. You think that using a checklist is a stupid requirement.

   d. You immediately grab the flap handle and add full flaps.

   e. You think, "It's all up to whether I get an updraft or downdraft now."

Response options:

   a. Invulnerable. "Nothing bad can happen to me." Go to situation 1 and select another option.

   b. Macho. When you're thinking more about impressing people on the ground than flying the airplane, look out! Go back to situation 1 and select another option.

   c. Anti-authority. Thinking that checklists are stupid is an invitation for disaster. Go back to situation 1 and select another option.

   d. Impulsivity. You're right. Immediately adding full flaps without thinking about the consequences is a clear example of an impulsive thought pattern. Go on to situation 2.

   e. Resignation. The answer's not blowing in the wind. Go back to situation 1 and select another option.

Situation 2:

Landing at an unfamiliar airport for fuel, you tell the lineman to "fill it up," and run inside the terminal to use the restroom. Returning, you pay the bill and take off without checking the aircraft, the fuel caps, or the fuel. Which of the following options indicates an IMPULSIVITY reaction?

   a. You feel that it's a silly requirement to preflight an aircraft which you've just flown.

   b. You just want to get underway, quickly.

   c. You know that you have skipped preflights before and nothing bad ever happened.

   d. You have every confidence that a pilot with your skill level could handle, in flight, anything that might have been overlooked on the ground.

   e. You feel that since you paid top dollar for the fuel, it's the responsibility of the lineman to ensure the airplane was refueled properly.

Response options:

a. Anti-authority. Thinking that regulations requiring a preflight inspection are non-sense suggests a definite anti-authority attitude. Go back to situation 2 and select another option.

b. Impulsivity. Bingo. Having that itch to get a move on shows great impulsivity. Go on to situation 3.

c. Invulnerability. Just because you got away with it before doesn't mean that it's safe. "It won't happen to me." Go back to situation 2 and select another option.

d. Macho. Even though you might think, "I can do it," you'll find yourself turning gray by your 25th birthday. Go back to situation 2 and select another option.

e. Resignation. Feeling that everything is up to someone else is a resigning attitude. Go back to situation 2 and select another option.

Situation 3:

After dark, two friends talk you into going for a short hop. You eagerly drive to the airport without checking the weather because it looks clear and you intend to stay in the pattern. After takeoff, you fly into a low-hanging cloud layer. Which of the following options best illustrates the IMPULSIVITY reaction?

a. You never check the weather because you always thought your instructor was overly cautious when it came to weather.

b. You figure that since you had several hours of hood time recently, flying in the clouds would be a piece of cake.

c. You think that you'll be out of these clouds soon because the sky looked clear from the ground. Besides, you have flown through light clouds before in daylight.

d. You figure that you can always get air traffic control to talk you down.

e. You want to immediately nose the plane over to get below the clouds.

Response options:

a. Macho. Revolting against a practice your instructor taught you is definitely a macho attitude. Go back to situation 3 and select another option.

b. Macho. Fooled you! Another macho attitude. Go back to situation 3 and select another option.

c. Invulnerable. "Things will work out, they always do" is an invulnerable thought pattern. Go back to situation 3 and select another option.

d. Resignation. The feeling that you can always rely on someone else is a resignation thought pattern. Go back to situation 3 and select another option.

e. Impulsivity. Correct. The key word that should have tipped you off was *immediately*. Go on to the next hazardous thought pattern exercise.

The invulnerability hazardous thought pattern

From the five choices following each situation, select the ONE option that is the best example of an invulnerability hazardous thought pattern. Check your answers with the response list and keep selecting until you have made the correct choice.

Situation 1:

You are making a pleasure flight with four friends, all of whom are drinking. You refuse to drink, but your friends remind you that you have flown this route many times and that the weather conditions are excellent. They begin to tease you for not drinking with them. Which of the following options best illustrates the INVULNER-ABILITY reaction?

a. You decide to drink, thinking that a little liquor will not have any bad effect on you.

b. You believe that the government is far too rigid in its regulations about drinking and flying.

c. You resent your friends' insults and start drinking, saying to yourself, "I'll show them."

d. You bend to their will, saying to yourself, "If my time is up, it's up whether I drink or not."

e. You suddenly decide to take a drink.

Response options:

a. Invulnerability. You are correct. Liquor affects everybody, and pilots who believe that it will not bother them, consider themselves invulnerable. Go on to situation 2.

b. Anti-authority. Considering the authority of the government as too rigid is another way of thinking, "Those rules are much more strict than they need to be, so I can disregard them." Go back to situation 1 and select another option.

c. Macho. The need to prove yourself, or show off to total strangers, is definitely a macho-thought pattern. Go back to situation 1 and select another option.

d. Resignation. Thinking that you have nothing to do with the outcome of a flight is a resigning attitude. Go back to situation 1 and select another option.

e. Impulsivity. Making the foolishly sudden decision to drink is an impulsive thought pattern. Go back to situation 1 and select another option.

Situation 2:

The control tower advises you to land on a runway other than the one you prefer. You see larger planes using the runway of your choice and wonder why you have been denied permission. Since the tower-recommended runway is on the far side of the airport, you radio the tower and ask for reconsideration. Which of the following options best illustrates the INVULNERABILITY reaction?

a. Before you receive a reply, you start making your approach to the unauthorized runway.

b. You feel that if other pilots can land their airplanes on the other runway, so can you.

c. You think that nothing dangerous will occur because you believe wake turbulence is very unlikely.

d. Regardless of what the tower tells you, you are going to do what you want to.

e. You figure there is no sense in waiting for instructions because the tower is going to do whatever it pleases, regardless of your wishes.

Response options:

a. Impulsivity. Rushing into an action without thinking about the consequences is an impulsive attitude. Go back to situation 2 and select another option.

b. Macho. Thinking that you can do anything, anytime, anywhere, with any configuration is a macho attitude! Go back to situation 2 and select another option.

c. Invulnerability. This is the correct response. Disregarding a potentially hazardous situation, like wake turbulence, and thinking there's nothing to worry about is an invulnerable thought pattern. Go on to situation 3.

d. Anti-authority. "I'll do what I want to do" regardless of the consequences, is an anti-authority thought pattern. Go back to situation 2 and select another option.

e. Resignation. Believing that nothing you do will make any difference is a resigning attitude. Go back to situation 2 and select another option.

Situation 3:

Because of strong headwinds on a cross-country flight, you land at an airport to refuel only to learn they are out of gas. A local instructor suggests you backtrack 40 miles to an airport that has fuel. Which of the following options best illustrates the INVULNERABILITY reaction?

a. You ignore this unsolicited advice. You feel flight instructors are always complicating matters.

b. You feel sure you can make it to the next airport because things always seem to work out well for you.

c. You continue your flight because your own instructor approved your flight plan.

d. Rather than taking the time to calculate your fuel requirements and analyze your alternatives, you hop in the plane and go.

e. You decide to go on, thinking how impressed your friends will be when they hear you beat the headwinds without refueling.

Response options:

a. Anti-authority. A pilot who disregards sound advice just because the flight instructor came up with it shows an anti-authority thought pattern.

b. Invulnerability. Right. Thinking things will always work out is an invulnerable attitude. Go on to the next hazardous thought pattern exercise.

c. Resignation. Feeling that enroute decisions are always the responsibility of others, such as your flight instructor, illustrates a resigning attitude. Go back to situation 3 and select another option.

d. Impulsivity. Making hasty decisions without looking at the alternatives is an impulsive thought pattern. Go back to situation 3 and select another option.

e. Macho. The old "I can do it." attitude. Go back to situation 3 and select another option.

The macho hazardous thought pattern

From the five choices following each situation, select the ONE option that is the best example of a macho hazardous thought pattern. Check your answers from the response list and keep selecting until you have made the correct choice.

Situation 1:

Visibility is barely more than three miles in blowing snow with a 1000 foot ceiling. Earlier you cleared the airplane of snow, but takeoff has been delayed for 15 minutes. Snow and ice are forming again, and you wonder if you will be able to take off. Which of the following options best illustrates the MACHO reaction?

a. You feel that there is no use getting out and removing the snow since it's only going to form again.
b. You believe that you can take off in these conditions and think of how impressed your friends will be when they hear of it.
c. You take off immediately, thinking that any further delay will worsen the problem.
d. You reason that you can do it because other pilots have done it and nothing happened to them.
e. You resent being delayed 15 minutes and decide you are not going to clear the snow and ice again for anybody.

Response options:

a. Resignation. When you don't think what you do affects what happens, you are displaying a resigning thought pattern. Go back to situation 1 and select another option.
b. Macho. Correct. You want to show off to others, and want to prove yourself. Definitely a macho attitude. Go on to situation 2.
c. Impulsivity. You take off immediately. No thinking and no planning show a great impulsive thought pattern. Go back to situation 1 and select another option.
d. Invulnerability. "Nothing happened to them, so nothing will happen to me." But something did happen to them: Remember Air Florida Flight 90? Go back to situation 1 and select another option.
e. Anti-authority. Pilots who resent using appropriate safety precautions show an anti-authority attitude. Go back to situation 1 and select another option.

Situation 2:

The weather forecast calls for freezing rain. Enroute you notice ice accumulating on the wings. You are not sure what to do because you have never encountered this problem before. Because the airplane is still flying well, you are tempted to do nothing. A passenger suggests you might radio for information. Which of the following options best illustrates the MACHO reaction?

a. You feel that there probably will not be any problem since you have always come out of difficult situations rather well.
b. You feel that there is nothing you can really do because radio information won't change the weather conditions.
c. You quickly tell the passenger to stop butting in.
d. You tell the passenger that you are the boss and will handle the problem your way.
e. You radio for information but decide to ignore the advice since the airplane continues to fly well enough.

Response options:

a. Invulnerability. When you think that since nothing has ever happened before, nothing will happen in the future, you're displaying an invulnerable-thought pattern. Go back to situation 2 and select another option.
b. Resignation. "What's the use?" Go back to situation 2 and select another option.
c. Impulsivity. Acting without thinking is impulsive. Go back to situation 2 and select another option.

d. Macho. This is the correct answer. "We'll do it my way," is a good indication of a macho attitude. Go on to situation 3.

e. Anti-authority. Those who ignore information or advice show an anti-authority attitude. Go back to situation 2 and select another option.

Situation 3:

The runway is short with high trees beyond the runway departure threshold, and a strong crosswind is blowing. You are asked to take an additional passenger, who will overload the airplane by about 170 pounds. The extra passenger is waiting for your reply. Which of the following options best illustrates the MACHO reaction?

a. You take the passenger, reasoning that if fate says you are going to crash, you will, with or without extra weight.

b. You take the passenger, fearing that you will lose respect if you do not.

c. You take the passenger, remarking to yourself that the weight and balance rules are unnecessarily strict.

d. Since the passenger seems friendly, you take him on board right away and do not give another thought about it.

e. You take the passenger, thinking that accidents happen only to others.

Response options:

a. Resignation. Trusting in luck is a resigning attitude. Go back to situation 3 and select another option.

b. Macho. Right. The pilot was more concerned about what others thought of him than he was of safety. Go on to the next hazardous thought pattern exercise.

c. Anti-authority. Disregarding safety precautions and practices, like not doing weight and balance computations, shows an anti-authority thought pattern. Go back to situation 3 and select another option.

d. Impulsivity. Making an immediate decision, which also shows poor judgment without any thought of the consequences, is impulsive. Go back to situation 3 and select another option.

e. Invulnerable. When you think that accidents happen to other people, especially those that obviously aren't as good of pilots as yourself, you have an invulnerable attitude. Go back to situation 3 and select another option.

The resignation hazardous thought pattern exercise

From the five choices following each situation, select the ONE option that is the best example of the resignation hazardous thought pattern. Check the answers from the response list and keep selecting until you have made the correct choice.

Situation 1:

You would like to arrive early for an important business meeting. If you stick to your flight plan, you will just about make it, assuming you have no problems. Or you can take a route over the mountains, which will get you there much earlier. If you choose the route through the mountain passes, it means you might encounter low-hanging clouds while good weather prevails over the planned route. Which of the following options best illustrate the RESIGNATION reaction?

a. You take the mountain route even though the weather briefer has advised against it.
b. You take the mountain route, thinking that a few clouds in the passes will not cause any trouble for this flight.
c. You feel it will be a real victory for you if you can take the mountain route and arrive early.
d. You tell yourself that there is no sense sticking to the planned route, because "There's nothing else to do to be sure to make it early."
e. You quickly choose the mountain route, deciding that you just must get there early.

Response options:
a. Anti-authority. Not accepting the advice of a weather briefer is an example of an anti-authority attitude. Go back to situation 1 and select another option.
b. Invulnerability. "It won't happen to me." Go back to situation 1 and select another option.
c. Macho. Making potentially dangerous situations into personal challenges is a macho thought pattern. Go back to situation 1 and select another option.
d. Resignation. Good choice. Thinking that there is nothing you can do is an example of a resigning thought pattern. Go on to situation 2.
e. Impulsivity. A quick decision isn't always the right decision. Go back to situation 1 and select another option.

Situation 2:
The weather briefer advises you of possible hazardous-weather conditions at your destination, but you elect to go anyway. Enroute you encounter a brief snowstorm and increasingly poor visibility. Although you have plenty of fuel to return to your departure point, you have a hunch that the weather will improve before you reach your destination. Which of the following options best illustrates the RESIGNATION reaction?
a. You feel there is no need to worry about the weather since there is nothing one can do about mother nature.
b. You immediately decide to continue, and block the weather conditions out of your mind.
c. You feel nothing will happen to you since you have plenty of fuel.
d. You think that the weather people are always complicating your flights, and sometimes, such as now, it's best to ignore them.
e. You fly on, determined to prove that your own weather judgment is better than the forecaster's.

Response options:
a. Resignation. When Doris Day sings the line, "What will be, will be," it's cute. If you sing it in the cockpit, it could kill you. Go on to situation 3.
b. Impulsivity. Quickly blocking important matters out of your mind is impulsive. Go back to situation 2 and select another option.
c. Invulnerability. Having plenty of fuel does not mean that all is well in the world. Go back to situation 2 and select another option.

d. Anti-authority. Disregarding sound advice is the same as ignoring regulations. They're both an anti-authority thought pattern. Go back to situation 2 and select another option.

e. Macho. Showing off again. Go back to situation 2 and select another option.

Situation 3:

On final approach at night, you fly into patches of ground fog, which severely limit visibility. Your altitude is 150 feet and you debate whether you can level off at the correct height and land properly, or whether you should abort the approach. Which of the following options best illustrates the RESIGNATION reaction?

a. You think the rules, in general, are too rigid.

b. You feel that the situation presents a challenge and that you are going to make the landing.

c. You begin to level off, immediately saying, "The heck with the fog."

d. You continue, feeling that the decision has already been made.

e. You say to yourself, "I'm going in because nothing is going to happen."

Response options:

a. Anti-authority. If all rules are too strict for you, then you have an anti-authority attitude. Go back to situation 3 and select another option.

b. Macho. Seeing a situation as a challenge, rather than a problem that needs to be solved, is a macho thought pattern. Go back to situation 3 and select another option.

c. Impulsivity. Acting without thinking first is impulsive. Go back to situation 3 and select another option.

d. Resignation. You picked the correct answer. When you believe a decision has already been made for you, then you exhibit a resigning attitude. You have just successfully completed the hazardous thought pattern exercise. Take a break and have some Junior Mints!

e. Invulnerability. The belief that "nothing bad will ever happen to me" is guaranteed to come back and bite you when you least expect it, which for the invulnerable types is all the time.

YOU CAN ALSO LEARN GOOD DECISION-MAKING SKILLS

A DECIDE model has been used in many disciplines for a lot of years and the FAA has been able to adapt this process to fit flying scenarios. Remember that the definition of a decision is: "The act of reaching a conclusion or making up one's mind." You'll find that the DECIDE model is a great guide in helping you reach those correct conclusions.

The steps to take

D—Detect: The pilot detects the fact that a change has occurred that requires attention. Collision-avoidance connection: traffic in the area.

E—Estimate: The pilot estimates the significance of the change to the flight. Collision-avoidance connection: What's the position of the traffic? Is it a potential threat? Is it an imminent threat?

C—Choose: The pilot chooses a safe outcome for the flight. Collision-avoidance connection: coordinating with ATC any heading changes. Coordinating collision avoidance with the other aircraft. Evasive maneuvers.

I—Identify: The pilot identifies plausible actions to the change. Collision-avoidance connection: Will my decision jeopardize my own safety or the safety of others?

D—Do: The pilot acts on the best options. Collision-avoidance connection: communicating your intentions in a clear, direct, and concise manner. Physically moving the airplane out of harm's way.

E—Evaluate: The pilot evaluates the effect of the action on the change and on the progress of the flight. Collision-avoidance connection: Did I make the right decision? Have I cleared the threat aircraft or do I have to make another fast decision? Did I handle the situation appropriately? What would I do differently next time?

How to use the DECIDE model

Later in this chapter you'll have the opportunity to do a DECIDE model exercise. Because the instructions could be a little confusing, I've included an example (Table 5-2), which relates to the following accident.

Table 5-2. DECIDE model example exercise. According to the chart, the "Ys" indicate that the task was completed and the "Ns" indicate that the task was not completed. The quick interpretation of the findings is as follows: A number of "Ns" are found in the "I" column suggesting that there was a failure of the crew to identify the correct action to counter the change. However, the crucial "Ns" occurred when the copilot reminded the pilot of IFR weather at Carbondale and got no response until it was too late. The copilot appeared to have the answer that may have avoided the accident but did not offer it to the pilot nor did he voice his concerns about the action the pilot was assertively pursuing.

Change	D	E	C	I	D	Action	E
Left gen fails after TO	Y	Y	N	N	Y	CP misidentifies failed gen and disconnects good gen	Y
CP tells Dep Con "slight" electrical problem	Y	Y	Y	Y	Y	Dep Con offers return to Springfield airport	Y
Crew gets Dep Con offer to return to Springfield	Y	Y	N	N	Y	Capt rejects offer and continues to Carbondale	Y
Right gen doesn't take electrical load	Y	Y	Y	Y	Y	CP tells Capt of loss of right gen	Y
CP tells Capt of right gen failure	Y	Y	N	N	Y	Capt requests lower altitude for VFR conditions	Y
CP tells Capt bat voltage is dropping fast	Y	N	N	N	Y	Capt tells CP to put load shedding switch off	Y

CP reminds Capt of IFR weather at Carbondale	Y	N	N	N	N	No reaction	N
CP turns on radar to get position	Y	Y	N	N	Y	CP tells Capt about dropping voltage	Y
CP tells Capt bat volt is dropping	Y	Y	Y	Y	Y	Capt turns off the radar	Y
CP warns Capt about low battery	Y	Y	Y	Y	Y	Capt starts descent to 2400	Y
Cockpit instruments start failing	Y	Y	Y	N	Y	Capt asks CP if he's got any instruments	Y

Derived from DOT/FAA/PM-86/46 , "Aeronautical Decision Making—Cockpit Resource Management," R. Jensen, 1989.

Air Illinois Flight 710—we have a slight electrical problem

Reported weather at time of accident: instrument meteorological conditions; cloud base at 2000 feet MSL, with cloud tops at 10,000 MSL; visibility below 2000 feet was one mile in rain. Scattered thunderstorms reported in the area.

On 11 October 1983, the Air Illinois Hawker Siddley 748-2A departed Springfield, Illinois, around 2020 CDT. The IFR-filed flight was already 45 minutes late. About 1½ minutes later, the crew of Flight 710 radioed Springfield departure control and reported they had just experienced a slight electrical problem. However, they informed ATC that they were continuing to their destination of Carbondale, Illinois, about 40 minutes away.

Although their intended cruise altitude was to be 5000 feet, they told departure control, "We'd like to stay as low as we can." Flight 710 was then cleared to maintain 3000 feet, and the controller asked if he could be of any assistance. The crew responded, ". . . we're doing okay, thanks."

At 2023, the first officer told the captain that "the left [generator] is totally dead, the right [generator] is putting out voltage, but I can't get a load on it." Seconds later, the first officer reported, ". . . zero voltage and amps on the left side, the right [generator] is putting out . . . [volts] . . . but I can't get it to come on the line." Shortly thereafter, he again told the captain that the battery voltage was going down "pretty fast."

By 2026, Flight 710 had left Springfield departure control's jurisdiction and had called into Kansas City Center with an "unusual request." The captain asked for clearance to descend to 2000 feet, ". . . even if we have to go VFR." He also asked the controller ". . . to keep your eye on us if you can." However, because 2000 feet was below Kansas City Center's lowest usable altitude and because the controller couldn't guarantee that he could maintain radar contact, the captain decided to remain at 3000 feet.

Two minutes later, the captain said, "Beacon's off . . . ," followed by "nav lights are off." The first officer then reminded the captain that Carbondale had a 2000 foot ceiling, and the visibility was two miles with light rain and fog.

The flight attendant eventually came forward to report that only a few lights were operating. The captain instructed her to inform the passengers that he had turned off the excess lights because the airplane had experienced ". . . a bit of an electrical problem . . . " and that they were proceeding to Carbondale. Their estimated time of arrival was in 27 minutes.

Only a few minutes after the flight attendant went back to the cabin, the first officer began to explain to the captain what he had found while troubleshooting the system: ". . . when we . . . started losing the left one [generator], I reached up and hit the right [isolate button] trying to isolate the right side . . . cause I assumed the problem was the right side but they [the generators] both still went off."

At 2045, Flight 710 had 20 volts left in its battery. But six minutes later, the first officer told the captain, "I don't know if we have enough juice to get out of this." The captain then asked the first officer to, "Watch my altitude, I'm going to go down to twenty-four hundred [feet]." He then asked the first officer if he had a flashlight, and if so, have it ready. At 2053, the first officer reported, "We're losing everything . . . down to thirteen volts . . .." A minute later the aircraft was at 2400 feet, and the captain asked the first officer if he had any instruments. The captain again repeated, "Do you have any instruments? Do you have a horizon [attitude director indicator]?"

About 2051, Kansas City Center had lost radar contact with Flight 710, presumably because they had already dipped below 2000 feet. And sometime after 2054:16, Flight 710 crashed 40 nm north of its destination airport. Three crewmembers and seven passengers were killed in the accident.

The NTSB determined that the probable cause of the accident was the captain's decision to continue the flight after the loss of dc electrical power from both airplane generators. The captain's decision was adversely affected by self-imposed psychological factors, which led him to inadequately assess the airplane's battery endurance after the loss of generator power. He also did not weigh the magnitude of risks involved in continuing to the destination airport.

Also contributing to the accident, according to the NTSB, was the failure of the airline management to provide a satisfactory company recurrent flightcrew training program. This failure subsequently led to the inability of the captain and first officer to cope promptly and correctly with the airplane's electrical malfunction. The failure of the FAA to assure such a program existed was also cited as a contributing factor.

Poor judgment and collision avoidance

This crew willingly flew into instrument conditions with an electrical problem that quickly turned into a full-blown emergency. So what does this accident have to do with collision avoidance? Two major issues. One is that the captain abandoned command of the airplane. Both pilots were so engrossed—head-locked—with their crisis that the actual flying of the airplane went unchecked. And two, the crew never effectively used ATC. They never declared an emergency or clearly asked for assistance. Because the pilots were unable to maintain their altitude, which they never directly explained to ATC, the jet descended through unassigned altitudes. And in the final moments prior to the crash, the jet flew out of radar coverage. Granted, traffic separation was not a big concern on that particular foggy night. But given the same emergency in VMC, one avoidable accident could have easily turned into two avoidable tragedies.

DECIDE model exercise

Now it's your turn. Closely study the events which led to the following accident, then jot down the appropriate responses on the provided DECIDE Model Exercise chart (Table 5-3).

Table 5-3. *DECIDE model exercise. Your assignment, if you choose to accept it, is to read the NTSB accident report on the crash of GP Express Flight 861. Use the example exercise as a guideline.*

Change	D	E	C	I	D	Action	E

Derived from DOT/FAA/PM-86/46, "Aeronautical Decision Making—Cockpit Resource Management," R. Jensen, 1989.

GP Express Airlines Flight 861—we're way off course

Pilot experience: The captain had been hired for that position, nine days prior to the accident. He had been a U.S. Army helicopter pilot with 1611 military flight hours, and a civilian flight instructor with 857 civilian flight hours. He had a total of 87 hours in the Beech 99—76 of which were simulated—and the day of the accident was his first day on the job. The first officer had 1234 total flight hours and had been flying the Beech 99 for about five weeks. He had flown approximately 90 hours as a GP Express first officer, all on Midwest routes. The day of the accident was his first day flying the airline's southern route structure.

Reported weather at time of accident: 700 feet scattered, estimated 1500 feet broken, 9000 feet overcast. Visibility was three miles in fog and haze.

On 8 June 1992, the crew of the GP Express Beech 99 had been on duty since 0400 CDT. By the time Flight 861 departed 27 minutes late from Atlanta, Georgia, for Anniston, Alabama, the captain and first officer had already flown two legs for a total of one hour and twenty minutes. The flight time between Atlanta and Anniston was estimated to be 50 minutes.

After the departure out of Atlanta, Flight 861 was cleared to maintain 6000 feet. Throughout the cruise phase, the captain and first officer had quite a bit of difficulty understanding each other because of noise on the intercom system. Additional conversations indicated that the first officer had noted several problems with the airplane's autofeather system and the battery. He even seemed to have trouble setting the radio frequencies.

At about 0841, Atlanta Center cleared Flight 861 to ". . . descend at pilot's discretion, maintain five thousand [feet]." The captain asked the first officer, to which he did not reply, "Does he want us to resume own navigation?" The captain then said, "I heard him say that. As far as I'm concerned, I'm still on vectors two eight zero [heading]." The first officer responded, "Yeah, two eight zero's fine. Because we're on course anyway, so let's just hold it." The captain remarked that he thought they were ". . . slowly drifting off [course]."

After a short conversation over whether the airplane was on course, the captain again asked, "What's the course?" The first officer replied, ". . . zero eight five inbound." The captain finally concluded that ". . . we're way off course."

In fact, 085 degrees was the outbound course from the VOR that they had been tracking. The inbound course, to which the aircraft was headed, was the reciprocal of 085, or 265 degrees.

Moments after this discussion, Atlanta Center informed the crew that radar contact was terminated, and they were to go over to Birmingham approach control. The first officer complied, but during the investigation, he testified that he believed the flight was continuing to receive radar vectors from ATC, even though Atlanta Center had terminated radar services.

At 0843, Birmingham approach instructed the flight to descend and maintain 4000 feet and to proceed direct to the [Talledega] VOR. They were also told to expect a visual approach into Anniston if they were able to see the airport. If that wasn't the case, then the crew was to set up for an ILS approach to runway five, from over the BOGGA approach fix. The first officer acknowledged the call.

Several minutes later, after receiving the latest Anniston weather, the crew decided to take the ILS. Before they could make that request, the controller notified them to "Proceed direct BOGGA, maintain four thousand 'til BOGGA, cleared . . . ILS runway five approach." Rather than ask the controller the distance to BOGGA, the first officer mentally computed the distance as being five miles.

As the first officer tuned in the localizer, he made the comment to the captain "Didn't realize that you're going to get this much on your first day, did ya?" By the time that the first officer had tuned in the correct frequency, the airplane had gone ". . . right through it." At that, the crew thought they were ". . . right over BOGGA . . . four and a half [miles] out . . .." The first officer told the captain to, ". . . go ahead and drop your gear . . . speed checks."

Seconds later, the captain stated that the glideslope wasn't even alive. He then asked, "What's the minimum altitude I can descend to 'til I'm established?" The response was ". . . twenty-two hundred [feet]." Because the company had provided only one set of approach charts in each airplane, only one pilot could review them at a time.

Therefore, the Board believed that was why the captain asked the first officer the question concerning the minimums.

By 0850, the weather was moving in their direction and was reported to be only two miles from the localizer outer marker. The first officer notified the controller that the ". . . procedure turn inbound [was] complete." But less than a minute later, the captain told the first officer ". . . we gotta go missed [approach] on this." The first officer replied ". . . there you go . . . there, you're gonna shoot right through it again . . . keep 'er goin' . . . you're okay." Within seconds, the captain called out ". . . there's the glideslope." Followed by the first officer saying "We can continue our descent on down. We're way high."

Almost immediately after they started their descent, they lost the glideslope. They were at 1100 feet when the captain asked the first officer to confirm that the correct ILS frequency had been tuned in. The answer was yes. But by this time, the captain had decided to go around. He asked the first officer "What's our missed approach point now?" His reply was "Twelve hundred [feet] . . . coming up . . .." One second later was the sound of impact.

The aircraft struck terrain a little more than 7 miles from the airport, at about the 1800 level. Although there were no witnesses to the crash, the area near the accident site was reported to be shrouded in fog and low-lying clouds. The captain and two passengers were killed, and the first officer and the other two passengers received serious injuries.

The NTSB determined that the probable causes of this accident were the failure of senior management of GP Express to provide satisfactory training and operational support for the startup of the southern routes, which resulted in the assignment of an inadequately prepared captain with a relatively inexperienced first officer. Additionally, the failure of the flightcrew to use approved instrument flight procedures resulted in a loss of situational awareness and terrain clearance. Contributing to the accident was GP Express' failure to provide approach charts to each pilot and to establish stabilized approach criteria. Other contributing factors were the inadequate crew coordination and a role reversal on the part of the captain and first officer.

Once again, history repeats itself

Have you noticed the similarities between all of the accidents that we've discussed so far? Intimidation, at varying degrees, between crewmembers, unsafe techniques or procedures, poor pre-flight preparation, loss of situational awareness (a big factor in collision avoidance), poor intra/inter-cockpit communication (another big factor in collision avoidance), and an overall lack of resource management (one more big factor in collision avoidance). History does repeat itself.

A DECIDE model for everyday flying and collision avoidance

For practice, think of your past experiences in a collision-avoidance environment, ones that have an element of uncertainty, such as weather forecasts, fuel remaining, engine or navigation system reliability, ATC clearances. Then go through the steps of the DECIDE model. As you repeatedly apply these steps to your own flying adventures, it will eventually become second nature to you. Applying the steps of the DECIDE model will help you make better and more timely decisions.

One last thought . . .

So far we've discussed the potentially disastrous results that can happen when a pilot's negative thought patterns and attitudes interfere with the flight. But now, let's take a quick look at the safe way to handle those external influences through sound judgment and good decision-making.

A young, recently hired pilot was flying a light plane with his new boss to attend a business meeting. The weather conditions at their destination, which was at a high elevation, was socked in with sky obscured and visibility at less than a ¼ mile. Another nearby airport was reporting marginal VFR and was unusually busy with arrivals due to the other field's conditions. Their alternate was clear, but 50 miles away. The boss desperately wanted to get to the meeting and told the pilot, "Go ahead, give it a try." The controller had informed them earlier that the only other airplane that had tried a landing that day had declared a missed approach.

The pilot was already well aware of his boss's macho attitude, but after thinking through the situation of bad weather, mountainous terrain, busy traffic area in marginal VFR, clear alternate, he decided while enroute to proceed to his alternate. The pilot had met guys like his boss before and was convinced that had he attempted an approach, his boss would have persisted with comments such as "I think I can see something," "Let's go lower," or "It doesn't look that bad to me," and so on . . . all the way down final.

With regards to the other nearby airport, the pilot felt uncomfortable with the thought of an active mix of VFR (untracked) and IFR traffic all vying for the same runway in marginal weather. Effective collision avoidance could be a bit perilous. Rather than risking a missed approach or landing short at his original destination field while his boss unrelentlessly needled him, he made the correct and timely decision to make a safe landing at his alternate.

The pilot proved three valuable points. One, he perceived the situation: bad weather, potentially dangerous collision avoidance environment, boss being a pain in the neck. Two, he distinguished between his available options: "I could try to land in unsafe conditions" or "I have plenty of fuel so I could safely land at my alternate." And three, he processed the information, did not succumb to external pressure, remained in command, and reached a successful conclusion.

CHAPTER 5 REVIEW

Good judgment
- Awareness
- Observation
- Recognition
- Understand differences between correct and incorrect alternatives to a solution

Hazardous thought patterns
- Macho. Must prove themselves
- Invulnerability. "Nothing bad can happen to me"
- Impulsivity. Acts too quickly
- Anti-Authority. Resents external control
- Resignation. "What's the use?"

DECIDE model
- DECIDE model helps reach a safe conclusion.

Chapter 5 references

Judgment Training Manual for Student Pilots. 1983. Federal Aviation Administration. Transport Canada. General Aviation Manufacturer's Association.

Jensen, Richard, Janeen Adrion. 1988. *Aeronautical Decision Making for Commercial Pilots.* U.S. Department of Transportation. Federal Aviation Administration.

Manning, C. K. May 1988. "Creeping Complacency." *Human Factor*: 22-24.

Nagel, David C. 1988. "Human Error in Aviation Operations." *Human Factors in Aviation.* Ed. Wiener, Earl L. and David C. Nagel. San Diego: Academic Press: 263-301.

Wickens, Christopher D. and John M. Flach. 1988. "Information Processing." *Human Factors in Aviation.* Ed. Wiener, Earl L. and David C. Nagel. San Diego: Academic Press: 111-155.

Yesley, Joel. 1990. A Study of the Relationships Between Near Midair Collisions, Midair Collisions, and Some Potential Causal Factors. U.S. Department of Transportation. Federal Aviation Administration.

6
Distraction: Confusion and chaos in the cockpit

. . . We were cleared to descend to 5000. I was doing the approach checklist.
Suddenly I saw the altimeter going through 4200. Before I could do
anything, a light airplane came over the top of us. We missed him by 200
feet . . .

Pilot report excerpt, NASA Aviation Safety Reporting System, Ames Research Center

WE'VE ALL BEEN DISTRACTED AT ONE TIME OR ANOTHER WHILE FLYING.
Sometimes we're lucky and wake up out of our purple haze before anything bad
happens. Other times, though, we find ourselves prying our white-knuckle fingers off
the yoke and trying to regain our normal speech pattern. What makes a distraction so
tragic is that most of the time we allow it to take over our flight, even when it goes
against our better judgment. Instead of taking charge as pilot-in-command, we permit
ourselves to be reduced to the status of a casual observer sitting in the back seat; the
one place in an airplane that's not conducive to scanning vigilance.

DISTRACTION

From reading the previous chapters you already know that no action, or lack of action, is isolated. Therefore, once we understand what distracts us both on the ground and in the air, we can more easily detect those traps, and through increased awareness, eventually eliminate some altogether. Remember, good situational awareness, competent decision-making, and judgment skills, which are all key factors in collision avoidance, are interrelated. All of it can go out the window in two seconds if you allow your mind to become muddled with disjointed thoughts.

A FEW THOUGHTS ON DISTRACTION

Ames (NASA) Research Center initiated a study on distraction because air carrier pilots identified that as being the most frequent cause for operational errors. The data were taken from 169 pilot reports and broken down into the following two groups: nonflight operations and flight operations. Nonflight operations consist of paperwork such as crew logs, engine logs, block/air times, public address announcements, passenger problems, and inappropriate cockpit conversations. Flight operations include crew coordination and, of course, actual flying tasks.

Distractions that can occur during an actual hands-on flight scenario show great similarity with those associated with the nonflight operations. In both types, you'll see how routine tasks and activities can be quickly mishandled or forgotten altogether.

If, as you read this chapter, the types of pilot errors start to sound like a broken record—they should. The same mistakes keep reappearing. The reason? Maybe it's because pilots don't always apply what they've learned.

Distractions: nonflight operations

Becoming distracted on climbout or descent is one of the most dangerous situations in which to be, yet time and time again pilots set themselves up for disaster when they have their heads buried in paperwork. In every incident that was reported to Ames, the crew had an altitude bust because at least one of the pilots was not paying attention to the instruments. The following excerpts are two telling examples of what can happen when vigilance is lost.

The crew of this first case had completed its initial climbout duties, and, most likely, was settling in for a routine flight.

> We were cleared to 11,000 feet by departure control. Once the workload diminished, I started to complete the logbook and time sheets. The F/O was flying and the aircraft leveled off and picked up speed. As I finished the paperwork, Center called and asked our altitude. I then noticed it was 10,000 feet.

According to the researcher's observations, the captain was obviously at ease with the skill of the first officer and was comfortable enough with the situation to become involved with paperwork. The first officer might have misunderstood the clearance, or

144

had gotten distracted with other tasks, but for those brief moments that aircraft was not where it should have been. Mere seconds is all it takes for two airplanes to collide.

This second report is an excellent example of how fast a crew can turn an otherwise routine flight into a nightmare, just by being distracted.

> We were climbing out of XYZ airport. The first officer was flying. I acknowledged a 7000-ft restriction, then went back to my paperwork. I didn't see the F/O set 17,000 in the altitude select window. As we passed 12,000, Center called, wanted to know where we were going.

This is one of those reports that can really make you squirm in your seat. The captain correctly hears the clearance and assumes the first officer did also. The first officer obviously misunderstood the clearance. The captain went back to being distracted and didn't monitor the other cockpit activities.

A simple task that is completed several times each day can easily become a distraction, one that is overlooked as inconsequential to the safety of the flight. Yet from this example, it was apparent that a lack of communication and crew coordination evolved from that simple distraction. Fortunately the flight had a happy ending. However, a 5000-foot altitude bust should send chills up your spine just thinking about what could have happened.

Lessons for general aviation

Avoid completing unnecessary paperwork, like filling in your logbook or jotting down any special notations required by the flight school, during critical phases of the flight. And don't assume anything.

This is your captain speaking

When one pilot's attention is devoted to a public address message, that pilot is often removed from the ATC communication loop. Misunderstood clearances are very common because the flying pilot is being distracted with the background talking and the nonflying pilot is not available to cross-check altitude or heading assignments. Add a system malfunction—which always happens at the most inconvenient time—and some bad weather, and three experienced crewmembers can easily be distracted away from the altimeter and from flying the airplane.

> The copilot was on the public address telling the passengers about the thunderstorm deviation. While climbing through FL 270 [assigned FL 280] the number four generator tripped the line. I asked the F/E to monitor the fault panel. The problem turned out to be a Generator Control Unit . . . When I looked back at the instrument panel, our altitude was 28,000. [We leveled off at 28,700].

As the crew flew through the assigned altitude, unbeknownst to them an aircraft on a head-on course was converging towards them at FL 290.

A simple distraction can take a perfectly good pair of eyes and hands away from flying the airplane.

Lessons for general aviation

Missed traffic or safety advisories and misunderstood clearances are just as common, and dangerous, anytime you're out of the ATC communication loop. Don't be shy about notifying ATC if you think you've missed a call.

Yak, yak, yak

There's nothing better than a light-hearted conversation or some juicy gossip to pass the time away on a long flight. Nevertheless, it's this kind of banter not essential to flight that causes pilots to miss ATC messages and clearances, clutter the airwaves because ATC has to repeat those missed clearances, forget checklists, land on wrong runways, and potentially lead to accidents. The call or action missed could be the one that saves your life.

Although personal conversations tend to be the most distracting because they're usually the most interesting, instructional conversations can also be hazardous. An instance was reported by a check airman, who explained:

> For 30 or 40 seconds we basically were not flying the airplane. The copilot was listening to me . . . I was talking. It was sure a reminder of how easy it is to be distracted.

Lessons for general aviation

Remember to not get carried away with distracting conversation. It's hard to not join in conversations when flying with friends, and no one expects pilots to fly in silence, but flying the airplane is still the primary responsibility. Maintaining altitude and heading while scanning for traffic, can be pretty difficult when one is in the middle of some hot story. Just as dangerous is when pilots on instructional flights and biennial flight reviews succumb to tunnel vision or head-lock in the cockpit. You're still in a collision-avoidance environment.

Captain, we have 10 passengers with tight connections

Cabin-related distractions can also take pilots away from their normal duties. The data collected from the Ames study indicate that 20 percent of the distractions experienced during nonflight operations in commercial airliners were caused by pilot-flight attendant interaction. Most of the cases occurred at the descent phase and pertained to travel connections, cabin conditions, and general problems of passengers.

Various errors have occurred as a result of these kinds of interruptions, including one pilot who misread the altimeter by 10,000 feet. Because these distractions happen at similar times during a descent profile, mistakes made in overshooting or undershooting altitude-crossing restrictions are frequently reported.

The following are excerpts from two such cases.

> Flight attendant discussing a cabin situation with captain. Clearance was received by first officer for flight to cross 15 DME at or below FL 230. Captain crossed 15 DME at FL 240 . . . [the] F/O failed to mention correct altitude.

146

A second example shows again what distractions can cause.

> We were at FL 230 and told to descend and cross ABC at 18,000. I hurried to fill
> out the engine readings. Just then a flight attendant came up front with a request
> for a wheelchair. Center asked us for our altitude. We were just west of ABC and
> still at FL 230.

In the first example, there was a glitch in communication between the crew that allowed a 1000-foot excursion of the assigned altitude. In the second case, the captain
was already rushing to complete a task when he was unexpectedly interrupted. A 5000-
foot discrepancy was the end result of that simple distraction.

Lessons for general aviation

A Turbo Arrow doesn't have flight attendants, but it can come equipped with an-
noying passengers. "What does that knob do?" "Where are we?" "May I talk on the radio?" "May I fly for awhile?" "Let me switch the fuel tanks." "Why is that clock hand
spinning?" "It's so hot in here, doesn't this thing have air?" "I think I'm getting sick."
Sound familiar? The bottom line is that you just can't afford to take your attention
away from scanning, navigation, communication, and flying the airplane in order to
deal with every distraction. Remember who's pilot-in-command. A simple "Just a
minute," or a polite "Be quiet," is sometimes all it takes to get the message across.

Call us in range

Altitude deviations caused by company communications were described nearly 30
percent of the time that errors were reported.

> We were coming into XYZ. We checked in with approach and were told to expect
> ILS. While F/O was calling in range to the company, I thought I understood Cen-
> ter having cleared us down to 4000. During the descent I was informed that I did
> not have clearance.

The mistakes are similar in nature to those occurring during PA announcements. It
takes one pilot completely out of the ATC loop; therefore, misunderstood clearances
are quite common. Pilots who mistakenly departed their assigned altitude went
unchecked for several minutes because the nonflying pilots were on the radio talking
to ops. The numbers are significant. Nonflying pilots caught an altitude deviation only
40 percent of the time.

This issue recalls the discussion in chapter 3 of the mid-air collision between
Wings West Flight 628 and a Rockwell Commander. Although the crew of Flight 628
did not deviate from the assigned altitude, having one radio tuned to the company frequency did hinder the ability to hear the Rockwell.

Lessons for general aviation

This is no different then when you call the FBO enroute to say you need a fuel
truck ready when you arrive. If you choose to do so, then be aware that you will be out
of the ATC communication loop for a few minutes. Be sure to get back into the loop as

soon as possible. The other option is to land, walk into the FBO, and request a fuel truck. You might save some time if you call ahead or you might not. The only thing you have done for sure is set yourself up for a possible missed traffic advisory.

DISTRACTIONS: FLIGHT OPERATIONS

It should be no surprise that the NASA study identified the task of reading a checklist while taxiing, climbing, or on approach as a common distracter, one that frequently leads to altitude deviations and missed ATC clearances.

Checked and set

We were cleared for an ILS approach and advised to contact the tower at the outer marker. At this time the crew became involved with checklists and inadvertently forgot to contact the tower prior to our landing.

Landing without clearance was surprisingly not uncommon. Nearly 30 percent of the flight operations reports specified that being distracted with checklists caused those types of errors.

There was also a close connection between checklist activity and other cockpit duties. During the busier times of a flight—climbout and descent—pilots were rushed to get through the checklists, which made them feel overloaded and stressed with tasks.

We had a light airplane and obtained a high rate of climb. Due to other distractions . . . rechecking SID, looking outside for traffic, resetting climb power, after takeoff checklist, changing frequencies, and selecting radials . . . we inadvertently passed through our assigned altitude.

Altitude deviations at these critical phases accounted for a little more than 40 percent of the reported cases.

Other cases of "excessive workload" in association with checklist activity included a near-miss on approach at 2500 feet. The crew reported being "very busy" with the landing checklist, studying the approach plates, and monitoring the airspeed.

At times, pilots have become so involved with these various activities that they even disregard their own altitude reminder system.

During climbout from XYZ we were assigned 6000 feet. At 5000 the bell and light altitude reminder worked as planned. The 1000-to-level call was made. Climb checklists were being completed, navaids tuned and identified. Center . . . and radar continuously monitored . . .. The 6000 foot altitude was missed.

Lessons for general aviation

General-aviation pilots can also become "very busy" with landing checklists, studying approach plates, and monitoring airspeed. Just like their professional counterparts, general-aviation pilots can get behind the airplane, bust altitudes, and make unnecessary missed approaches if they succumb to distractions. Stay alert and don't allow these distractions to overwhelm you. It's risky being a sloppy flier during a critical phase of flight and in a collision-avoidance environment.

System malfunctions happen

Of the 19 system malfunctions reported during the study, all were considered minor. But these minor distractions were enough to cause 12 flights to deviate from their altitude clearances, 3 flights to deviate from their routes, 2 flights to land without clearance, and 1 flight to penetrate restricted airspace. Only one flight won the prize and had no deviations. All 18 crews admitted being distracted to the point that they no longer monitored the assigned flight path.

> We broke out . . . at FL 190 (cleared to 16,000) and immediately lowered the nose . . . to 370 knots . . . rate of sink increased to 3000 to 4000 fpm. Crew began to troubleshoot anti-ice [malfunction] . . . noise level was high . . . didn't hear altitude warning bell. [Flying] pilot was troubleshooting switches . . . [nonflying] pilot didn't make the 1000-ft-to-level-off call out. An altitude overshoot of 2000 ft occurred before the captain noted the altimeter.

An interesting side note: Often the crews had the autopilot on. They then felt free to engage in protracted troubleshooting of the systems problem, taking their attention away from the instruments. Sounds familiar to a reduced state of vigilance, doesn't it? Pilot error, just like history, tends to repeat itself.

Lessons for general aviation

System malfunctions can be scary, even for those with four stripes on their sleeve, but what makes matters worse is when the pilot stops flying the airplane. Using the autopilot isn't the answer either. Remember the rule: Aviate, navigate, communicate. That should be your priority. Otherwise, the minor system malfunction that you thought was so important could easily become the least of your worries after you've collided with another airplane because you unknowingly deviated from your altitude or heading.

IT CAN HAPPEN TO THE BEST OF THEM

There's no better way to sum up this section than by briefly discussing the events surrounding two well-known airline crashes: Eastern Flight 401 and United Flight 173. Although both flightcrews were highly qualified and experienced, they each allowed themselves to become distracted over a system malfunction. The NTSB later determined that these distractions had gotten so out of hand that they were causal to both accidents. Ironically, these two accidents occurred within one day of being exactly six years apart, and the cause of the crews' distractions were nearly identical.

The following transcript excerpts are from the NTSB accident investigation reports. They should in no way be construed to portray the crews of Eastern Flight 401 or United Flight 173 negatively. Monday morning quarterbacking is always easier than being there. Whether certain scenarios actually took place or not are of little consequence. What is important, however, is learning from past events so the same mistakes are never repeated.

Case 1: Eastern 401—a moonless night over the Everglades

29 December 1972: Eastern Airlines Flight 401, a Lockheed L-1011, crashed in the Everglades, 18 miles northwest of Miami, Florida, International Airport.

Pilot Experience: Captain: 29,700 total hours, 280 hours in the L-1011. First officer: 5800 total hours, 306 hours in the L-1011. Second officer: 15,700 total hours, 53 hours in the L-1011.

Reported weather at time of accident: 2500 feet scattered. Visibility 10 miles. No moon.

Probable cause

The NTSB determined that the probable cause of this accident was the failure of the flightcrew to monitor the flight instruments during the final four minutes of flight and to detect an unexpected descent soon enough to prevent impact with the ground. The Board also noted that preoccupation with a malfunction of the system indicating the position of the nose landing gear distracted the crew's attention from the instruments and allowed the descent to go unnoticed.

The accident

Approximately 2330 EST, the crew of Flight 401 began the approach into Miami International. When they lowered the landing gear, the nose gear light failed to illuminate, which prompted the crew to tell Miami tower: ". . . we're gonna have to circle, we don't have a light on our nose gear yet." At 2334, Flight 401 was cleared to: ". . . climb . . . to two thousand [feet], go . . . to approach control . . ." Flight 401 checked in with approach, told them of their problem, and was instructed to maintain two thousand feet.

Within two minutes of reaching the assigned altitude, the captain directed the first officer, who was flying the aircraft, to engage the autopilot. He complied. As they continued to circle, the crew focused their full attention on the nose-gear problem. Because there was a possibility that the gear was really down and locked, and that the instrument panel light was actually the malfunctioning system, the captain and first officer spent nearly four minutes troubleshooting and discussing the panel-light lens assembly.

Meanwhile, the captain instructed the second officer to go down into the forward electronics bay, which is beneath the flight deck and can be entered from a trapdoor in the cockpit, to visually check the nose gear. This can be done through an optical sight positioned just forward of the nose-wheel well. When two specific rods on the landing gear linkage are aligned, the nose gear is fully extended and locked. At 2341, the second officer raised his head into the cockpit and said, "I can't see it, it's pitch dark . . .." An Eastern maintenance specialist, who happened to be riding in the jumpseat, then went down into the electronics bay to assist the second officer.

At 2340, an aural altitude alert sounded in the cockpit when the aircraft deviated 250 feet from the selected altitude, which had been set at 2000 feet. No crewmember commented on the warning.

About a minute later, the Miami approach controller observed Flight 401's altitude reading was at 900 feet, not the assigned 2000 feet. He then asked, "Eastern . . . how are things comin' along out there?" The reply was "Okay, we'd like to turn around and come . . . back in." The controller granted the request to change the heading. About 20 seconds later, the first officer said, "We did something to the altitude." The captain replied, "What?" Quickly followed by the first officer asking, "We're still at two thousand, right?"

The captain immediately exclaimed, "Hey, what's happening here?" In less than five seconds, the aircraft, which was in a 28-degree left bank, crashed into the Everglades.

The investigation

The question that needed to be answered was why did Flight 401 make a very slow, undetected, controlled descent into the ground? According to the investigation, four factors were at work. First, the altitude-hold function of the autopilot system had been inadvertently disengaged. Second, a combination of throttle reductions and control-column force inputs had caused the initial descent. Third, although ATC observed Flight 401's altitude on its data block as much lower than its assigned altitude, the controller did not pursue the situation. And fourth, the crew had become completely distracted with the nose-gear malfunction.

A slow, undetected descent. Few can dispute the usefulness of the autopilot in a crisis or abnormal situation. However, as discussed earlier in the NASA study, when pilots need to troubleshoot a system malfunction, they tend to shift their attention away from monitoring the flight instruments, leaving that job to "Otto." Beyond that, plenty of autopilot systems aren't entirely *human friendly.* The L-1011 system was one of those.

A disengaging experience. It was suggested by the Board that it was highly likely that the captain accidentally disengaged the autopilot. But how does that happen without it being noticed by at least one crewmember?

The system had been set with the altitude and attitude modes selected. It takes 15 pounds of pressure on the captain's side or 20 pounds of pressure on the first officer's side for the pitch computers to be overridden. Since the flight data recorder (FDR) readout showed a descent rate of 200 fpm at the same time the captain was telling the second officer to go down in the electronics bay, the Board believed that the captain might have inadvertently bumped the yoke when he had turned to the second officer. The bump could have been enough pressure to disengage the altitude-hold function. The autopilot was still on with the attitude-hold mode engaged even though it was not controlling the altitude.

This leads to a second point. When the altitude and attitude functions are on, two separate lights illuminate on the annunciator panel. In this case, when the altitude mode was disengaged, the light simply went out. This is what I meant by human unfriendly. According to the investigation, there was absolutely no indication, other than a light going out, to warn the pilots that a critical mode of their autoflight system had become disengaged.

The descent begins. Once the altitude mode was off, even a slight pressure against the yoke could cause a change in attitude. Because there was so much physical movement between the captain and first officer, the Board speculated that one or both of them might have accidentally bumped the throttles. Because the FDR readout showed several increases in airspeed, followed by a series of small adjustments in the throttle setting only 160 seconds before impact, it was believed that the crew noticed the higher airspeed and pulled back the throttles. It was also likely that they referred only to the airspeed indicators because they thought the autoflight system was still maintaining altitude. Therefore, the Board decided it was conceivable that no other instruments were cross-checked.

DISTRACTION

"Eastern four oh one, how are things comin' along out there?" That question was asked a few seconds after the controller noticed an altitude reading of 900 feet, instead of the assigned 2000 feet, on Flight 401's data block. The controller testified that he had no doubt concerning the safety of the flight, since momentary deviations in altitude information on the radar display are rather common. Because Flight 401 responded with an "Okay," this reinforced the controller's decision to not pursue the matter any further. He assumed the crew was on top of things.

The final distraction. Flight 401 is a perfect example of how the end result that leads to an accident is usually not the originating cause. Why did the autoflight system become disengaged in the first place? A distraction in the cockpit. Why didn't the first officer notice that the altitude-mode function had been turned off? A distraction in the cockpit. When the crew realized an increase in airspeed, why didn't they cross-check the other instruments? A distraction in the cockpit. And what took the third crewmember—a third pair of eyes and ears—out of the cockpit for the final five minutes of the flight? A distraction in the cockpit.

Case 2: United 173—engines are flaming out

If this accident seems familiar it is because details of it were recounted in chapter 4 as an example in the subject of crew resource management. To refresh: The DC-8 ran out of fuel and crashed on approach to the Portland, Oregon, International Airport. A highly qualified crew was concerned with a landing gear problem. Even greater concern was placed on emergency passenger evacuation. With these distractions, little attention was paid to other matters until too late.

Recall the excerpts from the transcript of the final seven minutes of the flight: the surprised questions, the comments when it was realized that engines were flaming out, the resignation that a crash was imminent.

Probable cause

The NTSB determined that the probable cause of the accident was the failure of the captain to properly monitor the aircraft's fuel state and to properly respond to crewmembers' advisories regarding the fuel burn. This resulted in fuel exhaustion to all engines. The captain's inattention resulted from preoccupation with a landing gear malfunction and preparations for a possible emergency landing.

The aftermath

Flight 173 had circled at 5000 feet for one hour and two minutes with the gear down and flaps set at 15 degrees. The plane had entered the holding pattern with about 13,334 pounds of fuel, but with the aircraft's configuration and altitude, the Safety Board calculated fuel burn to be approximately 13,209 pounds per hour, or 220 pounds per minute. According to the investigation, there was no evidence that the crew ever discussed the fuel remaining in relation to time and distance to the airport during the final 30 minutes of flight.

One distraction can lead to another

Oddly enough, the distraction caused by the possible gear malfunction was not what the crew devoted the majority of its time to. Instead, the crew concentrated a considerable amount of time and thought to evacuation procedures. According to the Board, there were numerous instances when the crew showed either a lack of concern or awareness over the fuel status. Just 17 minutes before the crash, with four thousand pounds of fuel remaining, the captain asked the first officer to check on the progress of the cabin preparations. Upon his return, four minutes later, the first officer told the captain the cabin would be ready in two or three minutes. But in the initial post-accident interview, the captain said that he felt the flight attendants wouldn't be in position for up to 15 minutes. Consequently, the fuel situation took a lessor priority, and at 1801, the crew accepted a vector that directed the plane away from the airport. Once the turn was completed, no one suggested heading back towards the airport. At that moment, because of the rate of fuel burn and the heading of the aircraft, it became physically impossible for Flight 173 to reach the airport.

Above all else, the Board believed that because of the crew's continuing preoccupation with the gear problem and landing preparations, the priority had long been shifted away from flying the airplane. An accident eventually became inevitable; it was just a matter of time. In this case, one hour and two minutes.

Tunnel ears. Although we already know that distractions can give pilots and controllers a tunneling effect of their visual senses, this particular accident revealed that one's hearing can also be significantly inhibited. About seven minutes prior to the accident, the captain was discussing the evacuation procedures with the first flight attendant. The first officer said, "I think you just lost number four . . ." The captain continued to speak with the flight attendant while the first and second officers tended to the emergency. It wasn't until the first officer repeated ". . . goin' to lose an engine . . ." that the captain responded.

It was apparent that the captain had tuned out the background conversation to the point that the words ". . . lost number four . . ." didn't even trigger a reaction. According to the investigation, the captain had not been monitoring the fuel situation, so when he heard the flameout was due to fuel exhaustion, it caught him totally by surprise.

DISTRACTIONS: TRAFFIC

Few ATC messages can create more lively and instantaneous cockpit activity as "Traffic at twelve o'clock, altitude unknown." Although pilots make a concerted effort to locate the threat aircraft, this distraction is frequently enough to cause altitude deviations, nonstabilized approaches, landings without clearance, and even near-misses with aircraft other than their target traffic.

"We were cleared to 8000 feet, passing 6000 . . . advised . . . VFR traffic at twelve o'clock, 4 miles. My copilot and I strained to see traffic but were unsuccessful . . . asked for vector away from traffic . . . [never saw traffic]. I [caught us] passing through 8700 ft."

The captain went on to say that poor visibility and target fixation by both crewmembers caused them to focus their entire attention outside. The pilot, however, should be praised for making the wise decision to ask for vectors as soon as it was apparent they were not going to visually detect the traffic. Reports from other pilots also indicated that when traffic advisories were called by ATC, the crew engaged in a lengthy search while disregarding the rest of their scan pattern.

An earlier traffic advisory had drawn the attention of the first and second officers toward one o'clock when a westbound light aircraft passed over from the nine o'clock position. As the old saying goes, " It's not the airplane that you're looking for that will hit you . . ."

The study also found that when traffic advisories were called by ATC, the entire crew literally dropped what they were doing in order to search for the traffic. During routine scans, however, only one pilot, maybe, was normally looking for traffic. If a crew was as vigilant with all of its duties as in a potential crisis situation, fewer distractions and errors would occur.

Lessons for general aviation

This situation is the reverse of head-lock in the cockpit. When one element of the flight is forgotten about, it comes back to bite you. Frantically looking for traffic tends to keep your eyes away from monitoring your instruments. You might have spotted the threat aircraft, but by the time you look back in the cockpit, you're off the assigned altitude by 500 feet—and still descending—and off course by 10 degrees—and still turning. Remain in control of your airplane. If you can't detect your traffic, then ask ATC—that untapped, available resource—for help. But don't deviate from your own assigned flight path just because you can't find your traffic.

HEADS IN THE COCKPIT

The study also showed that pilots with an inadequate or, worse yet, nonexistent visual search were involved in more near-misses because of heads in the cockpit than from any other form of distraction. It's also not surprising to note that there have been numerous reports of safety conflicts when both pilots have had their heads down, studying approach plates.

The following four incident report excerpts show classic examples of head-lock in the cockpit, especially during descent and approach.

Captain and F/O . . . eyes in cockpit . . . approach to ABC airport. S/O [sees] . . . light aircraft . . . 300 feet in front of us at our altitude moving right to left . . . captain increases nosedown attitude to pass under the light aircraft. Estimated miss . . . 50 feet.

One can only wonder what would have happened if there hadn't been that third pair of eyes in the cockpit.

An air carrier crew had just extended the flaps and gear while descending to 2500 feet. Both pilots' attention was in the cockpit when a light aircraft "flashed over engine nacelle at less than 200 feet separation."

The air carrier was slow, low, and at the perfect altitude that light aircraft like to suddenly appear. This is not a good time to be distracted.

Neither air carrier pilot had been in the area in the last 90 days. The two captains flying together had their heads down when a light airplane passed 200 feet over their aircraft.

Study time is the night before, that morning, or while sipping coffee at FL 350—not during the approach.

Descending through 9200 at 250 knots in a turn to the left as an aircraft came into view through the F/O's windshield . . . [no time to react] . . . other aircraft was behind us within two seconds of sighting. Estimated vertical separation . . . 100 or 200 feet as it passed directly over the right side of our aircraft.

Lessons for general aviation

Granted, the point about head-lock in a collision-avoidance environment has been beaten to death. Nevertheless, in a blink of an eye it can be over. And head-lock is one of those thoughtless actions that we've all done, but we can just as easily get out of the habit. Think for a minute. Are there certain times throughout a flight that you find yourself staring inside rather than scanning outside? Is there a specific task that routinely distracts you in this way? Then find ways to compensate for it, or better yet, avoid it altogether.

ONE LAST DISTRACTING TALE

Remember those times when you've been lost or you can't find the airport? You're frantically scanning the countryside for that big ol' slab of concrete. Vigilantly looking for other aircraft is not high on your priority list.

I remember the first time that I was really lost like it happened yesterday, even though it was actually 14 years ago. I was so distracted and focused on finding that darn airport that I thought about little else. It was a chilly November day, and I was flying my first solo cross-country. With only 26.5 total hours to my name (I don't have that number memorized—I dug up my old logbook), I was already a potential hazard by definition. This historic and dreaded flight took me from Pittsburgh's Allegheny County Airport north to Clarion, Pennsylvania, east along I-80 to DuBois, Pennsylvania, then direct back to home base. The first leg was uneventful. At DuBois, I made an unstable approach and humiliated myself by porpoising on my touch-and-go. I eagerly headed home. By now, my confidence level was barely registering, but I knew if I could just hang in there for a few more miles I would see familiar territory and this so-called enriching experience would be over.

With my map neatly folded open to display my intended route, I soon began looking for my landmarks. I should fly near a little uncontrolled airport and, to my relief, one was right in front of me. I double-checked the map, and although the runway layout wasn't the same as the one on the map, I convinced myself it was the right airport.

For those who have never flown in the Pittsburgh area, it's basically a no-brainer, or should be one. When you find one of the three rivers, turn until you see the smoke stacks and eventually you find the airport. With three rivers the hard part is knowing over what river you are flying.

I called Allegheny Tower, and reported over XYZ airport, inbound for landing. "Roger, Grumman 26401, report the river." That felt good.

Instead of seeing the river, I see farmland—miles and miles of farmland. Not good. However, I continue. Really not good. My map is now completely open and has filled half of the airplane. I start to fool around with the VOR. I hadn't yet really understood how to work it and even though my head was telling me to turn toward the needle, my gut was telling me not to get any further off course. Every five seconds I check my fuel gauge, look outside in hopes of seeing water, and glance at the map. Even when the friendly controller radioed, "Grumman 401, how ya doin' out there?" I shakily replied, "Okay." Now that's pride for you. What seemed like an eternity, I finally swallowed that pride. I figured admitting that I was lost would be less embarrassing than running out of gas and picking weeds out of the propeller. Meekly I called, "Allegheny tower, Grumman 401, um, that airport that I thought was XYZ, wasn't." In less than 30 seconds, I had squawked a new ident and was heading home.

Now that I was a little more relaxed, I started to scan for traffic. It wasn't really a conscious decision, but a natural one that evolved from being calmer and not as distracted. Within 10 minutes, I caught my first glimpse of the most beautiful steel mill I had ever seen, and I finally knew I was home free. I later discovered that I had flown right past the outskirts of Pittsburgh and was heading towards the Ohio—West Virginia border.

I learned some very simple, but valuable lessons that day.

1. I was not fully prepared. My knowledge and experience of dead reckoning and navaids was minimal and my general state of uneasiness set the tone for how the flight was going to progress, even before I got off of the ground. If it doesn't feel right, it probably isn't.

2. Poor navaid use. Instead of tuning in the DuBois VOR, I literally hung a right over Clarion, and followed I-80. Consequently, the airport came up a lot faster than I had anticipated, so I was still at my cruise altitude when I crossed the airport. I was so busy spiraling down to pattern altitude, with hopes of not killing myself, that see and avoid was definitely not in the plan. Besides, I thought DuBois tower would tell me if there was traffic.

   I was already nervous and so preoccupied with my upcoming approach that all I could focus on was the altimeter, airspeed indicator, and the runway. Some nonconformist pilot could have sliced right through my approach path, and I probably would never have seen him. And why would that have been the case? It goes back to not being prepared. Distractions are a dime a dozen when you're just along for the ride.

3. Poor map use. Can you believe I actually opened up the entire Detroit sectional chart in hopes of finding where I was? Not only was I being distracted with trying to locate my position, but part of the map was blocking the window. I cringe every time I recall that.

4. Poor ATC coordination. Why didn't I tell ATC of my situation sooner? I thought I could figure it out myself. Pride and stupidity. That's the only correct answer. I would rather have flown aimlessly than make a 15-second call for assistance. ATC is such a valuable resource if we'd only use it more often and more appropriately.

THE MORAL OF THE STORY

Lots of external forces can unexpectedly and temporarily distract us. Communication problems, deviations for weather, passenger and/or crew interaction, systems malfunctions, and a host of others. It's also apparent that flight hours and experience don't necessarily keep you from becoming distracted. Although the low-time pilot could be more vulnerable to distractions, the 20,000-hour, professional pilot can just as easily be lulled away from critical tasks, particularly when confidence leads to complacency.

As I stated earlier, the most frightening part of being distracted is the fact that we allow it to happen. Then we often continue, even against our better judgment. Remember, any interruption in the normal flow of cockpit duties creates the potential for serious, and even fatal, consequences.

PRACTICAL APPLICATIONS AND LESSONS LEARNED

1. Fly the airplane. No matter what, always remain in control of the airplane. Aviate, navigate, communicate.

2. Be decisive with the delegation of responsibilities. Who's going to fly the airplane? In the cases of Eastern Flight 401 and United Flight 173, there were no clear determinations or directions as to who would actually take over the duty of monitoring the flight. Flying solo? Refer to Number 1.

3. Don't complete nonessential tasks during critical phases of flight. It not only takes a good pair of eyes and ears away from traffic detection, it also removes a crewmember from monitoring the instruments. Remember those altitude busts.

4. Keep everyone in the loop. Immediately following ATC communications, make sure the flying pilot knows the exact clearance or message. Then cross-check.

5. Remain in the loop. Immediately following company communications or a PA announcement, ask what clearances or messages had been received while you were busy. Then cross-check the instruments for accuracy.

6. Don't tune out the rest of the world. Be aware of the activities going on around you. It's called having good situational awareness. It is particularly important when a momentary distraction takes you away from the tasks at hand. When the interruption has ended, promptly get back in the loop.

7. Prioritize your interruptions. There are going to be times when you just can't prevent an interruption; however, if you know the conversation is not essential to flight, and you're in the middle of something important, like finishing a checklist, ask the person to wait until you have time. And don't get suckered in thinking there's no harm in a 30-second conversation—you know what can happen from a 30-second distraction.

8. Maintain optimum time management. You would be surprised how much time you actually have for completing checklists when you don't allow unnecessary distractions to take over. Hack the clock.

9. Don't allow a minor distraction to turn catastrophic. Remember Eastern Flight 401 and United Flight 173.

10. One distraction can lead to another. Self-imposed distractions, like those on United Flight 173, can kill you. Whatever kind of distraction you might experience, isolate it.

11. Maintain vigilance at all times, not just when you hear "traffic at twelve o'clock, one mile."

12. Keep your head moving. Whether your head is in the full up or full down-and-locked position, remember, your SA has just been cut in half.

CHAPTER 6 REVIEW

- Distractions can negatively affect situational awareness, decision making, and judgment.
- Nonflight operations include paperwork, PA announcements, passenger problems, and inappropriate cockpit conversations.
- Flight operations include crew coordination, and actual flying tasks.

Distractions: nonflight operations

Paperwork keeps pilots' heads in the cockpit, preventing effective instrument and traffic scans. Common flight errors associated with paperwork include:

- Altitude deviations
- Misunderstood clearances

- Forgotten clearances
- Breakdown in crew communication

NASA Air Carrier Flight Operations Policy recommends that nonessential paperwork be delayed until the cruise segment of a flight.

PA announcements remove pilots from the ATC communication loop. Common errors associated with conducting public address messages include:

- Altitude deviations
- Misunderstood clearances
- Missed clearances
- Nonflying pilot is unavailable to cross-check altitude or heading assignments. NASA Air Carrier Flight Operations Policy recommends not to use the PA below 10,000 feet in the terminal area.

Common errors associated with nonflight-essential cockpit conversation include:

- Altitude deviations
- Misunderstood clearances
- Missed clearances
- No one flying the airplane

Professional cockpit discipline should be maintained at all times.

Most pilot-flight-attendant interaction occurs during the descent phase. Common errors associated with flight-attendant interruptions include:

- Misread instruments
- Altitude deviations
- Overshooting/undershooting altitude crossing restrictions
- Breakdown in crew communication

Common errors associated with company communication include:

- Altitude deviations
- Misunderstood clearances
- Missed clearances
- Nonflying pilot is unavailable to cross-check altitude and heading assignments.

Distractions: flight operations
Common errors associated with checklist activity include:

- Altitude deviations
- Missed clearances
- Landing without clearances
- Excessive workload

Common errors associated with system malfunctions include:

- Altitude deviations
- Route deviations
- Landing without clearances
- Penetration of restricted airspace
- No one flying the airplane

Troubleshooting can also lead to a reduced state of vigilance.

Traffic advisories

ATC-prompted traffic advisories can cause target fixation. Pilots tend to focus on the perceived threat aircraft and disregard the entire scan pattern. Pilots tend to suddenly become alert when a "traffic at twelve o'clock" advisory is issued and disregard all other cockpit duties. Common errors associated with traffic advisories include:

- Altitude deviations
- Nonstabilized approaches
- Landing without clearances
- Near misses with unknown aircraft

Request a vector away from threat aircraft when visual detection is not possible.

Heads in the cockpit

Inadequate and nonexistent visual search is the primary cause for near-misses. Both pilots concentrating on approach plates is a reason for an inferior visual search. Common errors associated with head-lock in the cockpit include:

- Near-misses
- Altitude deviations

Studying an approach plate during the approach is dangerous.

Getting lost
- Inadequate flight planning and preparation can lead to serious problems.
- Poor navaid use can cause pilots to become lost.

- Poor map use can cause unnecessary distractions.
- Poor ATC coordination can make a serious situation turn disastrous.

Conclusion
- Watch for sources of distractions that can suddenly and unexpectedly appear.
- Flight hours and experience does not guarantee a distraction-free flight.
- Distractions can lead to confusion and chaos in the cockpit.

Chapter 6 references

Foushee, H. Clayton, and Robert L. Helmreich. 1988. "Group Interaction and Flight Crew Performance." *Human Factors in Aviation.* Ed. Wiener, Earl L. and David C. Nagel. San Diego: Academic Press: 189-227.

Kantowitz, Barry H. and Patricia A. Casper. 1988. "Human Workload in Aviation." *Human Factors in Aviation.* Ed. Wiener, Earl L. and David C. Nagel. San Diego: Academic Press: 157-187.

Nagel, David C. "Human Error in Aviation Operations." 1988. *Human Factors in Aviation.* Ed. Wiener, Earl L. and David C. Nagel. San Diego: Academic Press: 263-303.

National Aeronautics and Space Administration. 1978. Aviation Safety Reporting System: Ninth Quarterly Report. Ames (NASA) Research Center, Moffett Field, California.

National Transportation Safety Board. 14 June 1973. Aircraft Accident Report: Eastern Air Lines, Inc., L-1011, N310EA, Miami, Florida, December 29, 1972. Washington, DC.

National Transportation Safety Board. 7 June 1979. Aircraft Accident Report: United Airlines, Inc., McDonnell-Douglas DC-8-61, N8082U, Portland, Oregon, December 28, 1978. Washington, DC.

Smith, Ruffell. 1979. A Simulator Study of the Interaction of Pilot Workload With Errors, Vigilance, and Decisions. National Aeronautics and Space Administration.

7

Welcome to the world of stress management

A superior pilot uses his superior judgment to avoid stressful situations that require the use of his superior skills.

Anonymous

STRESS MANAGEMENT BECAME A CATCH PHRASE FOR THE EIGHTIES, directed primarily at the high-powered, high-strung, stressed-out corporate captains of the world. In time, the rest of the population was introduced to stress inventories, life change units, exercise-to-relieve-stress programs, relaxation tapes, and so on. In this chapter, stress management is discussed a bit differently.

We already know that if we have a stress-filled and screwed-up life, every thought, action, decision, and even our health can be gravely affected. But what exactly does this all mean for us when we go out and strap on an airplane, or sit down at a radar scope covered with flickering lights? According to a study conducted by the Aviation

Psychology Laboratory at Ohio State University, the answer is that stress—including nervousness, anxiety, worry, uncomfortableness, fright, and panic—is one of the most significant forces affecting our ability to make logical decisions.

When we experience stress in any form, it can start an error chain in motion. Tunnel vision, a breakdown in the decision-making and communication process, distraction, poor judgment, excessive workload, physical fatigue, and a lack of situational awareness are all possible end results of stress. Conversely, allowing any one of these breakdown areas to take over a flight can easily cause additional stress. Information that might be staring us in the face can go unnoticed or unused simply because we don't have the big picture.

Even if we are able to partially come out of our stressful state, we have difficulty making the correct choice from the available options. We are easily distracted when operating under stress, which leads to a breakdown of communication and situational awareness. We can become mentally and physically overloaded by even the most mundane tasks.

Stress that goes unchecked can quickly turn into panic. Once panic enters the cockpit, appropriate and timely decisions are completely eliminated. It's a vicious circle that can rapidly lead to an accident. But as discussed in the introduction, the circle can be broken simply by removing one of the links to the error chain.

STRESS VS. STIMULATION

It has long been documented that everyone operates most effectively at a moderate degree of mental stimulation. Figure 7-1 depicts a simplistic illustration of what happens to our work performance at certain levels of mental stimulation and stress.

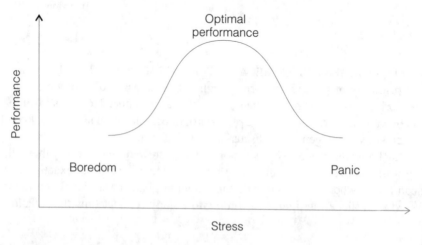

Fig. 7-1. *Relationship between stress and performance.*

It's not surprising to note that our work performance suffers when our level of mental stimulation, motivation, and attention are at their lowest points. By now you should be well aware of the hazards of a reduced state of vigilance. Boredom produces just that.

Boredom can be induced by one of two ways. First, very little or no mental stimulation tends to drastically slow down our capacity to think clearly—clearly is the key word—and to react quickly. A perfect example of this is the case where a mid-air collision occurred while the controller was monitoring only two aircraft.

Second, complacency can just as quickly produce boredom and poor work performance. Doing the same thing day in and day out is often thought of as the traditional means of becoming complacent. Repetition also causes complacency. Moreover, other ways to fall into this trap are rarely mentioned and frequently disregarded.

"With the amount of experience I have in this airplane, nothing surprises me anymore." A pilot with this kind of attitude no longer flies with an edge. He or she feels that it has all been seen and done before and, therefore, the pilot is more along for the ride than actually taking command of the airplane. Complacency and boredom are routine parts of this flying regime, but what is so disturbing is the fact that the pilot doesn't even recognize it.

Fighting boredom

Usually you can see boredom coming a mile away, so anticipate the possibility and do something to prevent it from entering into your work or flight environment. If you can take a break, do it. If you can't physically move away from the situation, then by all means keep your mind active. Take this time to perfect your visual scan, check your map, scan, calculate your groundspeed, scan, triangulate your position from VOR radials, scan, check your next GPS steerpoint, scan, get a weather update, scan, check your gas, scan, recheck your instruments, scan, ...

Top form

The appropriate degree of mental stimulation creates the mental and physical condition that is optimum for peak performance. Because everyone's best level of stimulation is different, there's no exact means of determining what the appropriate level is. For some, the line between stimulated and stressed-out is quite narrow. That's why some pilots have their most productive flights when being yelled at by their instructors.

I'm an example of the exact opposite type, and many of us are around. The second an instructor would turn into a raving maniac was the last time that person would have the pleasure of flying with me. The key to the proper level of stimulation is solely dependent upon what makes you feel comfortable and free of anxiety. Butterflies in the stomach or a case of the jitters is not stimulation, it's a form of stress.

Pushing that appropriate level of stimulation envelope too far can rapidly plummet an individual into a state of panic. Remember, the resultant difference between boredom and panic is usually only the speed in which the errors are made. Panic causes tunnel vision, poor decisions, poor judgment, a breakdown in communication, distraction, excessive workload, physical fatigue and exhaustion, and a lack of situational awareness. Instead of moving like a slug, you move like a crazed lunatic, which you no doubt are if you are trying not to die. Neither is very conducive to a safe flight.

Three stages of stress

According to an Ohio State study, the human body responds to stress in three stages: alarm reaction, resistance, and exhaustion. The research is based on the notion that our primitive ancestors used these responses in a fight or flight situation. Although there aren't many saber-toothed tigers left to wrestle nowadays, we still use the same instincts when confronted with stress.

The alarm stage

The alarm stage is triggered either by excitement or fear, each with very different results. We usually experience the initial phase of excitement on a daily basis. Operating in a busy airport area, maneuvering on the freeways, or even when sitting at a red light and noticing that the driver in the car next to us is pretty cute and looking back, can make us feel as if we had just run a 100-yard dash. This, of course, happens because the brain releases adrenaline, which in turn causes our hearts to beat faster and our breathing to quicken.

However, the way in which our bodies cope with fear—not panic—is the most significant. Think of the last time you experienced that nice little dose of excitement and stimulation in the traffic pattern. Felt good, until you had a close encounter with a Beech flying a right-hand pattern when the airport used a left-hand pattern. Your level of excitement just elevated to outright fear. Other than your eyes becoming the size of dinner plates, you most likely got a huge burst of energy and something you probably were unaware of—greater muscular strength and better hearing and vision.

The resistance stage

If the body is dealing only with being excited, such as flying in a busy airport traffic area, it slips into the resistance stage. After relatively brief moments of excitement, the stimulation caused by operating around a lot of traffic soon subsides. A body adapts to this sudden shock and, in time, repairs any damage caused by the stress.

However, if the stress continues, like being lost and running low on fuel, the body remains in a constant state of readiness. This is true also when a normal degree of excitement is rocket-boosted to a level of fear. Remember the near-miss with the Beech. We will, at least momentarily, be alert and seemingly keen-minded, but that soon disappears because we are just simply unable to keep up with such physical demands.

The exhaustion stage

The exhaustion stage then takes over, leaving us struggling with even the simplest of tasks. Because of this overload, we can quickly become fatigued. Decision-making, judgment, and communication errors are quite common, as are mistakes made in actual hands-on flying. Many pilots even succumb to a feeling of helplessness when the fight has gone out of them. They give up and literally stop thinking.

The resistance and exhaustion connection

The important point to remember is the next time you find yourself in an alerted state of readiness (advanced resistance stage), be fully aware that a period of exhaustion will follow. Instead of just going with the flow and ending up mentally and physically fatigued and good for nothing, try to slow the resistance process. It's up to you to calm down. Otherwise, your body will continue in overdrive until exhaustion sets in. With your newly found alertness, remain in command of the airplane, assess the problem, and make appropriate and timely decisions. Being excited or momentarily fearful doesn't have to be a bad thing. Use your increased abilities, and thwart off your own worse enemies: panic and exhaustion.

Stress and anger

Contrary to how the body reacts in a fearful state, when we experience anger, noradrenaline is secreted, which causes high blood pressure. In the short term, this condition retards our ability to think clearly and we find ourselves unable to make timely decisions or develop solutions to immediate problems. The next time you're on final and some jerk cuts you off, try to control those instincts of getting on the radio and going through some primeval screaming ritual. Likewise, if you're sitting there seething while picturing how therapeutic it's going to be when you confront this guy on the ramp, you have just stopped flying the airplane.

Time and stress

Time constraints are probably one of the greatest motivators in flying:

- I must get to my destination before the FBO closes for the night.
- Can I make it to the next town with the fuel remaining?
- I won't be able to make my meeting if the weather forces me to land at my alternate.
- I can do just one more pattern before sunset.

Demands often exceed the time available. This, coupled with the numerous other stresses associated with flying, can quickly produce a frazzled, weary-eyed pilot.

Just as being aware of our own personalities and attitudes helps when recognizing a potential hazard, the same is true concerning our individual vulnerability to stress. Although the following few questions pertain to situations in everyday life, the characteristics can also be found in the cockpit.

1. Do you have a rushed speech pattern?
2. Do you hurry or complete another person's conversation?
3. Do you hate to wait in line?
4. Do you feel as if you never catch up with your work?

5. Do you detest wasting time?
6. Do you become impatient if others are too slow?

Recognize yourself in any of the above questions? All of us, from time to time, fall into these categories, but if these characteristics are a way of life for you, then you are most likely functioning in a constant overload mode.

Now let's see how these questions pertain to flying.

1. Do you talk so fast on the radio no one can understand you? The answer is probably "yes" if you seem to hear an inordinate amount of "say agains" from ATC. Do you talk so fast that your fellow crewmembers catch only every third word? "What did he say?" "Are we cleared to 4000 or 14,000?"

2. Do you cut off other pilots who are talking on the radio? "They've had enough time to say what they needed to say, now it's my turn." Do you tune-out ATC when the information they are relaying seems to be impertinent chatter? "I've already got my clearance, why's he still talking? I'm busy with my checklist." Do you hurry your copilot's discussions and conversations? "Let's cut to the chase, what's your point?"

3. Do you hate being number four for takeoff? This question doesn't apply if you've ever flown out of Dallas/Ft. Worth at 5:00 p.m. just after a thunder-storm, and you're number 12 for takeoff. You're going to be stressed no mat-ter what. "I can't believe how many people are flying today. I'll be sitting in line forever. The plane has already flown once today, so I think I'll skip the pre-flight."

4. Do you feel like everything is going well and then, without warning, you're suddenly behind the airplane? "I don't know why I have so much to do at the most critical phase of every flight."

5. Do you detest wasting time prior to a flight? "I don't need to waste time get-ting a weather update, the earlier forecast is good enough." "Why did I bother getting to the airport early when the plane is still out on a cross-country? Somebody should've called me."

6. Do you get impatient when the FBO, refuelers, maintenance, weather fore-casters or ATC move too slowly? "All I want to do is buy a new sectional and these folks behind the counter move at a snail's pace." "Where did the fuel guy go? He said he'd be right out." "All I need is a quart of oil, and now the me-chanic disappears." "This is ridiculous. These weather guys sit around all day drinking coffee, but when I need a forecast the good ones go on break." "C'mon, c'mon. I don't have all day to wait for my departure clearance."

Anticipatory stress
Anticipatory stress can be helpful if used in moderate amounts. Preparing and plan-ning for a potentially stressful situation, like a checkride, an in-the-weather ILS approach, or a student facing a busy traffic pattern, can actually increase your level of attention and

awareness. However, what is just as likely to occur is that a pilot will focus on an event known to be stressful and disregard what currently is going on around him or her. This is when anticipatory stress can become more of a distraction and hindrance than a benefit.

Probably one of the best examples of how we react to anticipatory stress, and one to which most of us can relate, comes from a checkride experience. Although we basically know what to expect, there's still that element of the unknown. For instance, if we're most concerned about the pending simulated engine-failure segment, our focus shifts away from the other aspects of flying to "I can't stand this, let's get this over with."

A time for reflection

Once you have fallen prey to a bad case of anticipatory stress, you need time to think and learn from the experience. If there is not enough time to "come down" in order to relieve the tensions built up during the anticipatory stage, then the energy that surged during the experience will not be released and the body and mind will remain stressed.

PRACTICAL APPLICATIONS AND LESSONS LEARNED

1. Anticipate boredom. It's easy to know when boredom will strike, like on a long cross-country, or staring at a near empty radar screen, so:

2. Fight it off. Keep your mind active.

3. Know the difference between stress and stimulation. Whatever keeps you mentally alert and free of anxiety is your optimum level of stimulation. A case of the jitters is stress.

4. Recognize your panic threshold. Too much stress can quickly lead to panic. Stay stimulated without getting stressed and panic-stricken.

5. Excitement produces benefits. Use them. Use your newly found burst of energy, strength, hearing, and vision to get through that busy traffic pattern and safely on the ground. Guaranteed, you'll drive home from the airport with a smile on your face.

6. Fight off exhaustion. When you know you're in the resistance phase, calm down. If you don't, your body will. The problem with that is when your body shuts down, it also goes to sleep. Not good, when you are IFR and still 20 miles from the airport.

7. Suppress your anger. Yelling or a preoccupation with future yelling has no place in the cockpit.

8. Eliminate time crunches. This is different from time constraints. Here's an example. If you must be at your destination by 3:00 p.m., and it takes 50 minutes of flying time (your time constraint), don't arrive at the airport at 2:00 p.m. (your time crunch). You have weather to check, a flight plan to fill out, even if you airfile, and a pre-flight. Try to do all that in 10 minutes and you now have a big time crunch. Something will either be forgotten, thought about but disregarded as not being that important, or done half-way. Eliminating time crunches can usually be done quite easily. It might be setting the alarm 10

minutes earlier, or eating lunch in a half hour instead of 45 minutes. Such simple actions literally have the potential of meaning life or death.

9. Slow down your speech. Think about it. Do people really move any faster just because you are impatient? You waste more time having to repeat yourself than by speaking clearly and concisely the first time.

10. Make a concerted effort not to tense up or freak out if someone irritates you. This might be easier said than done, but it's this kind of behavior that can escalate to serious health problems. It's also just one more type of distraction that interferes with your flying. Either way, it's not a good situation to be in.

11. Anticipate anticipatory stress. Don't get so worked up that you focus on only one portion of the flight.

12. Take a breather. After a stressful experience, take some time to calm down and reflect. Wind the clock. You'll be amazed at what you can learn about yourself when you are thinking clearly. There's that "C" word again.

CHAPTER 7 REVIEW

Stress is a major enemy to clear thinking.

Stress management
- Stress significantly affects the ability to make logical decisions.
- Stress, in any form, can start an error chain in motion.
- Tunnel vision, a breakdown in decision-making and communication process, distraction, poor judgment, excessive workload, physical fatigue, and a lack of situational awareness can be caused by stress.
- Allowing any one of these areas to enter a flight regime can cause stress.
- Stress can be the cause or end result of an error chain.
- An error chain can be broken through awareness.

Stress vs. stimulation
- A moderate degree of mental stimulation is effective for producing peak work performance.
- Work performance suffers when mental stimulation is low.
- Boredom can produce a reduced state of vigilance.
- Little or no mental stimulation drastically reduces the capacity to think clearly and react quickly.
- Complacency can produce boredom.
- Repetition can cause complacency.
- Experience can cause complacency.
- Anticipate boredom.

- Keep the mind and body active before boredom sets in.

- Proper form of stimulation should be stress-, anxiety-, and tension-free.

- Panic can cause tunnel vision, poor decisions, poor judgment, a breakdown in communication, distraction, excessive workload, physical fatigue and exhaustion, and a lack of situational awareness.

The three stages of stress
1. Alarm stage triggered either by excitement or fear.
   — Brain releases adrenaline, which causes increased heart and breathing rates.
   — Fear can cause a momentary burst of energy, greater muscular strength, better hearing and vision.

2. Resistance stage allows the body to adapt to a sudden shock, and eventually repair any damage caused by the stress.
   — Continuous stress will keep the body in a constant state of readiness.

3. Exhaustion stage will take over when the body is no longer able to keep up with the stressful demands.
   — Errors in decision-making, judgment, communication, and hands-on flying are common.
   — Pilots can have a feeling of helplessness.
   — Slow down the resistance process before it turns into exhaustion.
   — Use the constant state of readiness to remain in command of the airplane, assess the problem, and make appropriate and timely decisions.

Anger and stress
- Noradrenaline is secreted which causes high blood pressure.

This condition retards ability to think clearly, make timely decisions, and develop solutions to immediate problems.

Time and stress
- Time constraints negatively affect thought process.

- Individuals with certain personalities and attitudes are vulnerable to stress.

Anticipatory stress
- Helpful in moderate amounts.

- Preparing and planning for a potentially stressful situation can increase level of attention and awareness.

- Anticipatory stress can be a hindrance when a pilot focuses on future events rather than current activities.

A time for reflection
- After an anticipatory stress episode, a time for reflection is necessary.
- Body will remain stressed, and performance will probably be reduced, if a calming down period is eliminated.

Chapter 7 references

Jensen, Richard S. 1989. Aeronautical Decision Making, Cockpit Resource Management. U.S. Department of Transportation. Federal Aviation Administration.
"Stress, Fatigue, and the Crewmember." May 1988. *Human Factor*: 26-8.

8
Traffic-alert and collision-avoidance systems

N O BOOK ON COLLISION AVOIDANCE WOULD BE COMPLETE WITHOUT A discussion on traffic-alert and collision-avoidance systems (TCAS). Very simply, a TCAS is a system in the cockpit that is independent of, but compatible with, the ground-based ATC network. With the use of an onboard computer, a TCAS processes transponder signals from other aircraft to determine their positions, altitudes, and rates of closure. These signals can be received and analyzed from up to 40 miles away. That information is then presented to the flightcrew on either the cockpit weather-radar scope or a specially designed TCAS color display.

With that basic understanding of how TCAS operates, let's briefly discuss the beginning of airborne collision-avoidance development. As you might have already guessed, the concept relies on a little mathematics and physics.

TAU PRINCIPLE

Besides transponder interrogation, virtually all airborne collision-avoidance systems designed in the past 30 years have used a mathematical equation known as the TAU principle. In 1955, Dr. J.S. Morrell, of the Bendix Communication Division, developed the TAU principle and applied his findings to learn more about the physics of collisions.

According to Dr. Morrell's concept, each aircraft flies inside an invisible envelope which varies in shape and size depending on speed of that aircraft and the speed of other airplanes. Figure 8-1 illustrates how the ratio of range-to-range rate represents the time period in which two aircraft on a collision course would intercept. A pilot's TAU is the minimum time needed to recognize the threat and take evasive action, typically about 25 seconds.

The TAU principle

Fig. 8-1. *TAU principle. Range divided by range rate equals time to closest approach point (CPA).* Bendix/King, Allied-Signal

Transponders

Transponder interrogation is integral to a TCAS. Let's take a quick look at the three types of transponders and see how each works, or doesn't work, with the system. A transponder is an onboard device that transmits a coded signal back to ATC. That numbered code appears as a distinct pattern on the controller's radar scope. The same transponder signal, however, provides slightly different information to TCAS.

Mode-A
The Mode-A signal shows only position, not altitude. Therefore, it reports only range and bearing information. Mode-A is sometimes referred to as Mode-3.

Mode-C
Mode-C transmits range, bearing, and altitude information.

Mode-S

Mode-S is the most sophisticated of the transponders and is an integral part of TCAS II. We'll get to TCAS II in a minute. In addition to the Mode-C capabilities, Mode-S provides two critical functions: discrete addressing and data linking. From ATC's viewpoint, Mode-S can be interrogated separately, eliminating garbled radar returns. The data-link function is actually two-fold. ATC is able to relay messages faster, via cathode ray tube (CRT) computer screen presentations, with less frequency congestion, and most importantly, TCAS II-equipped aircraft can detect each other's presence. Mode-S transmits a signal every second, known as a *squitter pulse,* making the interpretation of a traffic conflict nearly instantaneous. If both threat aircraft are equipped with TCAS II, the Mode-S data-link will coordinate the evasion maneuvers between the two.

TCAS I

TCAS I is a low-power, short-range (three to five nm) system consisting of a TCAS antenna, TCAS processor with a 100-watt peak-power transmitter, and a display unit. It does not have collision-avoidance logic and, therefore, cannot compute evasive maneuver courses. It does, however, locate aircraft in the immediate vicinity, display their locations within a given quadrant, and provide aural traffic advisories.

Although TCAS I is the least sophisticated of the airborne collision-avoidance systems, it does enhance a crew's situational awareness and their ability to visually detect their traffic.

TCAS II

The TCAS II, combined with a Mode-S transponder, scans a volume of airspace around the aircraft using two antennae: one on the top of the fuselage and the other beneath. Typically, the top-mounted antenna transmits interrogations on 1030 megahertz (MHz) at varying power levels in each of the four 90-degree azimuth segments. Mode-S transponder replies are received on 1090 MHz and are sent to the TCAS computer. The bottom-mounted antenna (the receiver) provides range and altitude data on targets that are below the TCAS aircraft.

The 1030/1090-MHz environment, in conjunction with the upper and lower antennae, optimizes signal strength and reduces multipath interference. The scanning area covers 14.7 miles to the front of the aircraft, 7.5 miles behind and 7000 feet above and 7000 feet below the aircraft. These distances are sufficient to handle an impressive 1200-knot closure rate off the nose and an altitude-closure rate of 12,000 feet per minute. The dual antenna feature also enables the aircraft to have full and continuous coverage even in a banking turn. Additionally, TCAS II is able to track up to 45 aircraft within a 15-mile radius and can display up to 30 aircraft at one time.

NOTE: The remaining discussion and illustrations pertain to TCAS II.

TCAS II operation

A TCAS II system monitors the airspace surrounding the aircraft by interrogating the transponders of intruding aircraft. The interrogation reply enables TCAS II to compute range, relative bearing, altitude, vertical speed, and closing rate.

TCAS II initial transponder acquisition

Figure 8-2 illustrates the initial phase of transponder interrogation. When an aircraft enters the *invisible envelope,* it is considered to be a potential threat. Therefore, TCAS II first determines the range of the intruder aircraft.

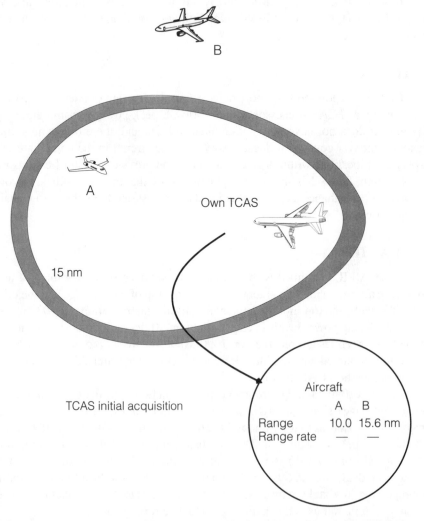

Fig. 8-2. *TCAS II initial transponder acquisition. The initial acquisition of a TCAS II's "invisible envelope" where own TCAS determines range of potential threats.* Bendix/King, Allied-Signal

TCAS II second phase of transponder interrogation

Once TCAS II measures the range of the intruder aircraft, it analyzes its track. Figure 8-3 shows that the determination of range rate, or closing speed, is the second phase of transponder interrogation.

TCAS II final phase of transponder interrogation

The final phase of transponder interrogation is illustrated in Fig. 8-4. It relies on mathematical computations that TCAS II automatically derives in determining the level of threat.

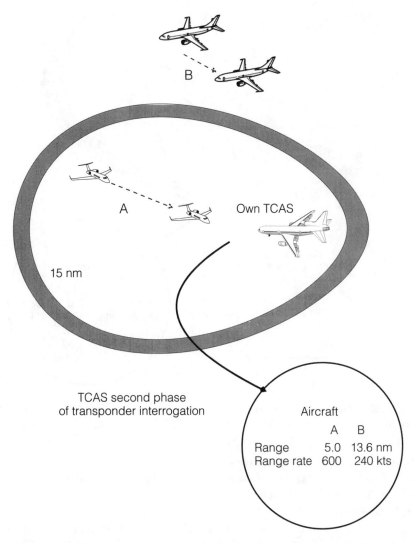

Fig. 8-3. *TCAS II second phase of transponder interrogation. Successive replies are used to establish range and closing speed.* Bendix/King, Allied-Signal

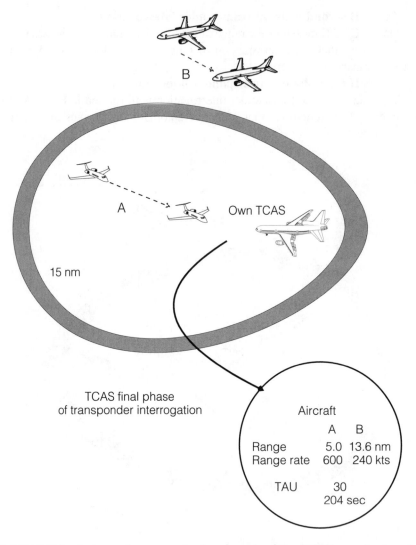

Fig. 8-4. *TCAS II final phase of transponder interrogation. The TAU for each aircraft is compared to a fixed threshold to determine the level of threat.* Bendix/King, Allied-Signal

Advisories and evasive maneuvers

TCAS II alerts the pilot with visual and aural warnings. The aural warnings advise the pilot what actions should be taken.

Traffic advisories

TCAS II issues traffic advisories (TA) when it predicts that a transponder-equipped intruder is within 45 seconds of its closest point of approach (CPA). The purpose of a TA is to notify the pilot that traffic is in the vicinity and to assist in visually detecting the intruder aircraft. An aural warning of "Traffic, Traffic," sounds in the cockpit. Because the intruder aircraft is not considered a threat, no maneuvers are required of the pilot.

Resolution advisories

TCAS II also issues resolution advisories (RA) when altitude-encoding intruders come within 30 seconds of CPA. For the evasive maneuver the computer calculates the vertical rate that must be achieved to maintain safe separation from the threat aircraft. When corrective RAs are required, the aural advisories include: "Traffic, Traffic," "Climb, Climb, Climb," "Descend, Descend, Descend," "Climb Crossing Climb," "Descend Crossing Descend," "Reduce Climb," and "Reduce Descent." These are considered normal RAs. If no evasive maneuver is needed, the alert is called a preventative RA. For preventative RAs the aural advisory is "Monitor Vertical Speed." After an intruder aircraft is no longer a threat, the aural message is "Clear of Conflict."

TCAS II hardware

The hardware, scopes, and displays of TCAS II (Fig. 8-5) are color-coded and use FAA-approved symbology. The center symbol on the display screen is the "own aircraft." A 2-, 5-, 10-, or 15-nautical-mile ring encompasses the center. The pilot selects the appropriate distance depending on phase of flight and volume of traffic in the area. This feature avoids false alarms when approaching congested airports during peak hours.

When an immediate threat aircraft enters the ring, a red square appears over the target to indicate an RA has been declared. A potential threat, or TA, is depicted as an amber circle. A proximity target, not a threat, is shown as an open white diamond. If a proximity target enters the ring and a TA or RA is already in progress, the proximity target is then displayed as a solid-white diamond.

Alphanumerics along with the symbols give the target's altitude, range, and bearing. Arrows next to the symbols show whether or not the intruder is climbing or descending at a rate of at least 500 feet per minute.

TURNING POINT FOR TCAS LEGISLATION

Throughout this book I've discussed numerous mid-air collisions. You might have been unfamiliar with a few, but I'm sure you recognized the more famous ones. But one more prominent accident is still left to mention: the mid-air between Aeromexico Flight 498 and a Piper Cherokee over Cerritos, California. That mid-air became the turning point for TCAS legislation.

I just lost contact with a DC-9

31 August 1986: Aeromexico Airlines Flight 498, a McDonnell Douglas DC-9, collided with a single-engine Piper Cherokee over Cerritos, California, which is in the greater Los Angeles Basin.

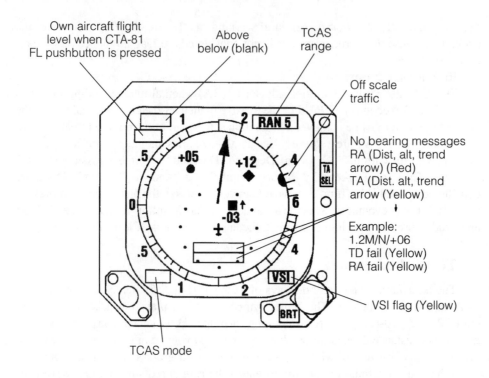

Own aircraft flight
level when CTA-81
FL pushbutton is pressed

Above
below (blank)

TCAS
range

Off scale
traffic

No bearing messages
RA (Dist, alt, trend
arrow) (Red)
TA (Dist. alt, trend
arrow (Yellow)

Example:
1.2M/N/+06
TD fail (Yellow)
RA fail (Yellow)

VSI flag (Yellow)

TCAS mode

TCAS mode/failure

Standard		Optional	
TCAS STBY	(blue)	NO TCAS (blue) TCAS system in standby	
TA/RA	(blank)	TA/RA	(blank)
TEST	(yellow)	TEST	(yellow)
TA ONLY	(blue)	TA ONLY (blue/yellow—when active TA)	
TCAS	(yellow)	NO TCAS (yellow) TCAS system failure	

Display message locations

Fig. 8-5. *Display screen of a Bendix/King TCAS II.* Bendix/King, Allied-Signal

Pilot experience: Aeromexico captain: 10,641 total flight hours, 4632 in the DC-9. Aeromexico first officer: 1463 total flight hours, 1245 in the DC-9. Piper pilot: 231 total flight hours.

Reported weather at time of accident: Clear. Visibility 15 miles.

Probable cause

The NTSB determined that the probable cause of this accident was the limitation of the air traffic control system to provide collision protection. Contributing to the accident was the inadvertent and unauthorized entry of the Piper Cherokee into the Los Angeles Terminal Control Area, and the limitation of the see and avoid concept.

The accident

Aeromexico Flight 498 was level at 7000 feet and setting up for the approach into Los Angeles International Airport when at 1150 PDT the controller advised the crew of "traffic, ten o'clock, one mile, northbound, altitude unknown." Although the crew acknowledged the advisory, they never advised the controller whether they had the traffic in sight. The traffic, however, was not the Cherokee.

At 1151, Flight 498 was cleared to descend to 6000 feet. Meanwhile, a single-engine Grumman Tiger had made an unauthorized entry into the TCA, and the controller was busy vectoring him out of harm's way. Less than a minute later, the controller noticed that Flight 498 had disappeared off radar and proceeded to make several unsuccessful attempts to contact it.

At approximately 1152, Flight 498 and the Cherokee collided over the city of Cerritos at about 6560 feet. All 58 passengers and a crew of six on the Aeromexico jet were killed, as were the Cherokee pilot and his two passengers. An additional 15 persons on the ground received fatal injuries.

The investigation

The air traffic controller at Los Angeles Center who was monitoring Flight 498 had a light-to-moderate workload. However, with a change in runways, evidence indicated that the controller's scan of his display was focused almost exclusively on an area that did not include the location of the Piper's target. According to the Safety Board, the Cherokee had entered the TCA inadvertently and because the controller was giving priority to IFR traffic, the Piper went undetected.

The NTSB also theorized that the Piper's radar antenna could have been partially inoperable, creating a much smaller than normal return on the controller's scope. Furthermore, Los Angeles Center had a history of inherent problems with radar signals ricocheting off of nearby mountain ranges and of signals being "swallowed" by the Los Angeles Basin area.

The angle of impact

The best in-flight scenario that can be determined is that the Piper initially appeared 15 to 30 degrees offset to the left of the captain's windshield and subsequently appeared in the same position through the first officer's windshield. With regard to the Piper pilot, Flight 498 was about 50 degrees to the right of the design eye reference point, and therefore, was visible out the far right-side window. Nevertheless, because the two aircraft were on a collision course, the relative motion of the Piper presumably would have been minimal, making it extremely difficult to detect.

At some point, the Piper moved off behind the Aeromexico and collided with the DC-9's vertical stabilizer.

TCAS legislation

In the wake of the mid-air between Flight 498 and a Cherokee, Congress and lobbyists went into action to pass TCAS legislation. On 30 December 1987, then-President Reagan signed an amendment to the Airport and Airway Safety and Capacity Expansion Act of 1987. It required a TCAS II to be installed on all commercial aircraft with at least 31 passenger seats operating in U.S. airspace. The amendment deadline for TCAS II was 31 December 1993. However, on 15 December 1989, then-President Bush signed a new law that allowed FAA to set new deadlines for phased implementation of TCAS II: 20 percent of the affected aircraft, approximately 1000, had to be equipped by 31 December 1990; a total of 50 percent by the end of 1991; and 100 percent by the end of 1993. In addition, a TCAS I is required for all commuter operators using aircraft with 10 to 30 passenger seats operating in U.S. airspace. That deadline is 5 February 1995.

Target acquisition flight tests

As a result of several years of flight tests, the FAA concluded that the search effectiveness of the TCAS II is such that one second of search equals eight seconds of physically looking for the traffic. Remember the 12.5 second recognition and reaction rule. Shaving eight seconds off a visual search is significant. Equally as important, the tests showed a marked improvement of pilots' visual acquisition times. After all, it is easier to locate traffic when the exact position and altitude are known.

The test programs at Lincoln Laboratories

The ability of pilots to sight other airplanes in flight was evaluated during two test programs conducted by the Lincoln Laboratories of the Massachusetts Institute of Technology (MIT). Each test was part of a general-research study and was not part of any accident investigation. However, during the investigation of the Aeromexico mid-air, the NTSB referenced these test flights to gain a better insight on target acquisition.

The test included evaluating unalerted visual acquisition. The purpose of the test was to evaluate the subject-pilot's ability to detect traffic during an unalerted search pattern. In the initial test, the subject pilot's only instruction was to fly three legs as if they were on a normal cross-country flight. Periodically, an FAA aircraft intercepted the subject, flying different collision courses. The FAA varied the aspect angle on the approach to simulated mid-air events to test various angles (Fig. 8-6) and the visual search/acquisition.

The test results were significant:

Data were obtained for 64 unalerted encounters. Visual acquisition was achieved in 36 encounters (56 percent of the total), and the median acquisition range for these 36 encounters was .99 nm. The greatest range of visual acquisition was 2.9 nm.

According to these findings, the subject pilots saw the threat aircraft a little more than half of the time. When they did see it, the conflict aircraft was between only one and three miles in range, leaving little time to react.

With regard to the Aeromexico mid-air, the heading-crossing angle between the two aircraft was nearly 90 degrees. The Piper hit the DC-9's tail section nearly head-on.

The second flight test evaluated the performance of pilots who had been alerted to the presence of an intruder aircraft. With the use of a TCAS II-equipped airplane, 66 encounters were collected. This time the subject pilots visually acquired the intruder 86 percent of the total encounters. The median range of the visual detection was 1.4 nm.

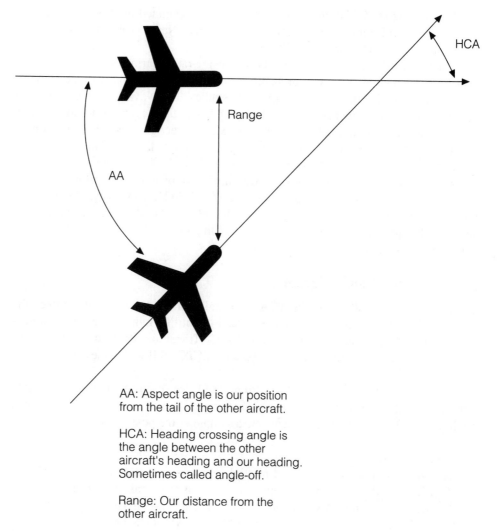

AA: Aspect angle is our position
from the tail of the other aircraft.

HCA: Heading crossing angle is
the angle between the other
aircraft's heading and our heading.
Sometimes called angle-off.

Range: Our distance from the
other aircraft.

Fig. 8-6. *Intercept angles.*

At the Safety Board's request, Lincoln Laboratories constructed two Probability of Visual Acquisition graphs founded on the extrapolation of pertinent flight data from the Aeromexico mid-air. The graphs were based on the closure rate between Flight 498 and the Piper and on the results achieved by pilots having an unobstructed view of the intruder.

The probability of the Aeromexico crew seeing the Piper, without TCAS II assistance, was only 35 percent at 15 seconds prior to collision. However, with TCAS II, the probability that the DC-9 flight crew would have seen the Cherokee was 98 percent at 15 seconds prior to collision.

Researchers at MIT's Lincoln Laboratories also examined the flight data involving a mid-air collision of a U.S. Army U-21 and Piper Navajo (refer to chapter 3 for details) to determine the benefits of TCAS II.

The following variables were calculated: closing rate, bearing of both aircraft, and visual area of both aircraft. The probabilities of visual acquisition without TCAS II continued to remain consistent with previous studies. The Navajo, with one pilot on board, had only a 27 percent chance of seeing the U-21 at 12 seconds prior to collision. Keep in mind the minimum of 12.5 seconds needed for recognition and reaction times. The U-21, with two pilots on board, had a slightly better chance at 33 percent.

Although the U-21 had a 48-square-foot-larger visual area than the Navajo, the increase in visual acquisition for the U-21 was attributed to having two pilots on board.

The exact data were then computed with a TCAS II alert capability. The probabilities of visual acquisition naturally jumped substantially. At 12 seconds prior to collision, the Navajo had a 91 percent chance of avoiding the U-21; and the U-21 crew had a 96 percent chance of avoiding the Navajo.

TCAS transition program

In conjunction with the initial TCAS II installations in the commercial fleet, the FAA, Air Line Pilots Association (ALPA), and the airline industry are conducting a joint evaluation program, known as the TCAS Transition Program (TTP). Their agenda is to assess and validate the safe operation of TCAS II within the air traffic control network.

In monthly updates, FAA's TCAS Program Office discloses the initial findings concerning various issues, analyses, and information collected from the operational environment. The following comments are a sample of the positive feedback from pilots and controllers.

ATC task saturation

A regional-airline crew reported multiple RAs on arrival at a northeast airport. The first RA called for a reduce descent, which was issued against an intruder departing the area. The second RA was issued shortly thereafter when the TCAS aircraft was at 4000 feet and was cleared to descend to 3000 feet. ATC called traffic at 11 o'clock, three miles, opposite direction, and at 3500 feet. As the TCAS aircraft passed through 3600 feet, the crew observed the aircraft passing clear to the left.

> While I was notifying ATC of the RA and that we were now climbing back to 4000 feet, we observed a second aircraft approximately 100 feet below our nose. If we had not followed the TCAS RA instruction there is no doubt in my mind that a mid-air collision would have occurred.

Another pilot report substantiates the capability of TCAS II in a busy-ATC environment.

> Ft. Worth Center was very busy, overloaded . . . but gave us a descent clearance to FL 240 at pilot's discretion. We weren't ready for the descent . . . so we main-

tained FL 290. TCAS was ON. Thirty seconds later the TCAS voice said "TRAF-FIC" [observed] opposite-direction traffic 1000 feet below. Sky conditions were clear and we watched a [Boeing] 767 pass across our nose at FL 280. After the conflict traffic passed, Ft. Worth Center asked us to maintain FL 290. TCAS definitely saved a potential mid-air collision."

ATC clearance coordination

A Continental Airlines McDonnell Douglas DC-10 was northbound at 33,000 feet southwest of Hawaii. A Quantas Airlines Boeing 747 was southbound at 31,000 feet and approaching the same oceanic waypoint. ATC authorized the Quantas to climb to 35,000 feet and cross vertically in front of the Continental flight.

The Continental TCAS alerted the crew that the Quantas was directly ahead and 1600 feet below. The Continental pilot started to turn 25 degrees off course when the TCAS issued a climb RA. Meanwhile, the Continental pilot had made radio contact with the Quantas jet on a common frequency to resolve the conflict. The Quantas maintained its altitude until the two aircraft had passed.

A TCAS-equipped air carrier was on a missed approach when the local controller cleared it to 3000 feet and to contact departure control. Departure then asked the local controller to have the air carrier maintain 2000 feet because of traffic. The local controller was unable to issue the revised altitude because the TCAS aircraft had already switched frequencies. The TCAS aircraft contacted departure stating, ". . . cleared to 3000 [feet] but descending for traffic." The controller reported that TCAS was beneficial in this situation because it perfectly coordinated the separation when ATC could not provide a quick assist.

See and avoid

All mid-air collisions share one common thread: the inability to see and avoid. Therefore, TCAS can be the extra third, fourth, and even fifth set of "eyes" that can fill the void between cockpit and radar scope.

A TCAS-equipped aircraft was on final approach at 4000 feet in VMC. During the approach, a TA was issued for an intruder at two o'clock, 500 feet below. As the crew of the TCAS aircraft commenced a visual search, a climb RA was declared when the intruder had closed to within two miles and at the same altitude. The intruder was not visually detected until it passed beneath the TCAS aircraft, at which time ATC advised the crew of its presence. In the report the pilot stated, ". . . the controller was extremely busy at the time of the event . . . TCAS saved us from a sure mid-air."

A DIFFERENCE OF OPINION

Although TCAS II has proved itself as a legitimate means of collision avoidance, many in the aviation community have valid concerns over the reliability of the system. In recent years, pilots and controllers alike have shown skepticism and even contempt for an airborne collision-avoidance system. The reasons have been numerous, but most center on the unpredictability of man and machine.

Unpredictable variables

By now we know that humans can be far more unpredictable than machines. Put the two together and then step back. Think of the person as a lit match and the machine as gasoline. Okay, so this might have been an overdramatization of the man-machine interface. However, when it comes to operating a system like TCAS, it might not be too far from the truth.

TCAS II is not a perfect system. It has had its glitches just like every other new piece of hardware and software that has come along. And since its conception, the manufacturers, ALPA, the National Air Traffic Controllers Association (NATCA), and FAA have continually and collectively upgraded and fine-tuned the system. Although few can dispute the TCAS II success stories, some remain skeptical. The unpredictability of the human element can sometimes be just too great for the system to withstand.

According to pilots and controllers, many airlines have inadequate TCAS II-training programs. Some consist of just a few hours, which can leave flightcrews still scratching their heads when they leave the classroom. An ill-trained pilot behind the yoke of an active TCAS can create a very dangerous situation.

Although the FAA has gone to several ATC facilities to teach controllers about TCAS, according to NATCA, active line controllers have had "very little" TCAS training. Their complaint is that staff members, procedures specialists, and inactive line controllers have received the majority of the training opportunities.

NATCA's bottom line

According to NATCA, controllers support the concept of an airborne collision-avoidance system. However, because of the number of inappropriate TCAS II-induced maneuvers, they do not believe the current system is the answer to the problem.

TCAS and general aviation

TCAS is not just an airline or corporate pilot's concern. TCAS affects every pilot, even those that fly Archers only on the weekends. But what has a TCAS II-equipped 727 got to do with a general-aviation pilot? Let's look at a couple of possible scenarios.

Say you're flying that Archer into an airport that has a mix of general-aviation and commercial aircraft. Approach reports your traffic as a United 727. You acknowledge with "traffic in sight," and go back to your pre-landing checklist. The next thing you hear is "United 123 climbing, RA." You quickly look out the window to see that your traffic has vanished. What started out as an uneventful approach has turned into you losing sight of your traffic during a critical phase of flight. Fortunately, you read this chapter and at least you know that the United pilot departed the flight path in response to a TCAS Resolution Advisory. The bottom line is that TCAS made an impact on your flight.

You just received a clearance to descend out of 6000 feet to 4000 feet. As you're descending you hear "United 123 descending, RA." Although you have no idea the position or altitude from where the United was starting its descent, you begin a vigilant scan of the surrounding airspace. Seconds later you see the silhouette of a 727 crossing your flight path, two miles off your nose. Did TCAS have an impact on your flight?

Absolutely. Although the 727 was not a threat, you suddenly had unexpected traffic crossing your flight path. The positive side is that thanks to the United pilot's radio call, you were able to acquire the traffic faster and have a much keener sense of situational awareness.

TCAS affects the entire flying community. Whether or not you think that TCAS is the best thing since sliced bread is immaterial. It exists, and it's here to stay. So, the more you learn and understand how the system is integrated into the overall ATC network, the safer you're going to become.

FUTURE OF TCAS

Although TCAS II is an overall outstanding feat of technological achievement, the system is hindered by the fact that the evasive maneuvers are only in the vertical. Because there are often times when a horizontal maneuver would be best suited for a particular situation, pilots have long been requesting a TCAS II version with horizontal-maneuvering capability.

TCAS with horizontal maneuvering capabilities

For years avionics manufacturers and the FAA have been trying to develop such a system. It had been referred to as TCAS III, but because of various issues, the name has recently been changed. At the FAA's Second International TCAS Conference, held in September 1993, an FAA representative announced the status of the TCAS III system. Due to the current antennae technology, a TCAS III version is unable to support horizontal maneuvers. Although the researchers have not had to go all the way back to the drawing board, a system with these advanced features will not be available in the near future. Therefore, the FAA is in the process of changing the name of the next generation of equipment to either TCAS IV or TCAS 2000.

TCAS: JUST ANOTHER RESOURCE

Just like every other resource that I've discussed in this book, TCAS has its limitations and is certainly not the be-all-end-all of collision avoidance. The concerns of NATCA and others in the aviation community are valid. Mix together man and machine and the outcome has the potential of being rather unpleasant.

However, when TCAS is used properly and conscientiously, it can enhance safety. The operative words here are properly and conscientiously. The system itself is impressive, but when a poorly trained pilot misunderstands the advisory commands or mishandles control inputs, TCAS becomes a detriment to safety instead of a benefit. Solid training programs for pilots and controllers seem to have slipped through the cracks. That's a shame because the system's true potential has yet be seen.

Meanwhile, TCAS does have its successes, many of them. However, it is just another resource. We know that no one resource ever stands alone. TCAS is meant to enhance a see and avoid environment, complement the air traffic control system, and increase situational awareness. But when it's misused, the negative effects can be far more detrimental to collision avoidance than you might realize.

CHAPTER 8 REVIEW

Traffic-alert and collision-avoidance systems (TCAS)
- TCAS is an airborne collision avoidance system.
- TCAS processes transponder signals.
- TCAS onboard computer determines other aircraft's position, altitude, and rate of closure.
- Signals can be received and analyzed up to 40 miles away.
- Information appears on cockpit weather radar scope or dedicated TCAS display.

TAU principle
- Ratio of range-to-range rate

Transponders
- Onboard device that transmits a coded signal back to ATC.
- Mode-A transmits position.
- Mode-C transmits range, bearing, and altitude.
- Mode-S transmits Mode-C functions, discrete addressing, and data linking.
- Mode-S transmits signals every second, known as a squitter pulse.

TCAS I
- Low-power, short range system
- No collision avoidance logic
- Displays position only

TCAS II
- Mode-S transponder and two antennae scan volume of airspace around aircraft.
- Top-mounted antenna transmits on 1030 MHz.
- Bottom-mounted antenna receives on 1090 MHz.
- Scanning area covers 14.7 miles to the front of aircraft, 7.5 miles behind, 7000 feet above and 7000 feet below.
- Can handle 1200 knot head-on closure rate and an altitude-closure rate of 12,000 fpm.

TCAS operation
- TCAS II initial transponder acquisition determines range of intruder aircraft.

- TCAS II second phase of transponder interrogation determines range rate.
- TCAS II final phase of transponder interrogation determines the level of threat.

Traffic advisory
- Predicts intruder within 45 seconds of CPA.
- Assists pilots with visual detection.

Resolution advisory
- Predicts intruder within 30 seconds of CPA.
- Provides preventive and corrective advisories.

TCAS hardware
- The displays are color-coded with FAA-approved symbology and alphanumerics.

The turning point for TCAS legislation
- The mid-air collision between Aeromexico Flight 498 and a Piper Cherokee over Cerritos, California, became the turning point for TCAS legislation.

TCAS legislation
- TCAS I: 10 to 30 passenger seats, 5 February 1995
- TCAS II: over 30 passenger seats, 31 December 1993

Target acquisition flight tests
- Unalerted visual acquisition
- Alerted visual acquisition
- Visual acquisition and Aeromexico Flight 498
- Visual acquisition and the mid-air collision of a U.S. Army U-21 and a Piper Navajo.

TCAS transition program
- Assess and validate the safe operation of TCAS II within the ATC network.
- ATC task saturation
- ATC clearance coordination
- See and avoid

Unpredictable variables
- Man-machine interface

- Pilot training
- Controller training

NATCA's bottom line
- Supports the concept of an airborne collision-avoidance system.
- Does not believe TCAS II is the answer.

Future of TCAS
- Horizontal maneuvers

Just another resource
- Used properly and conscientiously, TCAS can enhance see and avoid, complement ATC, and increase situational awareness.

Chapter 8 references

Bradley, Suzanne. 1992. *Simulation Test and Evaluation of TCAS II Logic Version 6.04.* Mitre Corporation.

Faville, Will. 9 September 1993. Statement. Federal Aviation Administration Second International TCAS Conference. Reston, Virginia.

Federal Aviation Administration Second International Conference on the Traffic Alert and Collision Avoidance System (TCAS). 8-10 September 1993. Reston, Virginia.

Mellone, Vincent J. 1993. TCAS Incident Reports Analysis. National Aeronautics and Space Administration.

Mellone, Vincent J. and Stephanie M. Frank. 1993. Behavioral Impact of TCAS II on the National Air Traffic Control System. National Aeronautics and Space Administration.

National Transportation Safety Board. Aircraft Accident Report: Collision of Aeronaves de Mexico, S.A., McDonnell Douglas DC-9-32, XA-JED and a Piper PA-28-131, N4891F, Cerritos, California, August 31 1986. 7 July 1987. Washington, DC.

Radio Technical Commission for Aeronautics. March 1989. Minimum Operational Performance Standards for Traffic Alert and Collision Avoidance System (TCAS) Airborne Equipment, Volume I. Washington, DC.

Radio Technical Commission for Aeronautics. 6 October 1989. Minimum Operational Performance Standards for Traffic Alert and Collision Avoidance System (TCAS) Airborne Equipment, Volume II. Washington, DC.

Steenblik, Jan. W. March 1991. "TCAS Pilot Alert!" *Air Line Pilot:* 33-4.

TCAS II: Collision Avoidance for Corporate Aviation, videotape, by Bendix/King

TCAS II Pilot Training Video, videotape, December 1990. Bendix/King.

TCAS II Proposal. 1987. Bendix-King. Allied Signal Aerospace, Inc.

TCAS Transition Program Newsletter. 29 April 1991. Federal Aviation Administration. Washington, DC.

TCAS Transition Program Newsletter. 3 June 1991. Federal Aviation Administration. Washington, DC.

TCAS Transition Program Newsletter. 12 September 1991. Federal Aviation Administration. Washington, DC.

Wapelhorst, Leo, Thomas Pagano, and John Van Dongen. 1992. The Effect of TCAS Interrogation on the Chicago O'Hare ATCRBS System. U.S. Department of Transportation. Federal Aviation Administration.

Williamson, Thomas and Ned Spencer. 1990 Development and Operation of the Traffic Alert and Collision Avoidance System (TCAS).

U.S. Department of Transportation. Federal Aviation Administration. Introduction to TCAS II. March 1990. Washington, DC.

U.S. Department of Transportation. 12 February 1991. Federal Aviation Administration. Advisory Circular: Air Carrier Operational Approval and Use of TCAS II, AC 120-TCAS. Washington, DC.

U.S Department of Transportation. 2 May 1991. Federal Aviation Administration. Memorandum. Immediate Distribution of a Traffic Alert and Collision Avoidance System (TCAS) Status Bulletin. Washington, DC.

U.S. House of Representatives. 1992. Report to the Chairman, Subcommittee on Investigations and Oversight, Committee on Science, Space, and Technology. Aviation Safety: Users Differ in Views of Collision Avoidance System and Cite Problems. Washington, DC.

9
Trends and issues that affect the collision-avoidance environment

AT WHAT POINT DOES PROGRESS COMPROMISE SAFETY? THIS EVER-changing world of technological advancements, economic, political, social pressures, and policy revisements begs the question: "Can the aviation community maintain an uncompromising level of safety in the face of progress?" Although there will always be endless debate over this issue, for the purpose of our discussion, the short answer is yes and no. Even in such a dynamic industry as aviation, some issues remain predictable.

We know that the airlines want to make money. We know that the airports want to accommodate their paying customers as best they can. Also, the federal government that provides the air traffic control system through the FAA recognizes the economic and social benefits of air transportation. Who's going to argue with free enterprise? But there are also the twin Tasmanian devils: politics and bureaucracy. Few places are more of a political hotbed than airports. Lastly, extremely vocal and very powerful community groups place stiff demands and pressures on the FAA and airport managers. Among these groups are the environmental activists that want all commercial airplanes to come equipped with a "Harrier" VSTOL function, farmers who threaten to shoot down the next jet that scatters their livestock, and angry homeowners who somehow missed noticing that the house they bought is two miles off the end of the runway.

The next set of issues concern new and revised policies. Economic, political, and social pressures change policies and procedures. Although the majority of changes and revisions are done with good intentions, and legally, at times a hasty revision is made just to get a bunch of protesters out of the airport manager's hair. Accidents have occurred because of these kinds of external pressures. One such mid-air is discussed later.

Few can dispute that technological advancements are usually great, but there is always a period of time needed for the bugs to be worked out and for the users to become confident and comfortable with the mechanism's intended purpose. The introduction of the traffic-alert and collision-avoidance system (TCAS) in the cockpit is a perfect example of the initial growing pains of a new system (chapter 8).

PROGRESS, PRESSURES, POLICIES AND COLLISION AVOIDANCE

Although progress can be the motivating force behind raising safety standards to greater levels, there can also be a down side. It's important to be aware of instances when policies and procedures are developed primarily from external pressures, leaving pilots and controllers to operate in a less-than-optimum environment. Noise-abatement programs and the various methods airports use to increase capacity are two such instances that immediately come to mind.

Every busy airport has its own Meadowood

Although Meadowood is a fictitious community in the novel *Airport*, there are plenty of real-life "Meadowoods" that pop up near busy airports, and whose citizens demand to live in peace, or at least in quiet. One such development exists outside the Oakland, California, International Airport. In 1987, the homeowners had enough. The circumstances that evolved from this "harmless" uprising was cited by the NTSB as a contributing factor to a tragic mid-air collision that claimed three lives.

Fly quietly

31 March 1987: A Cessna 172 and a Piper Lance collided at 1000 feet MSL, approximately one mile north of the departure end of Oakland International Airport's runway 33.

Pilot experience: Cessna pilot had a minimum of 1250 flight hours. Piper pilot: 1825 hours, 115 in the Lance.

Reported weather at time of accident: 10,000 feet scattered. Visibility 15 miles.

Probable cause

The NTSB determined that the probable cause of this accident was the failure of each pilot-in-command to see and avoid the other aircraft and the failure of the local controller to perceive the traffic conflict and issue traffic advisories. Contributing to the accident was the reduction in airspace separation between arriving and departing aircraft at Oakland's north-field runways. This reduction was caused by the failure of the FAA to exercise its authority over airspace management and the Oakland airport authority's establishment of noise-abatement departure patterns without FAA approval.

The sweet sound of jet engines roaring overhead

A noise-abatement plan had been in effect at Oakland International since 1983, when area residents had expressed their objections to the noise generated by aircraft departing from the north runways. The procedure originally called for pilots to:

> Make a 45-degree turn as soon as possible after takeoff [from runway 33]. Overfly center of San Leandro Bay, avoiding northwest shoreline. Fly to left of Green Tank [a prominent landmark used as a visual reporting point for Oakland's north-field operations], then establish departure heading.

Although these published procedures had been distributed to local pilots, Oakland's airport manager continued to receive a steady increase of complaints from citizens of the surrounding communities. Several months before the accident, a group of residents formed an activist group called the "Concerned East Alamedans for Safe and Quiet Environment" (CEASE). Alameda is a city west of the airport. The plan of this group was to keep pressure on the airport manager in order to get noise levels reduced even further. In January, the manager and the air traffic manager met with more than 100 angry CEASE members to once again hear their complaints. At that meeting, the airport-operations supervisor was overheard directing an assistant to post noise-abatement signs around the airport "even if he had to paint them himself." Obviously, the management staff was getting major heat from the community and had to do something—fast. Less than two weeks later, ten signs were installed around the north end of the field. The signs read, "Attention—For noise abatement turn right to 360 degrees until reaching freeway. Fly Quiet."

There was a noticeable difference between the procedures developed in 1983 and this revised plan. Pilots no longer turned 45 degrees shortly after takeoff, but rather waited to cross the San Leandro Bay before they turned to the northwest upon reaching the Nimitz Freeway. Consequently, under the new procedures, departing and arriving aircraft often flew east of or over the green tank, thus reducing the separation between arrivals and departures.

The accident

Approximately 0955 PST, a CFI and her student took off in a Cessna 172 enroute to the local practice area. The student was on his second instructional flight. They had been cleared for a "right turn out" after departing from runway 33.

At 0954, the Piper pilot reported that he was nine miles north of the airport. Seconds later, the Oakland-north tower controller told the Piper pilot to plan on a right entry to runway 27R. Two minutes later, the pilot radioed, ". . . over the green tank, turning downwind." The tower controller responded, "Northstar 1950 [the Piper's call sign] . . . not in sight. Cleared to land runway 27 right . . .."

Neither the Piper nor the Cessna was given traffic advisories. No further transmissions were received from either flight. According to witnesses, the two planes approached each other on a relatively head-on course and struck left wing to left wing.

The flight track

From recorded radar information, the investigative team was able to conclude that the Piper and Cessna had a closure rate of about 194 knots. This conclusion was based on the Piper's calculated true airspeed of 136 knots, the Cessna's true airspeed of 81 knots, and the collision angle.

The view from the cockpit

The radar data also determined that each airplane was within the viewing area of the other pilot for at least 20 to 30 seconds before the collision. However, the Cessna would have appeared about one degree to the right of the Piper pilot's eye-reference point, which put the 172 slightly above the Lance's engine cowl, in the propeller-rotation arc. Likewise, the Piper would have appeared just above the 172's engine cowl, also in the propeller-rotation arc. These positions would definitely not be easy places to detect head-on traffic.

From the specific damage caused by the impact, it was likely that the Lance pilot had just begun his left turn to enter the traffic pattern. As a result, he might have been looking toward the east to set up for his downwind leg. The 172 was still south of its position and climbing, placing the airplane below the Lance until just shortly before the collision.

The heart of the investigation

Besides the obvious problems with see and avoid, the Board focused its investigation on the issues of noise-abatement procedures, local air traffic control, and even pilot fatigue.

Noise abatement

Soon after the investigation got under way, it became apparent that the airport manager had changed the noise-abatement procedures without FAA approval. Furthermore, the signs that had been displayed around the north end of the field were very misleading because they did not indicate the new procedures were for guidance only, which meant they were not mandatory.

Even the local controllers weren't completely clear on the status of these procedures. Although the air-traffic manager told investigators that he believed most of the controllers saw the signs as strictly advisory, there were still others that viewed them as mandatory. There had been instances, one just the day before the accident, where a controller disapproved a request by a pilot for a straight out departure from runway 33. The reason he gave to the pilot was: "Unable due to noise abatement."

Subsequently, according to the accident report,

> . . . the Oakland airport manager was attempting to cope with what was certainly a great deal of community pressure . . . he exceeded his authority and directly and adversely affected air safety by placing the signs describing non-FAA approved noise-abatement procedures on the airport property . . .."

The Board, therefore, concluded that the manager's actions contributed to the mid-air collision.

Air traffic control

During the investigation, the tower controller testified that the reason he didn't provide traffic advisories to the two aircraft was because he thought the Piper was farther out than it really was, which made him believe the Cessna was not a potential conflict. Nevertheless, he was aware that the 172 was heading in the general direction of the Lance, and he also knew that the pilot of the Piper had called "over the green tank." And lastly, the controller cleared the Piper to land on runway 27R, even though he didn't have him in sight.

Therefore, the Board concluded that the failure of the tower controller to issue traffic advisories to the two airplanes was a primary cause of the accident.

Pilot fatigue

The pilot of the Lance had been up since the wee hours of the morning in preparation for a 0400 departure. Throughout the morning, he had delivered cargo to various locations in Northern California. By the time he was involved in the mid-air, he had been awake for more than nine hours and was just about to complete his fourth leg of the day.

Although the Board could not make a definitive conclusion concerning his level of fatigue, the evidence suggested that the pilot might not have been as vigilant or as quick to respond to the Cessna because he did not have a normal uninterrupted sleep pattern the night before. He left his house at 0145, drove more than an hour to get to the airport, and then flew off-and-on for the next six hours.

More concerns over noise abatement

This accident is just one example of how social pressures can affect safety, particularly collision avoidance. There are scores of other noise-abatement programs at airports across the country that also create a potentially unsafe flight environment for traffic detection. In California, Orange County's John Wayne airport has long been a concern in the aviation community because of the severe noise-abatement procedures that require airline pilots to take off at extremely steep angles of attack—23 degrees instead of the normal 15 degrees. These procedures make forward visibility extremely difficult—or nonexistent—thereby creating the increased potential for a mid-air collision.

Likewise, Washington National (DC) has a similar problem with steep climbout profiles. Turns to avoid a restricted area over the White House, Capitol, and tourist attractions, like the Washington Monument, while having to also reduce engine power for noise-abatement procedures, naturally increase the potential threat for mid-air collisions to occur.

Move 'em in and move 'em out for increased capacity

Airlines make money by hauling as many passengers in as many airplanes as fast as possible. But because airports usually don't have five active runways available, the airlines come knocking on the doors of the FAA and airport manager for help. The problem is how to increase capacity at a reasonable cost while maintaining a high level of safe operation.

How to move lots of airplanes in the shortest period of time

Capacity refers to the ability of an airport to handle a given volume of traffic. It is a limit that cannot be exceeded without incurring an operational overload in the form of increased delays.

The solutions generally advocated by airport administrators, airlines, and the FAA are to build additional facilities at crowded airports or to find ways to make more efficient use of existing ones. The latter course is usually viewed as the most attractive because it requires less capital investment and avoids many of the problems associated with increasing the size of the airfield and the resultant infringement upon the surrounding communities.

Developing closely spaced parallel runways and converging approaches is the direction most airports are taking to increase capacity levels. Safety concerns, particularly those of collision avoidance, have become a pressing issue that needs constant attention. Various means to cope with collision avoidance are being addressed, both at the pilot and controller level.

A fireside chat with the FAA

As airspace users, it's important for pilots to understand the viewpoints expressed by the FAA. It's those official viewpoints that tend to shape policy and procedures. Consequently, a few years ago, the Air Line Pilots Association (ALPA) interviewed then-FAA Administrator James B. Busey, IV. It was a revealing exchange of ideas as he shared his opinions on various aviation issues, including the see and avoid concept and how it applies to increased capacity.

The following is a paraphrased excerpt from that interview:

ALPA: FAA's use of visual separation and visual approaches to increase airport capacity has reached an all-time high, despite the proven limitations of the see and avoid concept. For example, at San Francisco, where the Runway 28L/R center-lines are only 720 feet apart, controllers are trying to bring in a pair of airplanes and send out a pair of airplanes, so they're trying to put airplanes wingtip-to-wingtip. In some cases, they're converging on head-on [opposite] base legs. Similar procedures have been implemented at Denver and Los Angeles and a couple of other high-density airports. . ... What does the agency plan to do to alleviate this problem?
Busey: Well, of course, what we're trying to do by using those procedures is to increase the arrival rate to handle the increased traffic. . ... In San Francisco . . . we're not after an exactly parallel type of approach . . . but we are trying to close up intervals. We will try to bring concurrent parallel approaches in where, at times, the airplanes are headed toward one another. Controllers will rely on the pilots if it's VFR conditions . . . they're trying to put that responsibility to 'see and be seen' back on the pilots in that case.

A few thoughts on the subject

The catch phrase that Administrator Busey spoke of was "Controllers will rely on the pilots . . . [and] put that responsibility to 'see and be seen' back on the pilots . . .." Although it's certainly not an ideal situation, it is, however, expected.

Remember that from a pilot's perspective, increased capacity boils down to two simple, yet key, points. First, you still must maintain vigilance at all times. And second, don't assume ATC will get you out of a bind; they might not even see you until it is too late.

ATC and the issue of increased capacity

Economic pressures led to another technological advancement. In a further development to increase capacity, a new system known as *Quick-Scan Radar* is currently being tested by the FAA at Raleigh-Durham, North Carolina, International Airport and Nashville, Tennessee, Metropolitan Airport. These locations were chosen as the testbed facilities because of their closely-spaced (approximately 3500 feet) parallel runways and converging approaches.

Quick-Scan, which is planned for operational use in the mid-1990s, more accurately depicts traffic position by scanning the final approach path once every half second, rather than every four seconds as conventional radar now does. The new system is so sensitive it can detect a 100-foot variation from a runway centerline by an airplane 10 miles away. If an aircraft on approach moves into a "forbidden zone" between runways, an alarm will sound on a special radar screen designed to monitor simultaneous landings.

According to the FAA, the benefit of such a system is safer tight separation of traffic under instrument approaches to closely spaced runways. It's not surprising that, nationwide, bad weather accounts for two-thirds of flight delays of more than 15 minutes. Therefore, the FAA estimates that the new radar could save more than a half-billion hours of delays and a billion dollars of delay costs per year at airports with parallel runways or converging approaches. Sounds like economic pressures could have been the driving force behind this technological breakthrough.

This chapter began with the question: At what point does progress compromise safety? It would be nice if the answer was "Never." But we know better. Fortunately though, progress tends to benefit safety more often than hinder it, but in those instances when the differences are hardly noticeable we must be fully aware of the potential pitfalls. Noise-abatement procedures and the various ways airports increase their capacity are two such circumstances that require constant attention and understanding. Each has its own purpose in the aviation community, but from the examples that have already been discussed, it is obvious that pilots don't always reap the benefits.

PRACTICAL APPLICATIONS AND LESSONS LEARNED

1. Find out if there's an active noise-abatement program at your destination airport. Not all noise-abatement procedures are published. In the Oakland example, the only notification to pilots was the posted signs—not much help for transient pilots or those pilots who weren't operating at the north end of the field.

2. Understand the flight profile of each noise-abatement procedure. Learn the specifics of the procedures and the exact flight profile for landing and departing traffic. Remember, noise abatement affects more than departures. Also, be aware if your plane can achieve the climb/bank gradients required for a specific noise-abatement procedure.

3. Don't assume anything. These are words to live by, literally. It's natural for pilots to assume all noise-abatement plans are FAA-approved; however, that is not always the case.

4. Don't expect traffic advisories. I know you've heard this before, but it is important to remember.

5. Maintain vigilance. Another broken record, but a valuable lesson. Being alert and vigilant about your visual scan is always crucial. This is particularly true when operating under noise-abatement procedures or around airports that use parallel runways with converging base legs.

CHAPTER 9 REVIEW

- Economic, political, and social pressures can drive revisions to policy and/or procedures.
- Technological advancements are sometimes a product of those external pressures.
- Noise-abatement procedures can create potentially unsafe flight environments.
- Capacity is the ability of an airport to handle a given volume of traffic.
- If capacity is exceeded, there will be operational delays.
- Closely spaced parallel runways and converging approaches are the least expensive and most common ways airports increase capacity.
- Even in high density airspace, ATC must still rely on pilots to see and avoid each other.
- Quick-Scan Radar is a new system being tested that will help detect traffic on final approach.
- Two-thirds of flight delays in this country are due to weather.
- The new Quick-Scan radar is expected to save passengers millions of delay hours and taxpayers billions of dollars in delay costs.

Chapter 9 references

Kane, Robert M. 1990. *Air Transportation, 10th ed.* Dubuque, Iowa: Kendall/Hunt.
National Transportation Safety Board. 27 October 1987. Aircraft Accident Report: North Star Aviation, Inc., PA-32-RT-300, N39614 and Alameda Aero Club Cessna 172, N75584, Oakland, California, Washington, DC.
"RDU Test of Radar in Works." 31 March 1989. *Raleigh News and Observer:* A5-6.
Wells, Alexander T., Ed., 1986. *Airport Planning and Management,* Blue Ridge Summit: TAB Books.

Conclusion

"Cessna two eight November, traffic two o'clock, two miles, type and altitude unknown."

Keying the headset-mike switch, you respond, "Approach, Cessna two eight November, traffic not in sight, request avoidance vectors." As you speak, you intently scan the right forward quadrant, rolling your right wing up to better see the full sector. Focusing your eyes on objects a couple miles distant, you fix, scan, fix . . .

"Cessna two eight November, turn left to three zero zero."

You quickly reply, "Cessna two eight November, left to three zero zero. Traffic in sight, white Tomahawk at 2500 feet, heading one eight zero.

"Roger, Cessna two eight zero, cleared own navigation."

The goal of this book is to give you practical information and guidelines to enhance air safety, particularly collision avoidance. I hope you agree that the implementation of good habits and enhanced situational awareness might just be worth the effort.

As you can see, there's a lot to a total mid-air collision-avoidance concept. Effectively and collectively using your available resources is paramount to the success of any collision avoidance discipline, both for general-aviation and commercial pilots alike.

CONCLUSION

In chapter 1, I discussed the myths and realities behind mid-air collision avoidance. The see and avoid concept was obviously a key point as a myth. How the eye functions, its strong points and limitations, and visual illusions were covered. The collision of TWA Flight 553 and a Beechcraft Baron illustrated the inherent problems in the see and avoid concept. The reality section provided some scanning techniques and a collision-avoidance checklist.

Chapter 2 explored the role of air traffic control in a collision-avoidance environment. I looked at the FAA's new airspace classifications and a summary of a commuter and general aviation aircraft mid-air in which an airspace incursion might have been causal. ATC's use, purpose, and relationship to the pilot were addressed. Also, I examined a bit of the operation of ATC radar and effective communications.

Again, myths and realities of avoiding mid-air collisions were discussed by way of example in chapter 3. Lessons learned from the three accidents in this section: Use clear, direct, and concise communication, notify ATC immediately when you lose sight of your traffic, and controllers should redirect communication if they don't get a clear response from a pilot.

In chapter 4 I looked at crew resource management in the airlines, and also how any general-aviation pilot can apply similar techniques to enhance safety. The well-known but frequently misunderstood accident of Air Florida Flight 90 was examined, as were several other incidents, which could possibly have been prevented if everyone involved had stood back and looked at the forest instead of seeing only a couple of trees. With pilot error attributed to 86 percent of all accidents and 90 percent of fatal accidents, correctly managing all of your available resources is obviously critical.

Pilot judgment and the process of decision-making stretch from the CRM discussion to chapter 5. This chapter discussed hazardous thought patterns, and the role of personal attitude was related to exercises that might help you avoid these thought patterns. The DECIDE model provides a system to make decisions. This was related to the Air Illinois Flight 710 and GP Express Flight 861 crashes and to ways to enhance the safety of everyday flying.

Chapter 6 delved into the dismal region of distractions. Several examples were related that showed danger of a crash increases as head-lock time increases, regardless of how big the sky might be. Some important lessons learned include: Fly the airplane. Be decisive and don't complete nonessential tasks during critical phases of the flight. Prioritize, and don't let down your guard, even for a minute.

Stress management was discussed in chapter 7. Types of stress, stress versus stimulation, and anger are things to which we can all relate. Every pilot has at some point been late to the airport, ran to grab coffee and a weather update on the way to preflight, and then realized that maybe something has been forgotten. Recognizing the three stages of stress—alarm, resistance, and exhaustion—can help make us aware when we are pushing it too far.

Chapter 8 examined the traffic-alert and collision-avoidance systems, long advised by the NTSB and FAA and only recently installed on air carriers that operate in

U.S. airspace. As an aid to the see and avoid concept, the TCAS legislation was written in blood. It is hoped that TCAS will prevent more loss of life.

Finally, chapter 9 discussed trends and issues that affect the collision-avoidance environment. Pressures on the aviation industry, airports, pilots, and controllers could run the risk of compromising safety to benefit certain special interests. Increased capacity

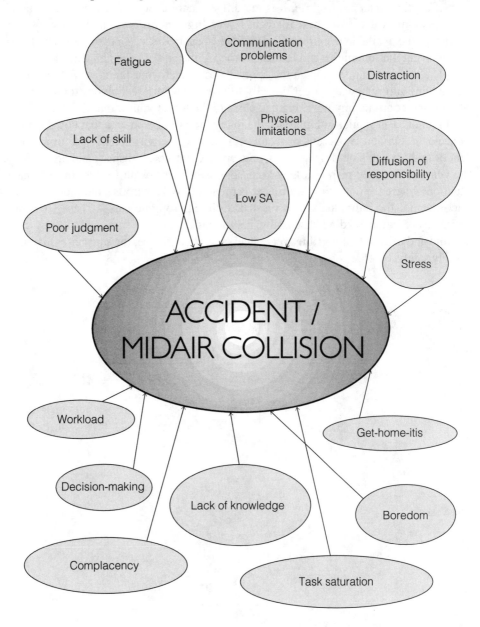

and noise restrictions are two examples of pressures on the whole collision-avoidance system. Some important lessons include researching noise-abatement programs at your destination, not assuming anything or expecting traffic advisories, and maintaining vigilance.

Obviously, no quick answers or magic solutions will always keep you safe. However, if anything can come close, it is the diligent application of any combination of these techniques that work best for you. Every flight is different and every pilot is unique, so the available resources vary for each scenario. Test yourself, now and then, by reviewing the summaries and lessons learned at the end of each chapter. Then try to complete the review questions in the appendix to refresh your memory. Add notes in the margins and review them periodically to keep your own techniques for scanning, talking, and coordinating in writing and close to the top of your mind.

Figure C-1 is a quick summary of the many important elements that could lead to an accident. Obviously, dozens of factors can create an environment ripe for an incident or mid-air collision. It is up to us, concerned aviation enthusiasts and professionals, who are not only responsible for our actions but who want to live, to recognize situations where the potential for disaster is great. Once dangerous situations are identified, we are the individuals who must take the appropriate steps. These steps are learned by research, reading, discussing, instructing, and experience, and must be used to avoid and diffuse that horrible, yet conceivable, occurrence, the mid-air collision.

Fly safely.

Appendix
Review questions

CHAPTER 1

1. State the see and avoid Federal Aviation Regulation (91.67).
2. Explain the side-by-side and front-to-side scanning methods.
3. Explain the physiology of the human eye.
4. Discuss the natural blind spot and how it affects your ability to visually detect other aircraft.
5. Discuss the findings of the 1966 Lockheed study on the physical limitations of pilots in a dynamic environment.
6. Discuss the connection between the Lockheed study and the recommended scanning methods.
7. Explain the problems associated with prolonged staring in one direction.
8. Discuss saccadic eye movement and how it affects your ability to visually detect other aircraft.
9. Discuss the difference between central and peripheral vision.
10. Discuss how our eyesight affects our ability to visually detect other aircraft.
11. Explain optical illusions and other related visual phenomena.
12. Discuss the importance of recognition and reaction times in a see and avoid environment.
13. Discuss the variables that could extend recognition and reaction times in a see and avoid environment.
14. Discuss the events that led to the mid-air collision of TWA Flight 553 and a Beechcraft Baron.
15. Explain the significance of the bar graph in Fig. 1-6.
16. Discuss how contrast affects your ability to recognize a target.
17. Discuss how a complex background affects your ability to recognize a target.
18. Explain the Minimum Visual Detection Angle Theory.
19. Explain the basic geometric principles of visual detection.
20. Explain how time-to-impact calculations can be misleading.
21. Explain the Minimum Visual Detection Area Theory.

22. Discuss scanning techniques that can be used when flying in a clear, feature-less sky.

23. Discuss how you can combine the FAA and U.S. Navy-recommended sector scan patterns into your personal see and avoid method.

24. Describe the importance of clearing turns, S-turns, and belly checks.

25. Explain the potential danger with visual illusions.

26. Refer to the collision avoidance checklist as a guideline. Develop a personal checklist, and explain how you could apply each area into your own flying regime.

27. Describe one of your own flights, and discuss how you could have applied the lessons from this chapter to that situation.

CHAPTER 2

1. Describe A airspace.
2. Describe B airspace.
3. Describe C airspace.
4. Describe D airspace.
5. Describe E airspace.
6. Describe G airspace.
7. Discuss the events that led to the mid-air collision of Skywest Flight 1834 and a Mooney M20.
8. Discuss the practical applications and lessons learned in the wake of the Skywest/Mooney mid-air.
9. Explain the complete definition of "radar contact."
10. Explain the purpose and benefit of radar flight-following services.
11. Describe the rules of VFR altitudes.
12. Discuss the intended purpose of ATC.
13. Discuss how a pilot flying VFR can most effectively use ATC services.
14. Explain diffusion of responsibility. Discuss how diffusion of responsibility can negatively impact a collision-avoidance environment.
15. Explain a reduced state of vigilance. Discuss how a reduced state of vigilance can negatively impact a collision-avoidance environment.
16. From a controller's perspective, discuss the similarities between runway incursions and mid-air collisions.
17. Explain how radar works.
18. Explain the difference between primary and secondary surveillance radar.
19. Discuss the limitations of radar and how those limitations negatively affect a collision avoidance environment.

20. Discuss the events that led to four near-misses discussed in the chapter.

21. Discuss the seriousness of ATC manpower shortages and how that can negatively affect a collision avoidance environment.

22. Discuss five ways to improve your radio voice.

23. Discuss the negative effect that ambiguous and indirect phraseology has in a collision-avoidance environment and an emergency situation.

24. Discuss the practical applications and lessons learned from the PSA/172 mid-air and the crash of Galaxy Flight 203.

25. Explain how to determine reciprocal headings.

CHAPTER 3

1. Explain the significance of the eye-brain tunneling phenomena (refer to the Ramachandran/Gregory study) as it pertains to collision avoidance.

2. Describe the main events which led to the Wings West/Rockwell Commander accident. Include communication and ATC factors.

3. Discuss how you can apply the lessons learned from this accident into your own flying regime. Feel free to come up with additional lessons.

Section review

1. Describe the events that led to the Piper Navajo/Army U21A mid-air.

2. Explain the relevance of the cockpit visibility study and the probability of visual detection.

3. Discuss how you can apply the lessons learned from this accident into your own flying regime. Can you think of any additional lessons?

Section review

1. Describe the events that led to the mid-air between the Cessna 340 and the North American SNJ-4.

2. Discuss the ATC and mid-air connection.

3. Discuss how you can apply the lessons learned from this accident into your own flying regime.

Section review

1. Describe the events that led to the PSA Boeing 727/Cessna 172 mid-air.

2. Explain the ATC and the mid-air connection.

3. Discuss how you can apply the lessons learned from this accident into your own flying regime.

CHAPTER 4

1. Explain the basic concept of crew resource management (CRM).
2. Discuss the relevance of the SHEL Model in a collision-avoidance environment.
3. Explain the goals of CRM.
4. Discuss the necessity of CRM.
5. Discuss the events that led to the crash of Air Florida Flight 90.
6. Discuss the practical applications and lessons learned from the crash of Air Florida Flight 90.
7. How can these lessons be applied to a collision-avoidance environment?
8. Discuss the events that led to the crash of Midwest Express Flight 105.
9. Discuss the practical applications and lessons learned from the crash of Midwest Express Flight 105.
10. How can these lessons be applied to a collision-avoidance environment?
11. Discuss the events that led to the crash of United Flight 173.
12. Discuss the practical applications and lessons learned from the crash of United Flight 173.
13. How can these lessons be applied to a collision avoidance environment?
14. Describe the main points of the awareness, practice and feedback, and continuous reinforcement phases of a CRM program.
15. Discuss how airline safety has improved since the introduction of CRM training.
16. Discuss the relationship between CRM training and the incident involving United Flight 663.
17. Discuss the relationship between CRM training and the crash of United Flight 232.
18. Discuss the ways in which CRM can be successfully applied to general aviation.
19. How can CRM methods and techniques be applied to a collision-avoidance environment?

CHAPTER 5

1. Explain the difference between judgment and decision-making.
2. Discuss, in detail, the five hazardous thought patterns.
3. How do these thought patterns pertain to collision avoidance?
4. Discuss how poor judgment affected the flight of Air Illinois 710.
5. Explain the benefits of the DECIDE model.

CHAPTER 6

1. Explain the types of distractions that can occur during nonflight operations.
2. Explain the types of distractions that can occur during flight operations.
3. Discuss the events that led to the crash of Eastern Flight 401.
4. Discuss the events that led to the crash of United Flight 173.
5. How can the lessons of this chapter be applied to a collision-avoidance environment?

CHAPTER 7

1. Explain the relationship between stress and work performance.
2. Discuss how boredom and complacency can have a negative effect in a collision-avoidance environment. Include the methods that can eliminate boredom.
3. Explain the three stages of stress.
4. Explain the relationship between stress and anger.
5. Explain the relationship between stress and time.
6. Discuss anticipatory stress.
7. Discuss how you can apply the lessons learned from this chapter into your own flying regime.

CHAPTER 8

1. Explain the principles behind an airborne collision-avoidance system.
2. Name the three types of transponders. Describe their relevance in a collision-avoidance environment.
3. Discuss TCAS I.
4. Discuss TCAS II.
5. Explain the three phases of transponder interrogation.
6. Explain the advisories and evasive maneuvers of TCAS II.
7. Discuss the events that led to the mid-air collision of Aeromexico Flight 498 and a Piper Cherokee.
8. Discuss TCAS legislation.
9. Discuss the target acquisition flight tests.
10. Discuss the concerns of NATCA.
11. How does the use of TCAS affect the entire flying community?
12. Discuss the future of TCAS.

CHAPTER 9

1. Explain how economic, political, and social pressures affect safety.

2. Discuss the events that led to the mid-air between a Cessna 172 and a Piper Lance near the Oakland (CA) Airport.

3. Discuss the relationship between noise abatement and collision avoidance.

4. Discuss the relationship between increased capacity and collision avoidance.

5. Describe the advantages of Quick-Scan radar in a collision-avoidance environment.

6. Express your personal opinion on the question "Does progress compromise safety?"

7. Discuss how you can apply what you've learned from this chapter into your own flying regime.

Index

Illustration page numbers in **boldface**